Cambridge Imperial and Post-Colonial Studies Series

The Cambridge Imperial and Post-Colonial Studies series is a well-established collection of over 100 volumes focussing on empires in world history and on the societies and cultures that emerged from, and challenged, colonial rule. The collection includes transnational, comparative and connective studies, as well as works addressing the ways in which particular regions or nations interact with global forces. In its formative years, the series focused on the British Empire and Commonwealth, but there is now no imperial system, period of human history or part of the world that lies outside of its compass. While we particularly welcome the first monographs of young researchers, we also seek major studies by more senior scholars, and welcome collections of essays with a strong thematic focus that help to set new research agendas. As well as history, the series includes work on politics, economics, culture, archaeology, literature, science, art, medicine, and war. Our aim is to collect the most exciting new scholarship on world history and to make this available to a broad scholarly readership in a timely manner.

More information about this series at
http://www.palgrave.com/gp/series/13937

Zoë R. Groves

Malawian Migration to Zimbabwe, 1900–1965

Tracing Machona

palgrave
macmillan

Zoë R. Groves
University of Leicester
Leicester, UK

Cambridge Imperial and Post-Colonial Studies Series
ISBN 978-3-030-54103-3 ISBN 978-3-030-54104-0 (eBook)
https://doi.org/10.1007/978-3-030-54104-0

Cover illustration: INTERFOTO/Alamy Stock Photo

This Palgrave Macmillan imprint is published by the registered company Springer Nature Switzerland AG
The registered company address is: Gewerbestrasse 11, 6330 Cham, Switzerland

Acknowledgments

This book would not exist were it not for the support and encouragement of many people. Thanks to Saul Dubow and Richard Drayton, and to the anonymous reviewers for their insightful comments on the proposal and the final manuscript. I am grateful to the members of the editorial team at Palgrave Macmillan who have enabled this process to go smoothly. *Tracing Machona* developed out of my Ph.D. thesis and doctoral research at Keele University, which was funded by the Arts and Humanities Research Council (AHRC). David Maxwell introduced me to Zimbabwean history as an undergraduate at Keele and inspired me to pursue African history to master's and doctoral level. I would like to thank David for his guidance and generous support throughout my academic studies and early career. I would also like to acknowledge the friendship and support of Shalini Sharma, my second supervisor at Keele, and many others from the Keele Postgraduate Association community.

Outside of Keele, I was immensely grateful to John McCracken for his advice and support when I began this research, and for introducing me to colleagues from the History department at the Chancellor College, University of Malawi. Kings Phiri, Hendrina Kachapila-Msosa, Wapulumuka Mulwafu and Wiseman Chijere Chirwa were welcoming and supportive during my visits to Zomba from 2007 onwards. This research would not have been possible without their support and guidance. Thanks to the staff at the Malawi National Archives in Zomba for their assistance on various trips to the archive reading rooms. Thanks also to the staff from the district offices who assisted Lucy Phiri and I with our oral history research. I would also like to thank my Chichewa teachers Alick Bwanali and Arnold Mboga. Learning Chichewa was a challenging but rewarding experience and taught me so much about Malawi, as well as enabling the research process to go more smoothly. Thanks to Lucy Phiri for being an excellent research assistant and for facilitating the interviews in Malawi in 2008. I am also grateful to Darlen Dzimwe for her enthusiasm and support with my research in 2018, for a 'behind the scenes' tour of Lilongwe market and for teaching me how to cook nsima. I look forward to working together again on future research projects.

In Zimbabwe, I would like to thank Gerald Mazarire, Joseph Mujere, Anusa Daimon, Nicholas Nyachega, Tinashe Nyamunda, Ushehwedu Kufakurinani and others from the History and Economic History departments at the University of Zimbabwe. Special thanks to Margaret Goreraza and Fortune Sithole for their research assistance and for conducting the oral history interviews in Harare. Nicholas Nyachega was a valued research companion during a later trip to Harare and I am grateful for his support and astute observations. Thanks to my Chishona teacher, Mickias Musiyiwa, at the University of Zimbabwe, and to the staff at the National Archives of Zimbabwe. Thanks also to Ngwabi Bhebe, Faith Ntabeni-Bhebe and Ropa for welcoming me into their family home on numerous visits to Harare.

Back in the UK, I would like to thank the staff and archivists at Rhodes House Library, the National Archives at Kew, the School of Oriental and African Studies library, the Centre for African Studies, Edinburgh University, and finally, the Institute of Education Archives at UCL. I am grateful to Kathryn Hannan from the Institute of Education Archives for her help in obtaining a copy of a photograph from the Margaret Read Collection that appears in chapter two.

Between 2011 and 2013, I was fortunate to spend two years as a postdoctoral researcher at Wits Institute for Social and Economic Research (WISER), in Johannesburg. During this time, I benefitted a great deal from discussions with my mentor Belinda Bozzoli, as well as members of the Zimbabwe Reading Group, colleagues at the African Centre for Migration and Society (ACMS), in the History Department and History Workshop group. Thanks to Sarah Nutall and Achille Mbembe for allowing me to stay in their house when I first arrived in Johannesburg, and big thanks to my housemates in Melville, including Nicky Falkof and Sophie Boullion. Thanks to everyone at WISER, and to Eric

Worby, Arianna Lissoni, Catherine Burns, Keith Breckenridge, Andrew Macdonald, Prinisha Badassy, Mucha Musemwa, Stacey Sommerdyk and Joel Quirk. Special thanks to Liz Gunner for her friendship and enjoyable walks and conversation on the Melville koppies.

Over the years that I have been researching the history of Malawi and Zimbabwe I have been privileged to be part of an engaged scholarly community and I am thankful to the historians, anthropologists and other scholars for their help in shaping the arguments in this book, especially Cal Biruk, Joey Power, Owen Kalinga, Wapu Mulwafu, Markku Hokkanen, Harvey Banda, Anna West, Mpalive Msiska, Bryson Nkoma, Mary Davies and Megan Vaughan. Also, Maxim Bolt, Blair Rutherford, Jocelyn Alexander, JoAnn McGregor, Debby Potts, Miles Larmer, Sara Rich Dorman, Timothy Scarnecchia, Wendy Urban-Mead, Terri Barnes, Francis Musoni, Mhoze Chikowero and Brian Raftopoulos. During my time in Cambridge from 2013 to 2017, I was grateful to work alongside supportive colleagues, especially Rachel Leow, Ruth Watson, Felicitas Becker, Joel Cabrita, Alison Bashford, Andrew Arsan and for a short time Leslie James and Saul Dubow. Special thanks to Jessica Johnson for moral support and to Rachel Leow for helping me to think through various aspects of this research.

More recently, I would like to thank my wonderful colleagues in the School of History, Politics and International Relations at the University of Leicester for warmly welcoming me when I joined the university in 2017. Special thanks to Clare Anderson, Richard Anderson (now in Aberdeen), Svenja Bethke, Richard Butler, Sophie Cooper, Andrew Johnstone and Zoe Knox for their feedback on draft chapters, and to Prashant Kidambi for his advice and encouragement. Special mention also to the Doctors Who Dine (you know who you are), and to Jan Vandeburie and Sophie Cooper for being great friends and colleagues in the final few months of work on this manuscript during the strange days of lockdown. Thanks to Scott (Michael O'Dane) for letting Paul Houghton and I stay in his house in Italy in summer 2016 for our writing retreat. Huge thanks to Paul Houghton for his friendship and expert writing advice. Thanks to Henry Dee for sharing his research and interesting archival material on Nyasas in South Africa. Thanks to family and friends in Suffolk. Biggest thanks of all to Mike Coll for his unwavering support and confidence in me.

Several people who helped me on this journey sadly are no longer with us. I dedicate this work to the memory of Patrick Harries and to John

McCracken, both of whom offered generous support and encouragement and believed that this research should be published as a book.

Finally, thanks to all those in Malawi and Zimbabwe who gave up their time to share their life histories. I take all credit for the shortcomings and limitations of this book.

Praise for *Malawian Migration to Zimbabwe, 1900–1965*

"Zoë Groves provides a carefully researched and compelling history of Malawian contributions to Zimbabwe's history. Her work illuminates how migrants transformed their cultural identities to successfully build a unique migrant culture. The narrative weaves between social, cultural, urban, and political histories that are well-grounded in personal and family migration stories. Groves presents a significant and compelling narrative of the key roles of many remarkable trade union and anti-colonial nationalists from Malawi in the establishment of Zimbabwe's nationalist politics. Groves' shows how the experiences of Malawian leaders with settler colonialism in Southern Rhodesia helped to solidify an anti-colonial solidarity, especially in the late 1950s. The final chapter covers the post-Independence period and demonstrates the collective pride, and legitimate citizenship claims, of the many former *Machona* and their descendants living in Zimbabwe today. Groves' book is a welcome revision of, and contribution to, the modern history of central and southern Africa."

—Timothy Scarnecchia, *Kent State University, USA*

"This is the first book-length study of Malawian labour migration focusing on the experiences of those who travelled and those left behind, also unique for its focus on migration between Nyasaland/Malawi and Southern Rhodesia/Zimbabwe (and particularly, Salisbury/Harare), contributing to a story long dominated by Malawi's ties to South Africa. Groves makes an important contribution to a historiography of

African migration often preoccupied with transoceanic movement into the Atlantic and Indian Ocean worlds."

—Joey Power, *Ryerson University, Canada*

"This compelling history of Malawian migration to Zimbabwe makes a major contribution to the growing literature on diasporas within the African continent. Groves' careful and sensitive research across the region brings alive the political, social and emotional dimensions of the migrant experience and ensures that the story of the Malawian 'lost ones' will be remembered."

—Megan Vaughan, *UCL, UK*

Contents

Abbreviations

ANC	African National Congress
BSAP	British South Africa Police
CAF	Central African Federation
CCAP	Church of Central Africa, Presbyterian
CYL	(Salisbury) City Youth League
DC	District Commissioner
FISB	Federal Intelligence and Security Bureau
ICU	Industrial and Commercial workers' Union
KAR	King's African Rifles
MCP	Malawi Congress Party
MNA	Malawi National Archives
NAC	Nyasaland African Congress
NC	Native Commissioner
NDP	National Democratic Party
NRANC	Northern Rhodesia African National Congress
PCC	People's Caretaker Council
RAR	Rhodesian African Rifles
RBVA	Rhodesian Bantu Voters Association
RHL	Rhodes House Library
RICU	Reformed Industrial and Commercial Workers' Union
RNLB	Rhodesia Native Labour Board
RNLSC	Rhodesia Native Labour Supply Commission
SOAS	School of Oriental and African Studies
SRANC	Southern Rhodesian African National Congress
SRBC	Southern Rhodesia Bantu Congress
TEBA	The Employment Bureau of Africa

UFP	United Federal Party
WNLA	Witwatersrand Native Labour Association
ZANC	Zambia African National Congress
ZANU	Zimbabwe African National Union—Patriotic Front
ZANU-PF	Zimbabwe African National Union
ZAOGA	Zimbabwe Assemblies of God Africa
ZAPU	Zimbabwe African People's Union
ZNA	Zimbabwe National Archives

List of Figures

List of Tables

CHAPTER 1

Introduction

Grey Areas was only 15 years old in 1949 when he left his home in Zomba to work as a cook for a white family on a farm in Marandellas, an area in the northeast of Southern Rhodesia.[1] After six years on the farm he made his way to the capital city of Salisbury. Reflecting on his life as a Malawian living in Zimbabwe in 2008, Grey Areas described the concept of *machona*:

> The *machona* are people who go to other countries and forget to return home. These people when they go back to Malawi, no one remembers them or wants them there. Most of them, they spend their money in these foreign countries and then go home poor, becoming a burden on those people at home. So usually the people at home would use *juju* to send them back to wherever they have come from so that they can live in peace. Just like me, I think that they are going to use *juju* to send me back here because they will say that I am *machona*. I can safely say now that I am a *machona*.[2]

[1] Southern Rhodesia later became Rhodesia, then Zimbabwe. Nyasaland became Malawi. See note on terminology and place names for a full explanation.

[2] Grey Areas used the term *juju* to refer to the practice and use of magic or traditional medicine including good and bad charms. Interview with Grey Areas conducted by Zoë Groves and Margaret Gororaza, Avondale, Harare, July 2008.

Z. R. Groves, *Malawian Migration to Zimbabwe, 1900–1965*, Cambridge Imperial and Post-Colonial Studies Series,
https://doi.org/10.1007/978-3-030-54104-0_1

In the 1950s, Grey Areas had moved to Waterfalls, a low-density suburb in the south of Salisbury where he met his wife. Her father was also from Nyasaland and worked as a 'garden boy' for a white family in the suburb. The couple later acquired a house in Dzivarasekwa, a residential area built to accommodate the growing African population in the racially segregated city. There, they raised their thirteen children. Throughout his time in Zimbabwe, Grey Areas maintained close connections with his original home in Zomba. However, it became increasingly difficult to travel back to Malawi from the early 2000s as the Zimbabwean economy spiralled into decline and standards of living worsened.

This book traces the history of migration of people like Grey Areas from Malawi to Zimbabwe, from the early 1900s to the mid-1960s. Under British colonial rule, hundreds of thousands of African men left Nyasaland to seek employment in the settler colony of Southern Rhodesia and elsewhere in central and southern Africa.[3] Women and children also went in search of better opportunities or to reunite with family members, in increasing numbers from the 1940s. Labour migrants, by definition, were only supposed to be temporary residents in Southern Rhodesia. Yet, in practice many stayed away from home for years or decades, while others never returned. 'Nyasa' migrants who lost contact with home became known as *machona*—'the lost ones'.[4] Popular beliefs about the fate of *machona* reinforced the expectation of return and put pressure on migrants to go back before it was too late. If one stayed away for too long, they could be marginalised by their kin in their home village. This book explores these stories and reveals the emotional costs of labour migration, as well as the relationships that were maintained across borders and the long-term legacies of colonial-era migration in the postcolonial period.

Malawi was a vital source of labour in southern Africa, providing one of the biggest and most consistent supplies of workers for the mines and

[3] Central Africa (or British Central Africa) was commonly used during the colonial era to refer to the British-controlled territories of Nyasaland, Northern Rhodesia and the settler-colony of Southern Rhodesia. These countries are more commonly defined in the postcolonial era as part of Southern Africa. In this book, Southern Africa is defined broadly to include Malawi, Zambia, Zimbabwe, Angola, Mozambique, Botswana, Namibia, Lesotho, Eswatini (Swaziland), and South Africa.

[4] This term is derived from the Chewa verb to be stuck/to get stuck 'kutchona'. It can also be spelt *mtchona*. Thanks to language teacher and friend Alick Bwanali for his translation and explanation of this term.

settler-owned commercial farms around the region for much of the twentieth century.[5] Yet surprisingly, Malawians are not so well represented in the vast historical literature on African labour migration. Few studies have explored migration between Nyasaland and Southern Rhodesia, despite both territories (along with Northern Rhodesia) being joined within the Central African Federation between 1953 and 1963. While most studies of southern African migration assume that workers were South Africa-bound, the extent of inter-regional migration has been largely underestimated.[6] By offering a new perspective on 'Nyasa' migration in the region, this book addresses this gap with a focus on the settler-colonial city of Salisbury, one of the most popular destinations for Nyasa migrants, from the 1920s to the mid-1960s. Furthermore, the history of Malawian migration is also relevant to wider scholarship on African and global migration history. Long-standing patterns of African continental mobility are rarely acknowledged beyond the Atlantic and Indian Ocean worlds, and such accounts are almost always focused on forced migration

[5] Previous work on Malawian migration includes: Jens A. Andersson, 'Informal Moves, Informal Markets: International Migrants and Traders from Mzimba District, Malawi', *African Affairs*, 105, 420 (2006), pp. 375–397; Harvey C. Chidoba Banda, *Migration from Malawi to South Africa: A Historical and Cultural Novel* (Bamendna, 2018); Robert Boeder, 'Malawians Abroad: The History of Labour Emigration from Malawi to Its Neighbours, 1890 to the present', PhD Thesis, Michigan State University (1974); Robert Boeder, 'We Won't die for fourpence': Malawian Labour and the Kariba Dam', *Journal of Modern African Studies*, 15, 2 (1977), pp. 310–315; G. Coleman, 'International Labour Migration from Malawi, 1875–1966', *Journal of Social Science*, 2 (1972), pp. 31–46; Robert E. Christiansen and Jonathan G. Kydd, 'The Return of Malawian Labour from South Africa and Zimbabwe', *Journal of Modern African Studies*, 21, 2 (1983), pp. 311–326; Wiseman Chijere Chirwa, 'Aliens and AIDS in Southern Africa: The Malawi-South Africa Debate', *African Affairs*, 97, 386 (1998), pp. 53–79; Wiseman Chijere Chirwa, "Theba is Power': Rural Labour, Migrancy and Fishing in Malawi, 1890s–1985', PhD Thesis, Queen's University, Kingston, Ontario (1992); Elios Petros Makambe, 'The Nyasaland African Labour *Ulendos* to Southern Rhodesia and the Problem of the African 'Highwaymen', 1903–1923: A Study in the Limitations of Early Independent Labour Migration', *African Affairs*, 79, 317 (1980), pp. 548–566; F. E. Sanderson 'The Development of Labour Migration from Nyasaland, 1891–1914', *Journal of African History*, 2, 2 (1961), pp. 259–271. On migration from Malawi in the early twenty-first century see Jessica Johnson, 'After the Mines: The Changing Social and Economic Landscape of Malawi-South Africa Migration', *Review of African Political Economy*, 44, 152 (2017), pp. 237–251. Mpalive-Hangson Msiska, '*Kujoni*: South Africa in Malawi's National Imaginary', *Journal of Southern African Studies*, 43, 5 (2017), pp. 1011–1029.

[6] A 'too South African' approach to regional labour migration is noted in Bill Paton, *Labour Export Policy in Southern Africa* (Harare, 1995), p. 12.

and slavery. This book instead draws attention to the voluntary movement of Africans within the African continent, at the same time raising important questions about the history and formation of diaspora communities in colonial and postcolonial Africa.

A widespread culture of migration developed in Nyasaland in the first half of the twentieth century. The British colony was central to the history of labour migration in southern Africa as the place of origin for so many migrant workers across the region. It was no exaggeration when the historian Robert Boeder claimed that: 'Virtually every Malawian who has ever lived in the twentieth century has been affected by labour migration, either as a participant or as a member of a migrant's family'.[7] Migration came to be pivotal to the experience of being a 'Nyasa' in the early twentieth century and migration continues to be a way of life for many Malawians in the postcolonial era.

Nyasas in Southern Africa

Migration to the mines and industrial centres of southern Africa was fundamental in shaping the wider region. Yet very few historical studies have looked beyond migration to South Africa or migration from the labour-sending countries of Lesotho, Swaziland and Mozambique, to explore the full extent of this regional history.[8] Focusing on Malawian

[7] Boeder, 'Malawians Abroad', p. 242.

[8] The historiography on migrant labour in (southern) Africa is vast. Early writings include Raymond Leslie Buell, *The Native Problem in Africa* (New York, 1928); H. E. Panofsky, 'Migratory Labour in Africa—A Bibliographical Note', *Journal of Modern African Studies*, 1, 4 (1963), pp. 521–529; Sharon Stichter, *Migrant Laborers* (Cambridge, 1985). Later reviews of labour migration in southern Africa include: Tshidiso Maloka, 'Mines and Labour migrants in Southern Africa: Review and Commentary', *Journal of Historical Sociology*, 10, 2 (1997), pp. 213–224; Lynn Schler, Louise Bethlehem, and Galia Sabar, 'Rethinking Labour in Africa, Past and Present', *African Identities*, 7, 3 (2009), pp. 287–298; Peter Delius, 'The History of Migrant Labour in South Africa, 1800–2014', *Oxford Research Encyclopedia for African History* (2017), https://doi.org/10.1093/acrefore/9780190277734.013.93. More recently, the edited collection and accompanying exhibition at the Wits Art Museum made clear the fundamental contribution of migrant labour to the making of modern South African society. What is less clear from this collection is the extent to which this was a regional story and one not limited to those from and within South Africa: Peter Delius, Laura Phillips and Fiona Rankin-Smith, *A Long Way Home: Migrant Workers Worlds 1800–2014* (Johannesburg, 2014). On Mozambican labour migrants to South Africa: Patrick Harries, *Work, Culture and Identity: Migrant Labourers in Mozambique and South Africa* (London, 1994). On

migration to Zimbabwe enhances our understanding of labour migration and draws attention to the understudied connections between two colonies in twentieth-century southern Africa—the white settler-controlled colony of Southern Rhodesia (from 1923) and the British Protectorate Colony of Nyasaland.[9] While South Africa is generally situated at the heart of the regional system of migrant labour, Malawi is often seen as peripheral, despite being one of the largest suppliers of labour for the mines and large-scale commercial farms in the twentieth century.[10]

Yet, the characterisation of Nyasaland as 'labour reserve', providing cheap migrant labour for South Africa is problematic for several reasons. Firstly, it overlooks the fact that migration and mobility were already features of the region before the development of the colonial economy. As well as sending its own migrants to other parts of southern Africa, Nyasaland was an important migrant-receiving territory before and during British colonial rule. Africans moved into the territory from the south and east, escaping persecution and looking for new opportunities and land on which to settle. Other groups came from further afield, including India, and parts of Europe besides Britain, such as Italy and Greece.[11] Chapter 2 discusses the wider context of pre- and early colonial migration in this area and complicates the simplistic portrayal of Nyasaland as a labour reserve. It argues that migration was already a part of life for many communities in Nyasaland before the introduction of 'push factors' like taxation during the era of British rule.

Lesotho migrants: David Coplan, *In the Time of Cannibals: The Word Music of South Africa's Basotho Migrants* (Chicago, 1995). On Swaziland: Hamilton Sipho Simelane, 'The State, Chiefs, and the Control of Female Migration in Colonial Swaziland, c.1930s–1950s', *Journal of African History*, 45, 1 (2004), pp. 103–124. The over-emphasis on migration to South Africa is briefly discussed in Bill Paton, *Labour Export Policy in the Development of Southern Africa* (Harare, 1995), pp. 12–14.

[9] Although I refer here to Zimbabwe as a former colony, I recognise that it was a different kind of political entity to most, or any other African colony. Luise White discusses the history of Southern Rhodesia (later Rhodesia, and for a short time Zimbabwe-Rhodesia) and its ambiguous, confusing constitutional status in the first chapter of her book, *Unpopular Sovereignty: Rhodesian Independence and African Decolonization* (Chicago, 2015), pp. 1–36.

[10] Southern Rhodesia was, in fact, the largest labour importer in the region prior to 1970. Paton, *Labour Export Policy*, p. 12.

[11] On migration to Nyasaland: Floyd and Lillian O. Dotson, *The Indian Minority in Zambia, Rhodesia and Malawi* (London, 1968); Landeg White, *Magomero: Portrait of an African Village* (Cambridge, 1987); and John McCracken, 'Economics and Ethnicity: the Italian Community in Malawi', *Journal of African History*, 32, 2 (1991), pp. 313–332.

Moreover, Nyasaland migrants made a wider impact on the region in ways besides their economic contribution. Recent work, for example, has shown how Christians engaged in cosmopolitan and internationalist urban society in 1920s Johannesburg.[12] More widely known are figures like Clements Kadalie, who founded southern Africa's first Black trade union, the Industrial and Commercial Workers' Union (ICU), in South Africa in 1919.[13] During the 1920s, the ICU under Kadalie's charismatic leadership became a highly influential mass-based movement across southern Africa, one which challenged conventional narratives of the time around race and gender.[14] Through mobility, religious and associational life, migrants came together in a number of arenas, not only the workplace. Nyasas influenced the transformation and spread of cultural styles, languages, and associations around the region. This book expands our knowledge of these trends in the important urban centre of Salisbury, a major attraction for migrant workers across the region, especially during the economically vibrant years of the federation period (explored in Chapters 5 and 6). It also shows the extent to which Nyasa men and women were involved in political, cultural, and religious communities and organisations beyond the colony, and later, the nation.[15] In doing so, this book challenges stereotypes about Nyasa migration. Migrants were not always the poorest members of their home societies as has been assumed. Indeed, it was often necessary to have some form of capital to begin one's journey. Equally, more migrants were relatively well-educated and highly skilled than is currently understood. As we have seen with Grey Areas, whose experience was mentioned at the start of this introduction, migration was not always temporary. Neither were migrants always single men. Despite greater restrictions on their movement, women and children were also among those who left Nyasaland for Salisbury and other locations around the region. Nyasa women migrated both as wives accompanying

[12] Henry Dee, 'Nyasa Leaders, Christianity and African Internationalism in 1920s Johannesburg', *South African Historical Journal*, 70, 2 (2018), pp. 383–406.

[13] Clements Kadalie, *My Life and the ICU: The Autobiography of a Black Trade Unionist in South Africa* (London, 1970).

[14] Henry Dee, 'I Am a Bad Native': Masculinity and Marriage in the Biographies of Clements Kadalie', *African Studies*, 78, 2 (2019), pp. 183–204.

[15] Another recent book that highlights the importance of networks and mobility in Malawi's colonial history is Markku Hokkanen, *Medicine, Mobility and the Empire: Nyasaland Networks, 1859–1960* (Manchester, 2017).

their husbands and as single independent women, but until now scholarship has focused overwhelmingly on male labour migration.[16] These gendered and generational experiences of migration are explored in Chapters 3 and 5.

Imperial historians have examined the lives of Europeans as migrants, settlers, and workers in all their complexity, but they often tell us little about the mobility of Africans beyond their role as labourers or slaves. Some of the best histories of labour migration in southern Africa portray Africans not just as passive victims in a dehumanising system, but as agents capable of expressing their grievances through various hidden struggles. For example, the classic labour history, *Chibaro*, explored how the Southern Rhodesian mining sector competed for and secured supplies of cheap African labour, as well as looking at worker behaviour in the larger mine compounds.[17] This study was pioneering for the attention it paid to topics including 'tribal' dances, football, and worker consciousness. Nonetheless, African voices are generally inferred in this work from European or colonial sources rather than analysed from empirical evidence. Also, like most regional labour histories, the focus is once again on the mines. While this book takes inspiration from these earlier histories it offers a new approach. Through an analysis of colonial-era migration from colonial and missionary archives, and the perspective of African migrants themselves—accessed through oral histories—this book captures a range of Nyasa migrant experiences and illuminates many important themes, namely, gender, ethnicity, class and urbanisation.[18] Much of the literature on Malawi suggests a homogenous experience of colonialism and labour migration. The life histories of Nyasa men and women discussed in the book present a different perspective.

Following earlier studies, migration is analysed here in a transnational framework, looking at both origin and destination to better understand

[16] One important exception to this is the study of Malawian women in Harare by Ireen Mudeka, '"We faced *Mabvuto*": A Gendered Socio-economic History of Malawian Women's Migration and Survival in Harare, 1940–1980', PhD Thesis, University of Minnesota (2011).

[17] Charles Van Onselen, *Chibaro: African Mine Labour in Southern Rhodesia, 1900–1933* (London, 1976).

[18] Benedetta Rossi cites some examples of new research on African migrations based on 'detailed, biographic and micro-historical studies of specific migrant networks and individuals' in a recent review article 'Migration History and Historiography', *Oxford Research Encyclopedia for African History* (2018), p. 23.

migrant experiences.[19] This approach enables us to see how migration from Nyasaland to Southern Rhodesia was a two-way process: wages were sent back and invested in home improvements, school fees, bicycles and clothes. Nyasa migrants returned to their villages with new ideas, commodities, and ways of thinking that in turn transformed the lives of others back home. The book reveals the long-term connections that migrants maintained with home through the life histories of former migrants like Grey Areas who still reside in Harare, as well as others who returned to Malawi. Unlike previous studies, it also highlights urban migration and the experiences of women and youth, many of whom migrated independently and through informal channels rather than signing up to the recruitment agencies that provided labour for the region's large-scale mines and commercial farms. Following migrants from origin to destination and in some cases back again, this book takes a multi-sited approach and explores life beyond the workplace.

Finally, looking at Malawian migration within the wider regional context brings important new insights to the politics of decolonisation. While the transnational nature of the liberation struggles in southern Africa is now much better understood, less is known about the interconnections between political movements in the territories of the Central African Federation, as well as the influence and activism of Nyasas beyond the nation.[20] Through their experiences of labour migration, Africans from Nyasaland were acutely aware of the harsh labour conditions, land

[19] Patrick Harries was one of the first scholars writing on labour migration in southern Africa to explore both home and destination in the same study: *Work, Culture and Identity: Migrant Labourers in Mozambique and South Africa, c.1860–1910* (London, 1994); Zachary Kagan Guthrie's book is a more recent example of using a transnational framework to study Mozambican migration in different parts of the region: *Bound for Work: Labour, Mobility and Colonial Rule in Central Mozambique, 1940–1965* (Charlottesville, 2018). A transnational perspective was also been applied to new global labour history, such as Philip Bonner, Jonathan Hyslop and Lucien Van Der Walt, 'Rethinking Worlds of Labour: Southern African Labour History in International Context', *African Studies*, 66, 2–3 (2007), pp. 137–167—African migrant labour from Nyasaland is briefly mentioned on p. 159.

[20] On the liberation struggles in southern Africa, see Hilary Sapire and Christopher Saunders (eds.), *Southern African Liberation Struggles: New Local, Regional and Global Perspectives* (Claremont, 2013); Jocelyn Alexander, JoAnn McGregor and Blessing-Miles Tendi, 'The Transnational Histories of Southern African Liberation Movements: An Introduction', *Journal of Southern African Studies*, 43, 1 (2017), pp. 1–12; See also the Part Special Issue: *Mobile Soldiers and the Un-National Liberation of Southern Africa* by Luise White and Miles Larmer (eds.), *Journal of Southern African Studies*, 40, 6 (2014).

alienation and racial segregation in Southern Rhodesia (and South Africa). Middle-class Nyasas were well travelled, pursued higher education and training opportunities abroad, and they created networks and exchanged ideas with other colonised peoples.[21] When the Federation was created against the wishes of the eight million African majority across all three colonies, more effective collaboration between political movements on both sides of the Zambezi became necessary and urgent to prevent the white settler minority from extending its reach further north.[22] Migration was central to political mobilisation and to the politics of the different territories in the Federation. Historians have begun to revisit the ideas of multiracial partnership, 'modernisation' and development that underpinned the proposals for the Central African Federation. They have considered the wider international context that led to and influenced federation, including Southern Rhodesia's complex relations with South Africa, the United States and the expanding United Nations.[23] Chapter 6 contributes to the revisionist historiography of African nationalisms in Central Africa and to more recent studies on 'the federal moment' by considering transnational migrant networks and political activism across the region. Previous revisionist histories depict federation as an alternative to colonial empire and the nation-state.[24] For white settlers in

[21] Ismay Milford highlights some important connections between anticolonial activists in Malawi and those in East Africa in her recently completed doctoral thesis 'Harnessing the Wind: East and Central African Activists and Anticolonial Cultures in a Decolonising World, 1952–64', European University Institute, 2019. See also Ismay Milford, 'Federation, Partnership and the Chronologies of Space in 1950s East and Central Africa', *The Historical Journal* (2020). https://doi.org/10.1017/S0018246X19000712.

[22] Ironically, the Central African Federation was argued for in British circles on the basis that it would prevent another group of white settlers from extending their control north of the Limpopo. See Philip Murphy (ed.), *British Documents on the End of Empire: Central Africa. Part 1: Closer Association, 1945–1958* (London, 2005), Introduction, pp. xxvii–cvii.

[23] Julia Tischler, *Light and Power for a Multiracial Nation: The Kariba Dam Scheme in the Central African Federation* (Basingstoke, 2013); Andrew Cohen, *The Politics and Economics of Decolonization in Africa: The Failed Experiment of the Central African Federation* (London, 2017); Robert Rotberg, 'The Partnership Hoax: How the British Government Deprived Central Africans of their Rights', *Journal of Southern African Studies*, 45, 1 (2019), pp. 89–110.

[24] For a recent historiographical review of the literature on 'the federal moment', see Merve Fejzula, 'The Cosmopolitan Historiography of Twentieth Century Federalism', *The Historical Journal*. https://doi.org/10.1017/S0018246X20000254.

Southern Rhodesia, federation was viewed as a step towards dominion status and independence from British control. For Africans in Nyasaland and Northern Rhodesia, federation was an act of betrayal by the British.

Nyasas in Salisbury

From the early 1900s increasing numbers of men left Nyasaland in search of work in the south. Besides the mines and farms, employment was also sought in the growing towns and cities of the region sometimes following a period of agricultural labour. For some, the goal was *Joni* (Johannesburg) and the mines and industries of the Witwatersrand known for their higher salaries. However, Johannesburg was more than a thousand miles from Nyasaland and many preferred to work closer to home.[25] Rather than setting their sights on Europe or America, Nyasa men and women aspired to make money in the cities of southern Africa. Salisbury, in particular, was seen as a place of opportunity, 'a land of milk and honey'—another city of gold.[26]

As a white settler city with a fast-expanding African population, Salisbury provides an important case study in the regional history of urban labour migration. The early to mid-twentieth century was a period of rapid urbanisation and enormous social and political change—with two World Wars, global economic depression, the end of colonial rule and independence for Malawi (1964), and the beginning of a long and bitter struggle for liberation in Zimbabwe (1965–1979). Already by 1912, an estimated 20,000 Nyasaland men were working in Southern Rhodesia—about 10,000 in the mines and the other half on farms and in urban areas where they were employed as domestic servants, clerks, and policemen. Salisbury, according to one colonial observer, was 'over-run by Nyasaland natives'.[27] From the 1920s, there were more Nyasas and other so-called

[25] Harare (formerly Salisbury) is about 500 miles from Malawi's central region.

[26] These were the words of Andu Pangani, one of the former labour migrants interviewed in Harare during this research.

[27] C. Knipe to Acting Governor, Zomba, 11 June 1908 enclosed in *Correlating to the Recruitment of Labour… for the Transvaal and Southern Rhodesian* Mines, 1908, quoted in John McCracken, *A History of Malawi, 1859–1966* (Woodbridge, 2012), p. 87. In 1912, the African population of Nyasaland was around 960,000 according to the Federation of Rhodesia and Nyasaland Census Report (1956), p. 3. By the late 1930s, Salisbury's total population was about 30,870. G. N. Burden, *Nyasaland Native Labour in Southern Rhodesia* (Zomba: Government Printer, 1938), pp. 4–5.

'non-indigenous' migrants (including from Mozambique and Northern Rhodesia) among Salisbury's African population than local Shona (the largest ethnic group in the Mashonaland area), yet their stories rarely feature in Zimbabwe's (urban) history.[28]

Salisbury underwent a period of enormous development and population growth in the 1940s, ushering in a new phase of urban politics. Nyasa workers were involved in labour strikes and trade union organisation, and they influenced and pioneered the development of new African political groups across the region. Migrant workers from outside of the colony had as much at stake in calling for better working conditions as those from within Southern Rhodesia. This was especially true during the years of the Central African Federation (1953–1963). As the federal capital, Salisbury experienced an economic and industrial boom, attracting larger numbers of migrant workers to the city than ever before. By the mid-1950s, the number of local Shona living in the African urban areas had substantially increased though migration from elsewhere in southern Africa continued. Migration flows to Salisbury were disrupted by political change as African nationalist movements were banned and their leaders called for an end to 'the stupid federation'.[29] Following the dismantling of the federation in 1963, Malawian independence in 1964, and the illegal declaration of independence (UDI) in Rhodesia in 1965, migration to Salisbury slowed from Malawi.

Throughout the period from the early 1900s to the mid-1960s, Nyasaland migrants shaped the African townships of Salisbury in distinctive ways that remain visible in Harare today. Nyasas established some of the first African churches and mosques in the city, and migrant cultural associations can still be found in areas known for their large and long-standing communities descended historically from Nyasaland. What this book refers to as the Malawian diaspora is evident in Mbare, the oldest African township in Harare (formerly known as Salisbury Native Location and later Harare African Township), from the languages spoken by

[28] Pioneering studies of Zimbabwe's urban history were published in Brian Raftopoulos and Tsuneo Yoshikuni (eds.), *Sites of Struggle: Essays in Zimbabwe's Urban History* (Harare, 1999). While a number of these essays do acknowledge the presence of migrants from outside of Zimbabwe, they fall short of a comprehensive investigation into their position in and contribution to the city.

[29] These were the famous words spoken by Hastings Kamuzu Banda, leader of the Nyasaland African Congress and later the Malawi Congress Party, also the first Prime Minister and (Life) President of independent Malawi.

residents in their homes and from the dances performed at weekends on the streets. Young people gather to watch the *Gule Wamkulu* (The Great Dance), a vibrant masquerade performance associated with Malawian (and Chewa) heritage, which is explored in Chapter 4.

The Malawian Diaspora

In 1966, the historian George Shepperson (known for his pioneering work on the African diaspora) called for historians to study 'the dispersal of Africans within Africa', and to think about this in the context of the African diaspora: 'Of course, not all the migrations of Africans inside Africa can be fitted into the concept of the African Diaspora. But some can and should'. He went on to give two examples to explain why he thought this was important, one of which was:

> the dispersal of Africans from Malawi, beginning in the 1890s – if not much earlier – and sending a stream of African soldiers, workers, clerks, preachers, trade unionists (such as Clements Kadalie), and politicians into many parts of South, Central and East Africa with important consequences for many aspects of life in those countries.[30]

Malawian migration to urban Zimbabwe is part of a much larger history of migration in southern and East Africa that should be considered beyond the confines of area studies, and in relation to global histories of labour, colonialism, urbanisation, and decolonisation.[31] This book therefore connects Malawian and southern African history with global history and with migration and diaspora studies. While labour migration was a major feature of colonies across Africa and other parts of the imperial world, the migrant labour system of southern Africa has generally been viewed through the very specific context of colonial, segregationist and apartheid South Africa.[32] More recently, scholars have noted the

[30] George Shepperson, 'The African Diaspora—Or the African Abroad', *African Forum: A Quarterly Journal of Contemporary Affairs*, 2, 1 (1966), p. 89.

[31] This point about the focus on South to North migration is made in a discussion about 'migrant novels': Rebecca Fasselt, 'Decolonising the Afropolitan: Intra-African migrations in post-2000 literature', in Moradewun Adejunmobi and Carli Coetzee (eds.), *Routledge Handbook of African Literature* (2019), ch. 6.

[32] Eddie Webster, 'Rethinking Migrant Labour' [Review article] *South African Historical Journal*, 28, 1 (1993), p. 292.

prospects for the comparative study of migrant labour in southern Africa and elsewhere around the world, as well as the value of studying labour migration in a transnational perspective.[33] By expanding on the history of Malawian migration in Southern Africa, this book highlights a different regional dynamic. Global migration history tends to underestimate the degree of inter-regional migration, focusing instead on movements across the Atlantic (often privileging the movement of Europeans), and from colony to metropole.[34] Asian indentured labour and migration into Africa has been widely noted, as well as European coloniser migration to Africa.[35] Yet the migration of African men and women in southern Africa is somehow seen as less 'global' than the movement of Africans or Asians across oceans, or even the movement of white Europeans within the continent. African migration usually features in global histories of migration with reference to slavery and forced labour (usually in reference to West Africa and the Atlantic Slave Trade). This is hardly surprising since it was enslaved Africans who experienced the largest forced migration in history.[36] However, 'free' or voluntary migration within Africa accounts for a large part of the continent's migration history—migration within the continent has always been greater than the numbers of Africans leaving it. As Dirk Hoerder puts it: 'Untold millions moved within Africa'.[37]

[33] Philip Bonner, 'Labour, Migrancy and Urbanisation in South Africa and India, 1900–1960', *Journal of Asian and African Studies*, 44, 1 (2009), pp. 69–95; Hyslop Bonner and Van Der Walt, 'Rethinking Worlds of Labour', p. 142. Bonner's comparative study on India and South Africa showed the remarkable similarity in patterns of labour migrancy between the two countries.

[34] This point is noted by Adam Mckeown, 'Global Migration, 1846–1940', *Journal of World History*, 15, 2 (2004), p. 155. For an important challenge to the dominant focus on the Atlantic word in Global History, see Sunil S. Amrith, *Crossing the Bay of Bengal: The Furies of Nature and the Fortunes of Migrants* (Cambridge, 2015). The Atlanto-centric approach is also noted by Dirk Hoerder, *Cultures in Contact: World Migrations in the Second Millennium* (Durham, 2002), p. 8. Important recent works which break with the colony to metropole paradigm include Andrew Arsan, *Interlopers of Empire: The Lebanese Diaspora in Colonial French West Africa* (London, 2014) and Sana Aiyar, *Indians in Kenya: The Politics of Diaspora* (Cambridge, 2015).

[35] See various chapters in Marjory Harper and Stephen Constantine, *Migration and Empire* (Oxford, 2000).

[36] Rossi, 'Migration History and Historiography', p. 1.

[37] Hoerder, *Cultures in Contact*, p. 436.

Yet, historians have been slow to explore the formation of new African diasporas created during the colonial period and subsequently.[38]

This book is a timely study of migration between two former colonies in a region where the legacies of the migrant labour system are still playing out in the present, through debates about citizenship, nationhood, xenophobia and belonging. Malawian history has generally been written through the lens of nation-building and underdevelopment, and its colonial history understood as the 'making of an imperial slum'.[39] However, these analyses fail to capture the significance of migration in the country's history, or the importance of Malawians in other national histories. Not only does the history of Malawian migration greatly enrich our understanding of a large inter-colonial labour diaspora, it provides an important corrective to 'patriotic history' in Zimbabwe, which neglects or simply denies the crucial role played by 'foreign' migrants in the country's history.

Migration from Malawi continued during the years of the Zimbabwean liberation struggle and after Zimbabwean independence in 1980. By this stage many Malawians had been in Harare for decades and they were welcomed as citizens in the newly independent African nation. Nevertheless, from the late 1990s and particularly during the fraught years of land reform in the post-2000 era, people of Malawian origin and descent found themselves pushed to the margins. Urban residents living in precarious informal housing in the city became vulnerable to government crackdowns on urban planning laws and were accused of lacking cultural ties to a rural home (*kumusha*) in Zimbabwe as was necessary for 'true' Zimbabweans. Similarly, farm workers in Zimbabwe, many of whom were of Malawian or Mozambican origin and descent, were evicted from their homes and left unemployed as a result of the post-2000 land invasions. Ambiguity surrounds the citizenship status of people of Malawian descent living in Zimbabwe, even those born in the country. Changes in citizenship law (and various interpretations of it) have rendered people 'aliens' in the only country they known as home.

[38] One exception to this is Francois Manchuelle, *Willing Migrants: Soninke Labour Diasporas, 1848–1960* (Athens, 1997). On African diasporas in the postcolonial period, see Oliver Bakewell and Naluwembe Binaisa, 'Tracing diasporic identifications in Africa's urban landscapes: evidence from Lusaka and Kampala', *Ethnic and Racial Studies*, 39, 2 (2016), pp. 280–300.

[39] John McCracken, *A History of Malawi, 1859–1966* (Woodbridge, 2012), p. 3.

Sources and Methodology

This work builds on long-standing fieldwork methodologies in African history.[40] It draws on research from multiple archives in Malawi, Zimbabwe, and the UK, and analyses oral history interviews conducted in rural Malawi and Harare. Colonial records, missionary papers and anthropological writings are used to contextualise migrant life histories and to explore government and missionary efforts to control and restrict labour migration and urban life. Together these accounts offer a broader perspective on colonial-era mobility and the experience of labour migration beyond the mine compounds, plantations and commercial farms that have traditionally been the focus of studies on southern African labour migration. African attitudes and experiences of urban life are captured in colonial reports on the living conditions of African townships, as well as newspapers, magazines and literature set in the settler-colonial city.[41]

Oral history interviews were conducted during a 12-month period of research in Malawi and Zimbabwe in 2007–2008, and later, on a follow-up visit in 2009. In total, 32 people were interviewed in Dedza and Ncheu in the central region, Thyolo in the southern region, and Nkhata Bay in the north (see Map 1.1). In some of these districts, entire villages were reputed for their high rates of migration to Southern Rhodesia. Lucy Phiri (a history graduate from the Chancellor College, University of Malawi) and I approached individuals and families on the basis of local knowledge. Interviews were conducted in Chichewa (Malawi's official language) and Chitonga (a language widely spoken in Nkhata Bay and other parts of the north among people identifying as Tonga) with 19 men and 13 women known to have lived and worked in Zimbabwe at some period in their lives. I was present at each of the interviews and together, Lucy and I transcribed and translated them into English. Members of the community and in some cases district administrators directed us towards those known to have lived and worked outside of Malawi.[42] Most of the

[40] See for example, Luise White, Stephan F. Miescher and David William Cohen (eds.), *African Words, African Voices: Critical Practices in Oral History* (Bloomington, 2001).

[41] One good example of a novel set in Salisbury is William Saidi, *Old Bricks Lives* (Gweru, 1988).

[42] Between 2007 and 2009, I was affiliated with the History Department at the Chancellor College, University of Malawi. In each of these areas permission to conduct research and interviews was granted by District Officials. The interviews were semi-structured around certain topics, including motivations for migrating, how they travelled, who with,

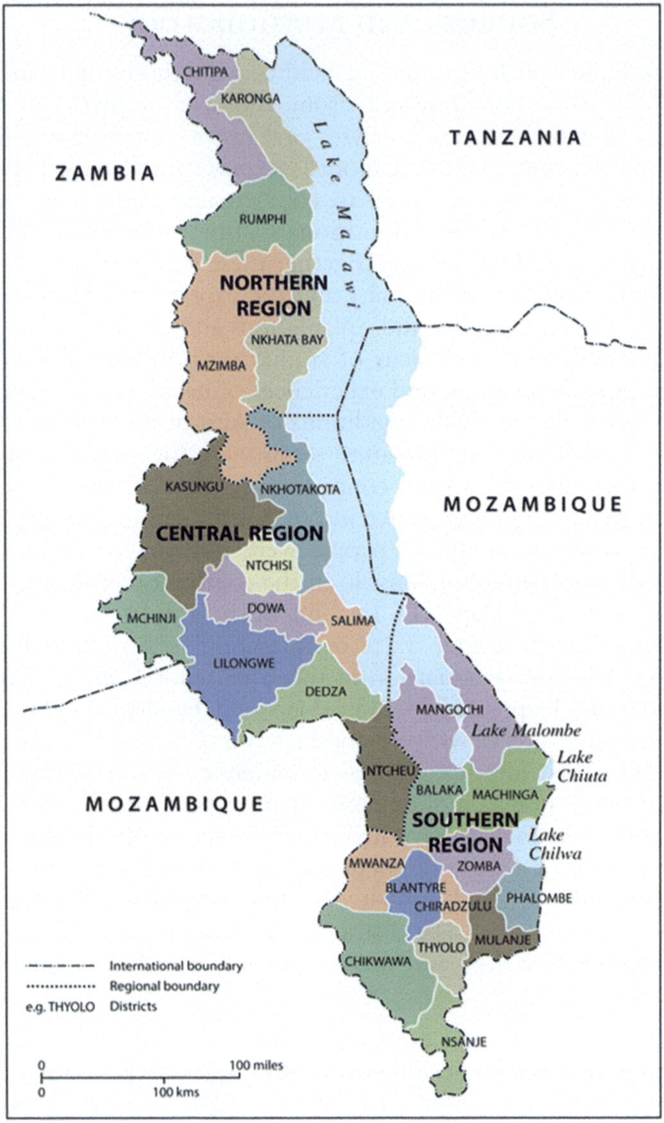

Map 1.1 Contemporary district boundaries in Malawi

Malawians interviewed were well known in their communities for having spent time in Zimbabwe although their experiences in Harare and their lives back in Malawi were similar in some ways and diverse in others. They had all migrated and returned at different times and for various reasons, having spent lengths of time abroad ranging from a few months to more than thirty years. Some lived notably more comfortably than others on their return to Malawi—there were stories of hardship, loss, nostalgia and regret.

Following a six-month period of research in Malawi, I arrived in Harare in April 2008 looking to conduct interviews with people of Malawian origin who had remained in Zimbabwe. Fieldwork and archival access in Zimbabwe were much more challenging than in Malawi due to the timing of this research. In 2008, Zimbabwe was approaching the worst period of hyperinflation while the country awaited the results of the critical Presidential and Parliamentary elections. For some time it looked as though the ruling party, the Zimbabwe African National Union-Patriotic Front (ZANU-PF), had lost to the opposition party, the Movement for Democratic Change (MDC)—this would have been a major upset for ZANU-PF had been in power since independence in 1980.[43] But it was not to be. Although the MDC did narrowly defeat ZANU-PF in the parliamentary elections the results of the presidential election were not announced until more than a month after the elections when it was declared that both candidates had failed to gain the majority needed to win in the first round. A Presidential run-off election was scheduled to take place in June 2008, and over the course of the following six weeks, the country rapidly spiralled deeper into economic and political crisis.[44]

experiences along the way, life in Salisbury and Southern Rhodesia, more generally, the type of work they found, associational life, including religious affiliation, political involvement, and reasons for returning to Nyasaland/Malawi. Interviewees were also asked to talk about their lives before they migrated and to share anything else that they wanted to about their life history.

[43] See 'Focus on March 29 Zimbabwe Elections', *The Daily Times* (Blantyre, Malawi), Monday 31 March 2008; 'Run off likely between Mugabe, Tsvangirai', *The Nation* (Blantyre), 31 March 2008; 'Impatience Grows over Zim Stalemate', *The Financial Gazette* (Harare), 8–14 May 2008; 'Smash Neo-Colonialism, Retain President Mugabe', *The Herald* (Harare), Thursday 5 May 2008.

[44] Zimbabwean historian Alois Mlambo described this period as the lowest point in the postcolonial era in 'Becoming Zimbabwe or Becoming Zimbabwean: Identity, Nationalism and State-building', *African Spectrum*, 48, 1 (2013), p. 62.

Being labelled 'Malawian' in Zimbabwe at this time had become a politically sensitive matter. The political climate had placed the politics of belonging, issues of citizenship and nation, and struggles for survival, top of the agenda. These issues are discussed in more detail in the final chapter of the book. But despite all this, some Malawians and their descendants were determined to share their life histories. With help from two history undergraduate students at the University of Zimbabwe—Margaret Goreraza and Fortune Sithole—17 people were interviewed in Harare (13 men and 5 women). These interviews were conducted in Chishona (Zimbabwe's official language) and transcribed into English.[45] The political context in Harare shaped the content of these interviews, particularly in the way that people looked back with a sense of nostalgia for the settler-colonial period and the early years of Zimbabwean independence.

These life histories offer insights into the diverse experience of migration that cannot be found in the colonial archives. While some recalled their migration story with enthusiasm, others were puzzled why their life might be of interest to a stranger (perhaps, especially, to a white woman researcher from the UK). The aim in drawing from their histories in this book is not so much to 'give voice' to the voiceless and powerless (something Sean Field described as 'outdated and at times patronising'[46])—although for some Malawians interviewed this was important—but to document and record the memories and accounts of ordinary people alongside other sources in the production of historical knowledge on African migration.

Organisational Outline

The chapters in the book are organised thematically and chronologically. The narrative shifts back and forth between Nyasaland and Salisbury, and occasionally other parts of Southern Rhodesia. Chapter 2 provides further historical context to labour migration from Nyasaland and traces

[45] I was present at some but not all of the interviews in Harare as some people felt more comfortable speaking to Margaret or Fortune on a one-to-one basis without me present. I interviewed 7 people from the Harare Central Church of Africa, Presbyterian (CCAP), in a group setting, without research assistance or translators. This interview was conducted in English.

[46] Sean Field, 'Doing Oral History in Africa' [Book Review: Paul Thompson with Joanna Bornat, *The Voice of the Past, Oral History*, fourth edition (Oxford, 2017)] *Journal of Southern African Studies*, 46, 2 (2020), pp. 384–386.

the development of the regional migrant labour system in the period leading up to World War Two. Far from being simply a colonial 'labour reservoir', this chapter shows that Nyasaland experienced a great deal of immigration as well as emigration, and it highlights the already high levels of mobility in the pre- and early colonial period. From the 1930s, more serious attempts were made by territorial governments, missionaries and European planters in Nyasaland to control migration, through labour legislation, taxation, and inter-territorial agreements. Importantly, the chapter traces these changes alongside African efforts to evade colonial government controls by choosing alternative routes, masquerading as Mozambicans, or simply taking advantage of the Nyasaland government's inability to control movement across colonial borders.

Chapter 3 explores social change, considering social mobility, gender, and family life in the villages of Nyasaland and the townships of Salisbury. Marriage, shifting gender relations, and the effects of mission-education are examined alongside the experience of returned migrants, noting how their new 'migrant' status back home altered their position in the community. Prestige as well as pressure was accorded to members of the community who migrated. The chapter also pays attention to the experiences of those who did not migrate themselves but who supported migration or were affected by it in other ways, for example, through care for family members and maintenance of land and property.

Chapter 4 considers identity among migrants in Salisbury. A spectrum of identities emerged in the townships, and these are explored through cultural practices and activities including dance groups, religious expressions and church congregations. These groups formed along common lines of migrant solidarity and not exclusively according to ethnicity or territorial origin. Broader cultural markers developed in Salisbury, including labels like 'Nyasa'. Language and local idioms, such as *MaBhurandaya* and *MaNyasarande*, literally meaning 'one from Blantyre' or 'one from Nyasaland' indicate the construction of new identities. Blanket terms such as 'northern migrants' when deconstructed reveal high levels of differentiation among non-indigenous migrant workers in the city. This chapter presents a more nuanced understanding of migrant identity by showing how migrants had multiple affiliations, diverse networks, and wider regional, rather than simply ethnic or national connections.

Chapter 5 looks at the transformation of the city from the 1930s and into the 1950s as more permanent African urban communities settled. As local Shona moved into the city in greater numbers, social and economic relations in the townships changed and more people came to view the townships as home. Nonetheless, entire areas of the townships remained known as the place where *MaNyasarande* lived. The representation of African urban areas by government officials is contrasted with an analysis of life histories and migrant experiences that show a stronger sense of urban community despite the hardships of township life.

The period from 1945 to 1965 was also one of increasing political change and these dynamics are examined in Chapter 6. Nyasa migrants played a crucial role in the formation and shaping of new African political organisations in Salisbury during the federation years (1953–1963). This chapter considers the experiences of Nyasa migrants in the context of increased social and political tensions, and in relation to the rise of African nationalism in the federation territories of Nyasaland, Northern Rhodesia and Southern Rhodesia.

The concluding Chapter 7 explores migration, citizenship and belonging after federation and independence. It argues that migration came to define the Malawian historical experience in the twentieth century as almost everybody was affected by migration in some form. One of the legacies of colonial-era labour migration in southern Africa has been the creation of new diaspora communities, some of which have struggled for access to citizenship rights and at times faced xenophobia and state-level discrimination because of their so-called 'foreign' origins. People of Malawian origin and descent in Zimbabwe have continued to assert their belonging in Zimbabwe, while others hope one day to return to Malawi.

CHAPTER 2

Labour Migration in Early Colonial Malawi

Although the central southern African region was highly mobile even prior to the onset of European rule, the nature and intensity of colonial-era labour migration was a new development.[1] Africans in nineteenth-century Malawi were connected through expanding economic, religious and kinship networks with East Africa. Yet by the early twentieth century, Nyasaland had been drawn more heavily into the southern African region through ties of 'finance, trade, political [and religious] influence, and especially migrant labour'.[2] With the discovery of large gold deposits on the Witwatersrand in 1886 and the extension of British imperial interests north of the Limpopo in the late nineteenth century, increasing numbers of migrant workers went from British Central Africa to work in the south. British Central Africa was declared a protectorate in 1891, following negotiations with the Portuguese who had long-standing trading interests in the area, and fledgling colonial administrations were established in Southern and Northern Rhodesia in the 1890s, under the control of the British South Africa Company. By 1911 the boundaries of the central and southern African state system had been set.

[1] Stephen Rockel argues that labour migration and wage labour predate colonial intervention and that African porters were drawn into the orbit of international capitalism well before the mines opened on the South African Rand: *Carriers of Culture: Labour on the Road in Nineteenth Century East Africa* (Portsmouth, 2006).

[2] Leroy Vail, *The Creation of Tribalism in Southern Africa* (Berkeley, 1989), p. 7.

Z. R. Groves, *Malawian Migration to Zimbabwe, 1900–1965*, Cambridge Imperial and Post-Colonial Studies Series,
https://doi.org/10.1007/978-3-030-54104-0_2

This chapter situates the history of Malawian labour migration in the context of regional mobility and the development of a migrant labour system in southern Africa, in the period from the late nineteenth century leading up to World War Two. Nyasaland experienced a great deal of immigration as well as emigration in the early decades of colonial rule. More concerted efforts were made by the colonial government to control labour migration from the mid-1930s in response to increased concerns by missionaries and European planters. The decision to re-establish labour recruitment for the major industries of South Africa and Southern Rhodesia in the late 1930s heralded a series of inter-territorial labour agreements between Nyasaland and its neighbours. African efforts to evade colonial government controls continued, by boycotting recruitment, risking alternative routes and modes of transport to the south and masquerading as Africans from other colonies (who were not subjected to the same controls as Africans from British colonial territories).

Precolonial Mobility and the Origins of Migrant Labour

European missionaries, traders and explorers arrived in Malawi in the mid-nineteenth century at a time of widespread social, political and economic upheaval. New African groups migrating from the south settled in the area.[3] Others came with the expansion of East African trade routes from the Swahili coast.[4] Incursions by Yao-speaking peoples from the east, and Ngoni settlers from the south, forced entire villages in precolonial Malawi to disperse and relocate. Yao settlers arrived from east of Lake Nyasa and established a presence through a process of negotiation with existing indigenous inhabitants and more direct conquest. Common clan affiliations were used to forge initial contacts with Nyanja and Mang'anja chiefs, and people from these villages were incorporated into Yao communities

[3] On the period known as the *Mfecane*, which led to mass migrations in southern Africa, see Carolyn Hamilton (ed.), *The Mfecane Aftermath: Reconstructive Debates in Southern African History* (Pietermaritzburg, 1995).

[4] Edward Alpers, *Ivory and Slaves in East Central Africa* (Berkeley, 1975). For a summary of nineteenth century Malawi, see John McCracken, *Politics and Christianity in Malawi, 1875–1940* (1977), ch.1. See also important work on precolonial Malawi by Kings M. Phiri, 'Chewa History in Central Malawi and the Use of Oral Tradition, 1600–1920', PhD Thesis, University of Wisconsin (1975).

through intermarriage, pawnship and bondage.[5] Gradually, Yao villages increased their numbers through slavery and further immigration, and came to dominate the Upper Shire Valley and the Shire Highlands in the southern part of the territory.[6] Mang'anja villages in the Shire Highlands and Lower Shire Valley were especially badly hit by the raids. Men fled targeted villages leaving women and children to be captured after their houses were burnt. Captives were marched to Sena or Tete where they were sold for ivory.[7]

Ngoni groups arrived from the south in the 1850s, seizing people, cattle and agricultural resources along the way. The Ngoni eventually settled and created four main kingdoms within, or bordering Malawi.[8] Immigrants also moved into the Shire Valley in the south hailing from the Zambezi region. They travelled in small family collections representing several different ethno-linguistic groups. Kololo from Barotseland had accompanied the missionary David Livingstone on his journey to Tete and settled in 1861 in the area that would become Chikwawa district. By the early twentieth century, the term Sena was used to describe those originating from the Sofala and Tete Provinces of Mozambique and eastern Zimbabwe.[9] Lowme migrants (known at the time by the pejorative term 'Anguru') arrived in large numbers during the first three decades of British rule, and continued to enter the colony right up until 1945. New arrivals were attracted to the area by the agricultural prospects of the land, high rainfall and permanent water supplies. But there were many reasons for Lomwe to leave Mozambique. Some were fleeing slave-raids, or outbreaks of famine. Others sought sanctuary from the Portuguese wars of 'pacification' in the late 1890s. Escape from the harsh forced

[5] Megan Vaughan, *Creating the Creole Island: Slavery in Eighteenth Century Mauritius* (Durham, NC, 2005), pp. 119–120.

[6] J. Clyde Mitchell, 'The Political Organisation of the Yao of Southern Nyasaland', *African Studies*, 8, 3 (1949), p. 142.

[7] Elias Mandala, *Work and Control in a Peasant Economy: History of the Lower Tchiri Valley in Malawi, 1859–1960* (Madison, 1990), pp. 72–73.

[8] On the history of the Ngoni in Malawi, see Margaret Read, *The Ngoni of Nyasaland* (London, 1956); T. Jack Thompson, *Christianity in Northern Malawi: Donald Fraser's Missionary Methods and Ngoni Culture* (Leiden, 1995); Giacomo Macola, *The Gun in Central Africa: A History of Technology and Politics* (Athens, 2016), especially part III.

[9] Mandala, *Work and Control*, p. 95. Initially they were known as *Chikunda*, a term applied to the armed slaves employed on Portuguese estates (*prazos*) in the Zambezi region. John McCracken, *A History of Malawi, 1859–1966* (Woodbridge, 2012), p. 20.

labour regime operated by the Portuguese colonial state was another factor influencing migration into Nyasaland.[10] Yet, Lomwe immigration also occurred because of the active and often forcible recruitment by Blantyre-based settlers working on behalf of the African Lakes Company (previously the Livingstonia Central Africa Company), a British company set up by Scottish businessmen looking to eradicate the slave trade and replace it with 'legitimate trade'.[11] From 1875, villages in the south had been organising labour to act as porters (*amtenga tenga*) for European missionaries and traders. As greater numbers left in search of work outside of the territory, Ngoni labour became scarce and the shortfall was resolved by the large 'influx' of Lomwe.[12]

By the mid-1890s, the Protectorate of British Central Africa had become a more tangible entity at least in the minds of the colonisers.[13] Several mission stations had been founded in Nyasaland and their influence would shape experiences of colonial conquest as well as migration opportunities. The Scottish Presbyterian Mission established in the north at Livingstonia in 1876 was arguably the most remarkable for its impact on local people (see Map 2.1).[14] Scottish missionaries soon established good relations with the lakeshore Tonga and Tumbuka (in contrast

[10] On Portuguese rule in East Africa, see: Allen Isaacman and Anton Rosenthal, 'Slaves, Soldiers and Police: Power and Dependency Among the Chikunda of Mozambique, ca.1825–1920', in Suzanne Miers and Richard Roberts (eds.), *The End of Slavery in Africa* (Madison, 1988), pp. 220–253; Eric Allina, *Slavery by Any Other Name: African Life under Company Rule in Colonial Mozambique* (Charlottesville, 2012).

[11] Landeg White, '"Tribes" and the Aftermath of the Chilembwe Rising', *African Affairs*, 83, 333 (1984), p. 514; McCracken, *History of Malawi*, pp. 48–50.

[12] According to White, the term Anguru comes from the name of the mountain closest to where most immigrants originated in Mozambique. It came to be used as a derogatory term and was eventually replaced with Lomwe. Ibid.

[13] McCracken, *History of Malawi,* p. 66. McCracken describes the character of the British administration, referring to the Protectorate as 'a hybrid', legally subordinate to the will of the imperial government but in practice functioning as a semi-autonomous body, with much important decision-making being left to the Commissioner'. Ibid., p. 69.

[14] The Free Church of Scotland Mission at first went to Cape Maclear along the southern end of the lakeshore, but conditions there were not suitable for permanent settlement, so they moved northwards to Bandawe where the climate was slightly more amenable. Finally, the Livingstonia Mission was permanently established in the Northern Province (see Map 2.2). McCracken, *Politics and Christianity in Malawi*. On the Church of Scotland Mission in the Southern Province, see Andrew Ross, *Blantyre Mission and the Making of Modern Malawi* (Blantyre, 1996).

Map 2.1 Nyasaland showing district boundaries c.1910 (*Source* Adapted from McCracken, *Politics and Christianity*, p. 226)

with the more difficult encounters between the Yao and the Universities Mission to Central Africa in the 1860s).[15] The Tonga welcomed the presence of the mission as protection against invading Ngoni groups. In contrast, the Yao and Ngoni resisted British rule and missionary influence into the early years of the twentieth century. Entire Tonga and Tumbuka villages soon converted to Christianity, and literacy spread through Ngoni villages in the north. Mission-educated migrants were encouraged to look for wage-earning opportunities in the Shire Valley and beyond. Others went to work as missionary servants elsewhere in the region, while a few early converts left the colony in disgrace having broken church rules.[16]

Within Nyasaland, labour migration initially took the form of southward movement to the plantations of the Shire Highlands where areas of land had been alienated by white settlers for coffee and cotton production. In 1897, the British Central Africa Gazette recorded 1,000 'Anguru', 9,000 Ngoni and 2,000 Atonga working in the Shire Highlands.[17] Male migrant workers travelling from the northern part of the colony soon grew dissatisfied with the offerings of wage labour within Nyasaland. Working conditions and wages were more attractive further south, and men from as far north as the Congo, Angola and Tanganyika ventured to the mines in Southern Rhodesia and South Africa.[18] By the early 1900s, thousands of Nyasa men were heading south for employment outside of the colony.

Following the end of the South African War, the Transvaal Chamber of Mines experienced an acute shortage of labour.[19] Subsequently, in 1903, the Nyasaland Governor agreed for one thousand men to be recruited by the Witwatersrand Native Labour Association (WNLA) for employment on the gold mines, thus marking the beginning of formal labour

[15] A. E. Anderson-Morshead, *History of the Universities' Mission to Central Africa, Volume I, 1859–1909* (London, 1955).

[16] Robert Boeder, 'Malawians Abroad: The History of Labour Emigration from Malawi to its Neighbours, 1890 to the Present', PhD Thesis, Michigan State University (1974), p. 5.

[17] Cited in White, '"Tribes" and the Aftermath of the Chilembwe Rising', p. 514.

[18] David Beach, 'The Shona Economy: Branches of Production', in Robin Palmer and Neil Parsons (eds.), *The Roots of Rural Poverty in Central and Southern Africa* (London, 1977), p. 58. See also, Jonathan Crush, Alan Jeeves, and David Yudelman, *South Africa's Labour Empire: A History of Black Migrancy to the Gold Mines* (Oxford, 1991).

[19] McCracken, *A History of Malawi*, p. 85.

recruitment in Nyasaland. The agreement was short-lived, however, as recruitment was later suspended in 1907 after a dispute between the Nyasaland government and the Chamber of Mines over terms of employment. The Nyasaland government was concerned by high mortality rates on the mines, as well as potential shortages of labour at home. Nonetheless, migrants continued to find their way across the Limpopo, partly through the assistance of recruitment agents stationed over the border in Portuguese East Africa, just south of Dedza. The high death rates from pneumonia and tuberculosis suffered by 'tropical natives' meant that recruitment by the WNLA was banned anywhere north of 22 degrees south in 1913. Nonetheless, Nyasa men continued to cross the border into South Africa to seek work. Limited measures were introduced to control 'foot traffic' entering from the north and continued demand among industrial and agricultural industries for cheap labour meant Nyasas were still welcomed by many employers despite the official ban on recruitment. Farm work and employment at the smaller mines outside of the control of the Chamber of Mines remained relatively easy to find.

In the early 1930s it was thought that ten thousand 'prohibited immigrants' from Nyasaland were in the Witwatersrand, Pretoria and Durban, although one estimate suggested the number was even higher at around twenty thousand.[20] The emigrant labour committee claimed that 'Hundreds, if not thousands [of Nyasaland Africans] were thought to enter the Union annually'. Migrants had varying experiences on doing so, with some reportedly able to enter without difficulty, others were known to cross by 'devious routes' at night: 'Hundreds apparently have been caught and imprisoned and then given contract labour or freedom to look for work'.[21] Some Nyasa migrants caught by the authorities were allowed to remain for six months if they paid 5/- for a pass. The South African Immigration policy in the 1930s seemed to be one of regulating rather than restricting immigration.[22]

[20] Report of the Committee appointed by His Excellency the Governor to Enquire into Emigrant Labour, 1935 (Zomba, 1936), p. 13.

[21] Ibid., p. 13.

[22] Andrew MacDonald, 'Colonial Trespassers in the Making of South Africa's International Borders, 1900 to c.1950', PhD Thesis, University of Cambridge (2012), p. 245.

Table 2.1 Comparison of Africans Employed in Southern Rhodesia, 1921–1936[a]

Country of origin	*1921*	*1926*	*1931*	*1936*
Southern Rhodesia	52,527	78,233	76,184	107,581
Portuguese East Africa	17,198	13,068	14,986	25,215
Northern Rhodesia	31,201	35,431	35,542	46,884
Nyasaland	44,702	43,020	49,487	70,362
Other Sources	1,688	2,218	2,983	2,440
Total Males	147,316	171,970	179,092	252,482

[a]Figures compiled by the Chief Native Commissioner for Southern Rhodesia and quoted in, J. C. Abraham, *Nyasaland Natives in the Union of South Africa and in Southern Rhodesia* (Zomba, 1937), p. 3

Like South Africa, Southern Rhodesia was also highly dependent upon foreign migrant labour (see Table 2.1). The continued viability of peasant agriculture in Mashonaland into the 1920s meant that new mining companies struggled to secure adequate labour supplies from within the colony. Again, Africans were acutely aware of the higher wage-earning opportunities across the Limpopo. Workers from Nyasaland, Portuguese East Africa, Northern Rhodesia and, to a lesser extent, Tanganyika and the Belgian Congo came to work on gold, asbestos, chrome and other mineral reefs in the settler colony, sometimes as a stepping-stone on their way to the Rand. In 1908, the Rhodesian Native Labour Bureau (RNLB), a parastatal organisation partially funded and backed by the British South Africa Company, was granted permission to recruit a thousand men from Nyasaland, following an agreement between both colonial authorities.[23] The agreement did not work out according to plan, however, as the organisation struggled to recruit the required numbers in part due to suspicions over contract labour and the association with forced labour.[24] RNLB recruiters would wait for Africans at the 'free' ferry crossing points along the Zambezi, offering food and transport for workers in return for

[23]McCracken, *A History of Malawi*, p. 86.

[24]The RNLB came under criticism from white commercial farmers in Southern Rhodesia who had difficulty securing enough labour because it was forcefully diverted to the mines. 'Rhodesia Native Labour Bureau', *Hansard* 23 November 1908.

Table 2.2 Africans in Wage-Earning Employment in Southern Rhodesia, 1921–1956[a]

Year	*Non-Indigenous*	*Indigenous*
1921	92,302	47,347
1926	93,737	78,233
1931	102,908	76,184
1936	144,901	107,581
1941	168,106	131,404
1946	202,412	160,932
1951	246,772	241,683
1956	310,000 *x*	300,000 *x*

x—provisional figures
[a]It is likely that these figures represent male migrants only. MNA 14239II Nyasaland Government Representative Salisbury 'Migrant Labour Legislation', Report from 1956

contracts.[25] By 1909 all recruitment from Nyasaland was banned, except for the construction of the Trans-Zambesia Railway.[26] This remained the policy of the colonial government until 1934. Despite the ban on contract recruitment, the numbers of people leaving Nyasaland continued to rise. By 1928, approximately two-thirds of Southern Rhodesia's work-force originated from outside its borders (see Table 2.2).[27] One-third of Southern Rhodesia's mine workers in 1934 were recorded to be from Nyasaland but Nyasas were known to prefer other types of work: 'The Nyasaland Native does not as a rule like mine work. It would appear that for every one employed on the mines four are employed in other work'.[28]

The southern African regional economy developed zones of high and low wages. Farms near the ports of entry in northern Mashonaland and

[25]'The free ferry service often only worked in exchange for the dreaded *chibaro* contract…', Charles Van Onselen, 'Black Workers in Central African History: A Critical Essay on the Historiography and Sociology of Rhodesia', *Journal of Southern African Studies*, 1, 2 (1975), p. 241.

[26]For a detailed account of the awkward relationship between the Southern Rhodesian and Nyasaland governments, from the early 1900s to the 1930s, see E. P. Makambe, 'The African Immigrant Factor in Southern Rhodesia, 1890–1930: The Origin and Influence of External Elements in a Colonial Setting', PhD Thesis University of York (1979), chapter 6.

[27]See R. L. Buell, *The Native Problem in Africa* (New York, 1928), p. 228; U. Weyl, *Labour Migration and Underdevelopment in Malawi: Late Nineteenth Century to the mid-1970s* (Masvingo, 1991), p. 50.

[28]Report of the Committee appointed by His Excellency the Governor to Enquire into Emigrant Labour, 1935 (Zomba, 1936), p. 14.

the northern Transvaal became known for their poor remuneration but provided a convenient stopping point for those intending to reach Salisbury or the Witwatersrand, and they often paid better salaries than the plantations in the south of Nyasaland. Poor wages in Southern Rhodesian mines made them less appealing to Shona and Ndebele men, who were acutely aware of the better opportunities further south and in the growing urban centres of Salisbury and Bulawayo. The Deputy Governor of Nyasaland wrote candidly about the competition for labour in the southern territories in the 1930s: 'Of course, the truth of the matter is that if Southern Rhodesia wishes to compete against the Rand on equal terms, she must improve her conditions of labour'.[29] The same was true, of course, for Nyasaland where the colonial government justified lower wages on the basis that it was an agricultural colony arguing that African labourers could not expect to receive the same wages as they might in industrial colonies. European missionaries and planters highlighted what they called the 'moral benefits' of work in an agricultural colony like Nyasaland, in contrast to towns like Johannesburg, Beira and Salisbury that offered 'inducements in vice and drink which were not found in agricultural country'.[30]

Not all Nyasa migrants went south for wage labour. Huge mineral deposits developed in the Belgian Congo and Tanganyika attracted increasing numbers of Nyasa men in the 1920s.[31] Consequently, flows of labour to the south were interrupted and competition for labour in central southern Africa intensified.[32] Labour migration to Katanga from Northern Rhodesia and parts of Nyasaland frustrated the British South Africa Company, which preferred to keep labour within British territories. A policy of 'containment' was intended to discourage migration

[29] MNA S1/174Ai/35 Letter from K. L. Hall, Nyasaland Deputy Governor to W. Ormsby-Gore, Secretary of State for the Colonies, 24 July 1936.

[30] A petition presented in 1900 by the British Central Africa Chamber of Commerce—representing secular planters of the Shire Highlands and Dr Alexander Heatherwick's Church of Scotland Mission—to Sir Alfred Sharp, Commissioner and Consul-General of British Central Africa, cited in Makambe, 'The African Immigrant Factor in Southern Rhodesia, 1890–1930', p. 574.

[31] Approximately 20,000 Nyasaland Africans were estimated to be working in Tanganyika in 1935 and numbers were expected to increase. MNA S1/174/35 'Committee to Investigate the Question of Labour Supplies', 22 August 1935.

[32] ZNA S235 The Rhodesian Native Labour Bureau, Salisbury 4 February 1925. This is mentioned in a draft speech by Mr D. Hawksley, managing director of the RNLB.

to the north.[33] Nevertheless, higher mortality rates in the Congolese mines worked in the favour of British colonial interests, and the mines of Southern Rhodesia and South Africa proved more popular with Nyasa migrants as a result. Southern Rhodesia experienced labour shortages in the 1930s when Northern Rhodesia began to expand its mining industry and migrants close to the Northern Rhodesia-Nyasaland border looked to the Copperbelt for employment, while many from Northern Rhodesia, who had previously worked in Southern Rhodesia, began to seek work closer to home.[34] Even so, the numbers of Nyasaland workers heading to Southern Rhodesia continued to grow, and colonial governments and industries attempting to direct labour to where it was needed most, continued to be frustrated (Map 2.2).

European Settlement and Taxation

European settlement was anticipated to bring economic development to the Nyasaland Protectorate. However, settler numbers remained small when compared with neighbouring Northern and Southern Rhodesia (see Table 2.3) and economic developments in some parts of the colony were barely seen. Scottish and English coffee planters were concentrated around the commercial centres of Blantyre and Zomba in the south; in the early days of the colony the interests of missionaries and new 'legitimate' European trading companies were sometimes hard to distinguish. The Colonial Office was determined to spend as little money as possible 'developing' the colony and the economic under-development of Nyasaland only discouraged further European settlement. Racial discrimination in government policy protected white interests in Nyasaland's industry and agriculture, and was in contradiction with Colonial Office proclamations of 'African paramountcy'. Nonetheless, this policy distinguished the 'northern territories' of Nyasaland and Northern Rhodesia from those, south of the Zambezi, and this distinction was fundamental in defining settler support and African antagonism towards proposals for 'closer association' or amalgamation, and later, federation between the Rhodesias and Nyasaland.

[33] Bill Paton, *Labour Export Policy in the Development of Southern Africa* (Harare, 1995) p. 75.

[34] Buell, *The Native Problem*, p. 228.

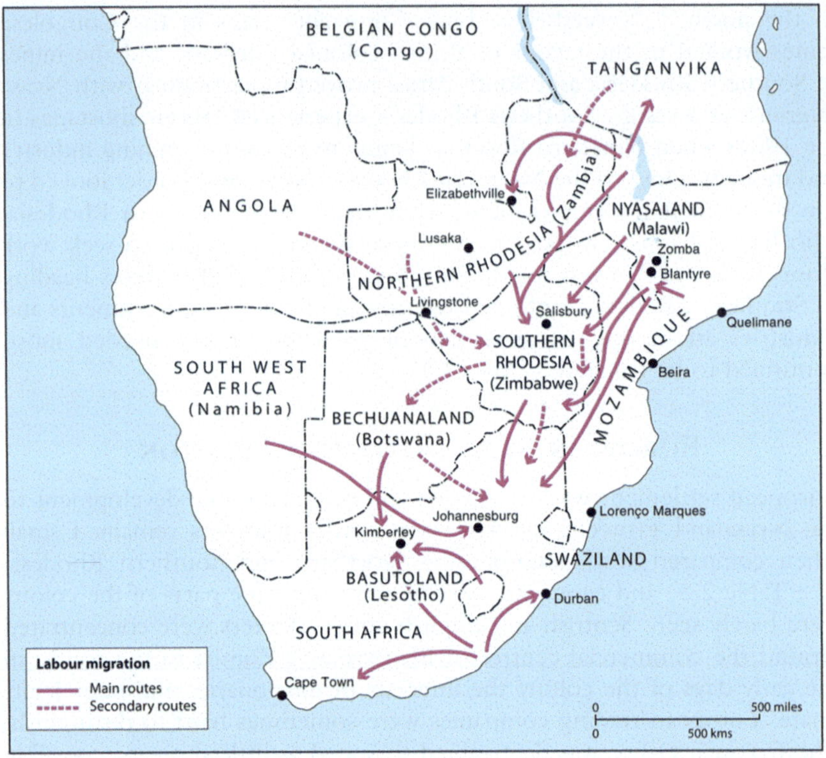

Map 2.2 Labour Migration Routes in Central and Southern Africa (*Source* This map is adapted from Van Onselen, *Chibaro*, p. 238)

Table 2.3 Population of Nyasaland at Census Dates, 1901–1956[a]

Census date	*Europeans*	*Coloured persons*	*Asians*	*Africans*	*Total population*
1901	314		706,000		706,314
1911	766	481		960,000	961,247
1921	1,486	563		1,175,000	1,180,000
1926	1,656	850		1,245,000	1,250,000
1931	1,975	1,591		1,545,000	1,550,000
1945	1,948	455	2,804	2,044,707	2,049,914
1956	6,732	1,199	8,504	2,570,000	2,590,000

[a] Both the African and total population figures are estimates. *Federation of Rhodesia and Nyasaland: Census Report, 1956* (Salisbury, 1956), p. 3

Most European plantations were established in the southern part of Nyasaland and the Northern Province was largely neglected in terms of agricultural and industrial development. Many came to refer to the sparsely populated region as 'the dead north'[35] and there was little sign of the colonial administration until after the District Administrative (Native) Ordinance of 1912. Hut tax was introduced in the north in 1896, four years later than the southern and central districts.[36] Labour shortages were acutely felt by the European planters in the south and tax in the north was meant to help resolve this. In practice, it proved to be an inefficient device, not because people were reluctant to go into wage labour, but because they chose where and when to go, on their own terms. Even prior to the introduction of hut tax, migrant workers in the north had begun to introduce cash to the local subsistence economy, alongside new commodities, such as soap, bicycles and sewing machines.[37] Wages earned from periods in Southern Rhodesia or South Africa could be reinvested in local communities, rather than spent solely on tax. Fishing was also a major source of income for families around the lakeshore and provided the means for many to pay their taxes. Under British South Africa Company rule in Southern and Northern Rhodesia, tax collection and labour coercion were especially harsh. District officers punished those unable to pay by burning down their huts or by imposing heavy fines and administrators demanded periods of compensatory labour for tax defaulters.[38] As such, it was common for men to resort to labour migration to meet their tax demands, although labour migration could also be a means of tax-avoidance. Taxation in Nyasaland was no less punitive.[39]

[35] See, for example, MNA S1/174AI/35 Report of the Committee to Enquire into Emigrant Labour from Nyasaland—preliminary observations from the 1935 Report by the Travers Lacey Committee.

[36] The exception was Northern Ngoniland, where taxation was not imposed until 1904 because of continued resistance from Ngoni chiefs to British rule. Robin Palmer, 'Johnston and Jameson: A Comparative Study in the Imposition of Colonial Rule', in Pachai (ed.), *The Early History of Malawi*, p. 306.

[37] J. Clyde Mitchell, *The Yao Village: A Study of the Social Structure of a Malawian People* (Manchester, 1954), pp. 19–20.

[38] Paton, *Labour Export Policy*, p. 75.

[39] A tax rebellion in Northern Ngoniland in 1907 prompted the authorities to burn villages, make arrests and issue beatings: Markku Hokkanen, *Medicine and Scottish Missionaries in the Northern Malawi Region, 1875–1930: Quests for Health in a Colonial Society* (New York, 2007), p. 73.

The Nyasaland Governor refuted the idea that the need to pay taxes was the main motivation for migration from the Protectorate:

> It may be asked, why do so many of our natives emigrate to Southern Rhodesia and South Africa? I have put this question to many, including missionaries and administrative officers of experience and they all reply that the chief reason now-a- days is that the young men of the emigrating tribes are brought up to the adventure of travel. It is becoming a tradition with them that they must go out and see the world, and they look forward to coming back and entertaining the village with their traveller's tales. I have never heard it seriously suggested that they cannot earn their tax in this country if they wish...[40]

The governor romanticised the 'tradition of migration', yet there was some truth in his comments—a tradition of migration was emerging. For some communities, travel had long been an important part of their identity. The Emigrant Labour Committee report in the mid-1930s described the Ngoni as 'wanderers' by nature and referred to 'the love of travel and desire for adventure' which characterised Nyasaland 'tribes'.[41] The hut tax of six shillings per annum introduced by Sir Harry Johnston in the 1890s undoubtedly persuaded more African men into waged employment away from home. But taxation also failed to resolve the problem of adequate labour supplies on the poorly paid plantations in the south of the colony where some still paid their workers in calico or other trade goods, rather than cash, which certainly did not help to raise the cash needed for tax. Labour migration to the Shire plantations was mostly seasonal and short term. Tonga and Tumbuka migrants coming from the north found work as domestic servants and gang foreman. Those with a mission education were able to work for the colonial administration as interpreters, messengers and police irregulars. Many of those who did work in the colony often stayed in European employment for a short period of one month or long enough to earn the required sum, before returning to their own fields. Labour was especially short in supply during the rainy season when Africans were busy planting their own crops at the same time as European

[40] MNA S2/4/31 'Government Labour Policy', Letter from the Governor Shenton Whitelegge Thomas to Secretary of State for the Colonies, 7 May 1931.

[41] Report of the Committee Appointed by His Excellency the Governor to Enquire into Emigrant Labour, 1935 (Zomba: Government Printer), p. 23.

planters were looking to extend their coffee fields.[42] After consultation with the planter community in 1900, a new labour incentive tax was devised. The tax reduced the amount payable by Africans if they could prove that they had worked for a European for a period of at least one month every year.

In the southern province, planters used a system of labour known as *ganyao* which entitled workers to accommodation and food in return for their labour.[43] The scheme was initially introduced to accommodate Lomwe migrants looking to settle in Mlanje and the surrounding districts, and tended to be a mutual agreement between Lomwe incomers and Yao chiefs. *Thangata* was a slightly different system used among the Mang'anja in the area, prior to the arrival of the European planters.[44] Formalised and corrupted by Europeans, the system forced tenants—those who settled on the estates—to work for their landlords for two months each year. Planters were regularly accused of withholding signatures from work certificates, forcing their tenants to work for prolonged periods. *Thangata* naturally became a source of violent clashes between Africans and the Nyasaland government, at different points throughout the colonial period, culminating in massive protests during the early federation years. Nonetheless, Europeans continued to use the system to secure labour in the Shire Highlands, despite strong criticism from Africans and missionaries that it was 'a crude method of exploitation'.[45] *Thangata* also provided a further push factor for labour migration outside of Nyasaland, as men would escape beyond the borders in an effort to avoid the excessive demands of the system. Some temporarily crossed the border into

[42] White, *Magomero: Portrait of an African Village*, p. 86.

[43] The name *ganyao* arrived with immigrants from Portuguese East Africa and is based on the Portuguese term meaning 'bonus'. On the meaning and history of *ganyao* (sometimes spelt *ganyu*) see White, *Magomero*, p. 88; Deborah F. Bryceson, 'Ganyu in Malawi: Transformation of Local Labour Relation Under Famine and HIV/AIDS Duress', in J. Abbink (ed.), *Fractures and Reconnections: Civic Action and the Redefinition of African Political and Economic Spaces* (Leiden, 2012), pp. 37–59.

[44] *Thangata* means 'help' among the Mang'anja people in the south. It was an old system used by chiefs when labour was needed to complete a task in their village. For a good description of how *thangata* used to work prior to its corruption by the European planters see: White, *Magomera*, pp. 89–91.

[45] B. S. Krishnamurthy, 'Economic Policy, Land and Labour in Nyasaland, 1890–1914', in Pachai (ed.), *The Early History of Malawi* (London, 1974), p. 391.

Mozambique, while others sought more permanent employment in the economies further south.[46]

African cash crop production in Nyasaland was considered by the British administration from the early 1900s. African agriculture seemed a viable alternative to large scale migrant labour at a time when there was increased demand for cotton in Britain. Tobacco and cotton cultivation were encouraged among Africans in Port Herald and Karonga and supported by the British Cotton growing Association which formed in 1911. In contrast, cash cropping was generally discouraged in the areas around Zomba and Blantyre, where European settlers were short of labour. Africans in the Lower Shire and Mlanje districts were able to grow small quantities of cotton for tax purposes, but it was difficult to acquire enough land to produce any significant quantities of cash crops for export.[47] The problem had first been raised on the Legislative Council in 1910, following warnings from missionaries and colonial administrators that land shortages and alienation created great dissatisfaction among the African population.[48]

The First World War and the global depression exacerbated the land and labour situation in the Southern Province. The cotton industry went into decline with falling demand from Britain in the 1920s and by the 1940s cotton was only produced in Nyasaland on a small scale and solely by Africans.[49] Generally, there was little scope for Africans to produce cash crops and Lomwe immigration, conveniently for the planters, allowed local wages to be reduced even further. Without access to land, Lomwe migrants had no option but to accept the terms and conditions offered to them on arrival. Insecurity of tenure was a real threat to Lomwe residents; they were trapped on European plantations, subjected to the *thangata* system and women were liable to eviction if their husbands sought work elsewhere.[50] For Yao and Mang'anja men from Fort Johnston, Blantyre and the Lower Shire, Southern Rhodesia became by far the better option

[46] Melvin E. Page, *The Chiwaya War: Malawians and the First World War* (Oxford, 2000), pp. 5–6.

[47] For more on land shortages in the Southern Province, see Krishnamurthy, 'Economic Policy, Land and Labour, 1890–1914', pp. 384–404.

[48] Ibid., p. 387.

[49] Mandala, *Work and Control*.

[50] McCracken, 'British Central Africa', pp. 604, 609.

for wage labour, and they left in greater numbers than ever before in the 1930s (see Table 2.4).

In the late 1920s, the government proposed the expansion of an African grown tobacco industry in the Northern and Central Provinces of Nyasaland.[51] Lilongwe produced more tobacco than any other district and had the most fertile soil in the region, but by the 1950s it had become one of the largest migrant sending districts in the Central Province. Most district officials in Nyasaland fully supported the development of small-scale peasant production, but the position of the state on settler and African peasant interests was ambiguous. Ncheu was the most densely populated district of the central region and suffered from extreme land overuse and soil deterioration. Ngoni and Chewa migrants again sought cash earning opportunities across the border. The 1930s saw a brief slump in the migration rate due to the economic depression. Thousands of Africans were repatriated and many more deterred from going south following reports of work shortages at key labour centres.[52] Some of the more successful migrants returned and were able to secure enough land (five acres or more) to become prosperous farmers. Others went back to work on the land as tenants.[53] By 1935 the labour market in the south had largely settled following the depression.[54]

Situated between German East Africa (Tanganyika) to the north, and with major British interests in Southern Rhodesia to the south, Nyasaland experienced significant upheaval during the First World War. Wage workers were engaged in recruitment as carriers (*tengatenga*) and passes to seek work outside of the colony were withheld in several districts due to wartime military requirements.[55] The First World War came to be known as the 'War of *Thangata*', reflecting frustrations over excessive demands

[51] John McCracken, 'Peasants, Planters and the Colonial State: The Impact of the Native Tobacco Board in the Central Province of Malawi', *Journal of Southern African Studies*, 9, 2 (1983), pp. 172–192.

[52] Rev Dr W. Y. Turner, 'A Visit to Nyasaland Natives', *Central Africa: News and Views*, 1, 1 (July 1935), p. 17.

[53] McCracken, 'Peasants and Planters', p. 185.

[54] MNA S2/4ii/31, 'Nyasaland Treasury Minutes', 5 December 1934 and February 1935.

[55] This was usually the case in districts with the highest levels of out-migration, including: Ncheu, Dedza, Lilongwe, Fort Manning, Dowa, and West Nyasa District. MNA S21/2/1/7 'Passports', 28 November 1942.

Table 2.4 Nyasaland African Absentees, before and after 1939[a]

	Left before September 1939		*Left after September 1939*		*Serving in forces*	*Total Absent From the Protectorate*			*Absent working or visiting other districts in the Protectorate*		
	M	*F*	*M*	*F*	*M*	*M*	*F*	*Both sexes*	*M*	*F*	*Both sexes*
Karonga	790	105	3,283	453	599	4,672	558	5,230	398	153	551
Chinteche	4,533	474	5,788	910	429	10,750	1,384	12,134	292	142	434
Mzimba	1,928	250	11,319	607	1,434	14,681	857	15,538	948	401	1,349
Total Northern Province	7,251	829	20,390	1,970	2,462	30,103	2,799	32,902	1,638	696	2,334
Kasungu	2,124	313	1,881	153	516	4,521	466	4,987	1,482	973	2,455
Dowa	923	58	4,050	123	658	5,631	181	5,812	1,062	552	1,614
KotaKota	1,087	170	2,900	249	624	4,611	419	5,030	1,339	702	2,041
Fort Manning	1,944	648	1,680	620	894	4,518	1,268	5,786	909	659	1,568
Lilongwe	2,332	118	4,449	111	1,139	7,920	229	8,149	386	242	628
Dedza	2,050	118	5,498	198	1,367	8,915	316	9,231	2,287	977	3,264
Ncheu	1,451	85	4,925	443	1,053	7,429	528	7,957	3,079	1,754	4,833
Total Central Province	11,911	1,510	25,383	1,897	6,251	43,545	3,407	46,952	10,544	5,859	16,403
Fort Johnston	2,375	295	5,149	866	1,382	8,906	1,161	10,067	4,075	1,165	5,240
Liwonde	812	72	1,668	168	2,236	4,716	240	4,956	698	152	850
Zomba	1,203	161	1,565	208	5,843	8,611	369	8,980	2,062	643	2,705
Blantyre	911	140	2,161	301	1,409	4,481	441	4,922	1,825	797	2,622
Neno	398	31	926	79	262	1,586	110	1,969	863	356	1,219
Chikwawa	490	8	1,348	50	253	2,091	58	2,149	361	110	471
Chiradzulu	800	137	2,449	262	1,504	4,753	399	5,152	2,558	1,105	3,663
Cholo	524	75	1,853	191	701	3,078	266	3,344	2,448	719	3,167

	Left before September 1939		*Left after September 1939*		*Serving in forces*	*Total Absent From the Protectorate*			*Absent working or visiting other districts in the Protectorate*		
	M	*F*	*M*	*F*	*M*	*M*	*F*	*Both sexes*	*M*	*F*	*Both sexes*
Mlanje	740	2	4,066	113	2,380	7,186	115	7,301	3,812	1,286	5,098
Port Herald	1,457	12	2,794	69	553	4,804	81	4,885	1,675	778	2,453
Total Southern Province	9,710	933	23,979	2,307	16,523	50,212	3,240	53,452	20,377	7,111	27,488
Grand Total	28,872	3,272	69,752	6,174	25,236	123,860	9,446	133,306	32,559	13,666	46,225

[a] *Nyasaland Protectorate Census Report, 1945* (Zomba, 1945)

for African labour as well as food and resources. It also brought to the surface some of the tensions of early colonial rule as Africans grappled to understand why they should sacrifice so much for the white man's cause.[56] Grievances over the demands of the First World War added to pre-existing hardships. Nowhere was this expressed more clearly than in John Chilembwe's famous letter to the *Nyasaland Times*, published in 1914.[57] As the number of casualties increased, greater pressure was felt on Nyasaland communities and many fled to Southern Rhodesia to avoid recruitment.[58] The First World War also interrupted government plans to curb migration levels from the Protectorate. Missionaries later highlighted again the moral and social consequences of widespread male absence from villages, pointing to the deterioration of family life, and the dangerous influence of educated and 'detribalised natives' who worked in the industrial south, and later returned to Nyasaland frustrated by the lack of opportunities, and politicised through their contact with cosmopolitan communities in the south. By the 1930s, pressure from planters and missionaries was again mounting:

> The question of emigration overshadows and is ultimately connected with almost every problem in the district, affecting especially such matters as agriculture, education, health, labour and revenue. Many of the emigrants never return, whilst others do so only after very long intervals of absence.[59]

Annual reports from 1929 to 1935 showed that between 800 and 1,000 passes were issued each year in the north, and it was estimated that close to 5,000 were absent at any one time. Many left without reporting to district officials.[60] In 1934, more than eighty per cent of Nyasaland's labour migrants originated from the northern region, mainly from

[56] Melvin Page, 'The War of Thangata: Nyasaland and the East African Campaign, 1914–1918', *Journal of African History*, 19, 1 (1978), pp. 87–100.

[57] The letter is reproduced in full in George Shepperson and Thomas Price, *Independent African: John Chilembwe and the Origins, Setting and Significance of the Nyasaland Native Rising of 1915* (Edinburgh, 1958), pp. 234–235.

[58] Van Onselen, *Chibaro*, p. 122.

[59] MNA NNC 3/1/4 Annual Reports for Chinteche, West Nyasa District, Report for the year ending 31 December 1929.

[60] MNA NNC 3/1/4 'Annual Reports', Chinteche, West Nyasa District, 1931.

Chinteche and Mzimba Districts.[61] District reports called for stronger measures to be taken by the Colonial Office and Nyasaland government. The Provincial Commissioner for Nkhata Bay wrote to the Governor Thomas in 1930: 'I must lay stress on the great loss sustained by Nyasaland, particularly in the Northern parts, through native emigration'.[62] Hut tax was difficult to collect owing to absenteeism, and Tonga, Tumbuka and Ngoni men were especially noted for their absence.[63] The government finally heeded to concerns in 1934 and commissioned the Emigrant Labour Committee to investigate 'the conditions now prevailing with regard to the exodus of natives from the Protectorate for work outside, the effect on village life and the probable future effect on the Protectorate'.[64]

Recruitment and Independent Migration: *Mthandizi*, *Wenela* and the *Madobadoba*[65]

The 1930s ushered in a new era of inter-territorial 'bureaucratic bargaining' over migrant labour in the region. Labour agreements were drawn up between colonial governments essentially concerned with six key areas: identification and control of migrant workers; repatriation of workers after an agreed period; maintenance of families and dependents in the absence of workers; deferred payment systems; adequate medical facilities, housing and 'feeding' (*en route* and at the workplace); and the provision of migrant labour inspectorate staff, or labour bureaux. Policies were revised as regional and territorial circumstances changed during wartime

[61] Weyl, *Labour Migration and Underdevelopment in Malawi*, p. 45.

[62] MNA S2/4/31 Letter from the Provincial Commissioner, Nkhata Bay, Nyasaland 23 October 1930.

[63] Henga and Ngonde resided in the most northern districts of Nyasaland, Karonga and Mzimba. They were more likely than any other ethnic group to migrate to Tanganyika than the south because of the proximity of the border.

[64] Report of the Committee appointed by His Excellency the Governor to Enquire into Emigrant Labour, 1935 (Zomba, 1936), p. 5.

[65] *Mthandizi* was the local name in Nyasaland for the Rhodesian Native Labour Supply Company (RNLSC). *Wenela* was the local name for the Witwatersrand Native Labour Association. The *madobadoba* were independent and unofficial recruiters of labour—see glossary for a fuller explanation of these terms.

or in light of domestic issues, such as famine or drought.[66] The main aim of the colonial governments was to control the flow of labour towards the desired locations and prevent as far as possible any increase in independent (*selufu*) or 'clandestine' migration.[67] A pass system to regulate labour migration had first been introduced in Nyasaland under the Native Labour Ordinance in 1894.[68] The idea was to supervise emigration through registers and passes issued to independent migrants by the district authorities. This became more practical following the Native Authorities Ordinance in 1912, which returned a degree of authority to the 'traditional' village headmen and chiefs.[69] The early pass system largely failed as most people leaving simply ignored the regulations. Moreover, the administrative resources to police such a system were too meagre. But in the mid-1930s the system was replaced with one where potential migrants were required to get passes from their village headman before collecting identity certificates from the District Office at the nearest Boma (administration centre). Village headmen sometimes demanded gifts (or bribes) or else refused to cooperate over personal grievances. Migrants promised gifts of clothes or other goods on their return in order to get their endorsement.[70]

After decades the ban on contract labour was lifted and recruitment rights for the mines in South Africa and Southern Rhodesia were reinstated in 1935. That same year the London and Blantyre Supply

[66] Paton, *Labour Export Policy*, p.85. Agreements were reached in 1936 in Salisbury and Johannesburg.

[67] On the notion of *selufu* migration, see Harvey Chioda Banda, 'The Dynamics of Labour Migration from Northern Malawi to South Africa since 1974', PhD Thesis, University of the Witwatersrand (2019).

[68] Robin Palmer, 'Johnston and Jameson: a comparative study in the imposition of colonial rule', in *The Early History of Malawi*, p. 309.

[69] Chiefs and headmen played a part in the collection of taxes and general administration. In the 1920s the British looked to introduce a more formal system of indirect rule and in 1924 the District Administration Native Ordinance was passed strengthening the African role in controlling village society. In 1933 a full system of Indirect Rule was established with the Native Authorities and the Native Court Ordinances. See L. Vail and L. White, 'Tribalism in the Political History of Malawi', in Vail (ed.), *The Creation of Tribalism*, pp. 158–159.

[70] M. M. J. Sakala, 'The Experiences of Ex-Migrant Workers in Mzimba District, 1956–2006', History Seminar Paper, Mzuzu University (2006); Ireen Mudeka, 'Gendered Exclusion and Contestation: Malawian Women's Migration and Work in Colonial Harare, Zimbabwe, 1930s to 1963', *African Economic History*, 44 (2016), pp. 18–43.

Company was granted a permit to recruit workers from the Northern Province for employment on farms in the Rhodesias and the Union of South Africa.[71] The first formal 'tripartite agreement' (hereafter 'the Salisbury Agreement') was signed between Northern and Southern Rhodesia and Nyasaland in 1936 and later that year an agreement was reached between Nyasaland and the Union of South Africa ('the Johannesburg Agreement'). In 1942 a revised agreement further tightened measures to prevent independent migration and a 'two-year clause' was introduced, which meant 'emigrant natives [are required] to return to their homes after working for an economic period which should not exceed two years...after two years they should be repatriated and should not be allowed re-entry into the territory of employment until a further period of six months has elapsed.' [72] Exceptions were made for those who had found specialised employment of a permanent nature, or who had taken their wives and families with them (see Chapter 3). The revised agreement remained in place until March 1947 when a new accord was signed by representatives of the Central African Council in Lusaka.[73]

Under the new inter-territorial agreement, the Southern Rhodesian authorities began to demand passes at the border. Southern Rhodesia had agreed to establish a (Foreign) Migrant Labour Department to supervise placement and repatriation of Nyasaland workers, and collection of taxes and voluntary deferred pay.[74] The Native Registration Act in Southern Rhodesia encouraged a more effective monitoring of migrants entering the colony and the Nyasaland Labour Office placed their own government representatives in Salisbury to help control and supervise migrants entering the colony and their working conditions. Nyasa migrants hated pass laws. They were reminiscent of the racist legislation and regulations they had to endure in South Africa and Southern Rhodesia and they resented these controls being forced upon them in Nyasaland.[75] Just as in

[71] MNA S1/174/35, 'Committee to Investigate the Question of Labour Supplies', 27 June 1935.

[72] MNA S21/2/1/4, 'Migrant Native Labour', Provisional Revised Agreement between the Governments of Southern Rhodesia, Northern Rhodesia and Nyasaland, 1942.

[73] Rhodes House Library (RHL), MSS.Afr.S.997 Hoole Papers, Labour Department, 'Memorandum on the Labour Migration from Nyasaland to other Territories in Africa', Acting Labour Commissioner, Zomba, 26 October 1948.

[74] Paton, *Labour Export Policy*, p. 36.

[75] Boeder, *Malawians Abroad*, p. 212.

colonial and later apartheid South Africa, Nyasa men and women found numerous ways to subvert the pass laws and other government controls over their movement. Mr Chimayo described how, 'You could stay for two years and then you were supposed to leave but you used to be able to find someone to endorse your stay. You could always find a way to get a stamp in your book'.[76] Through forgery of documents or simply travelling back across the border from Southern Rhodesia to Portuguese East Africa, one could re-enter under the identity of a Mozambican.[77]

The idea behind the inter-territorial labour agreements was to create a controlled system of circulatory labour migration to enable the administration to meet their tax demands, while preventing the burden falling on the state of having to support deserted wives and children. The struggling administration benefitted from the money brought into the protectorate from migrant remittances and fees from large scale recruitment agencies. Recruitment, the government argued, would allow for tighter control over labour migration, something the earlier pass system had failed to do. After the ban was lifted the number of contracts rose sharply each year reaching more than 8,000 by 1940. In 1955, 12,407 contract workers were signed up in Nyasaland. The figure peaked in 1970 with 78,492 Malawians employed through labour recruitment, although independent migration rates were thought to be even higher.[78] In reality, the Nyasaland government could never prevent independent migration as it lacked the resources to patrol the territory's borders and prevent men and women from leaving on their own terms.

The largest labour recruitment company operating in Nyasaland was the Rhodesia Native Labour Supply Commission (RNLSC), known locally in Nyasaland as *Mthandizi* (helper).[79] The other major company was the Witwatersrand Native Labour Association (WNLA) or *Wenela*. Tonga, Tumbuka and Ngoni men from the north went to great lengths to avoid recruitment agents and contracts. Recruitment was more successful

[76] Interview with Mr Chimayo, CCAP Harare Synod, August 2009.

[77] MNA Transmittal files 14239 Secretariat 'Nyasaland Government Representative, Salisbury-Labour Inspection, 1957.' This issue is discussed further in Chapter 4.

[78] Paton, *Labour Export Policy*, p. 27. Jonathan Crush, 'Migrations Past: An Historical Overview of Cross-Border Movement in Southern Africa', in D. A. McDonald (ed.), *On Borders: Perspectives on Cross-Border Migration in Southern Africa* (New York, 2000), p. 15.

[79] The RNLSC later replaced the RNLB after it ceased operations in 1933.

among the Ngoni in Mzimba District where there were more people and even fewer local employment opportunities than other northern districts. Africans throughout the territory were usually highly suspicious of any contract work, regarding it as *chibalo* (slave or forced labour) and the government was aware of this:

> The majority of Nyasaland natives who live in districts from which migration has been prevalent for some years are well aware of the activities of recruiters and are usually strongly averse to becoming 'chibalo' a term of opprobrium originally denoting 'forced labour' and now indiscriminately applied to all recruited or attested labour. The result of this aversion is that of the immigrants attested by recruiters, the majority are from tribes unaccustomed to emigration such as anguru [Lomwe] or amanganja from the Lower Shire districts or consist of those who lack the initiative or physical strength to proceed any further on their own.[80]

Poorer men with less resources signed labour contracts. Contract workers were bound by fixed periods of service and many deserted on arrival or before the expiration of their contracts if they were unhappy with pay or working conditions. News spread through migrant networks about which mines or farms to avoid due to the harshest conditions or cruellest managers. Those unfortunate to end up in a bad workplace wrote letters home warning others from their village.[81] One note found pinned to a tree in 1925 along a well-trodden labour route to Southern Rhodesia read:

> Dear Brothers, I have gone but I want to tell you one word; that you must not agree if any 'chibalo' or anybody calls you to his hut to eat food. You had better refuse – or take meat, do not receive it [sic]. I tell you

[80] MNA Report of the Nyasaland Labour Department, 1937, p. 2. *Chibaro* or *chibalo* was a widely used term across southern Africa to describe contract, forced or migrant labour. For a discussion, see Makambe, 'The African Immigrant Factor in Southern Rhodesia, 1890–1930: The Origin and Influence of External Elements in a Colonial Setting', PhD Thesis, University of York (1979), chapter 6 and Van Onselen, *Chibaro*.

[81] Bryson Nkhoma, 'The Competition for Malawian Labour: Wenela and Mthandizi in Ntcheu District, 1935–1956', MA History Dissertation, Chancellor's College, University of Malawi (1995), p. 26.

who wants to hear he can hear, and if you do not heed you will see. I am Jabez.[82]

Warnings were issued for migrants to avoid farms or mines because of poor quality mealie meal and violent bosses who withheld wages. Contracts were deserted and workers occasionally walked out in groups in protest. Work certificates that enabled migrants to be signed off from their contracts could be forged before they had officially expired.[83] These measures gave labourers greater freedom and control within the oppressive recruitment system.

Ultimately, *Mthandizi* and *Wenela* relied heavily upon strong networks of local agents, including village headmen and chiefs, to fulfil their quotas. In 1947 *Mthandizi* began to recruit workers from centres in Ncheu and Dedza districts in the Central Province, and from Fort Johnston in the south. Similarly, the WNLA (*Wenela*) set up depots in Dedza, Lilongwe, Salima, Fort Manning, Dowa and Mzimba, competing with *Mthandizi* for workers.[84] The RNLSC was the main recruiter of labour for the building of the Kariba Dam in 1956 and signed up more than 2,000 workers from southern and central Nyasaland.[85] The organisation and its treatment of contracted labour was heavily criticised by the Nyasaland African Congress and recruits deserted their contracts amidst complaints of poor conditions of service.[86] Henceforth the RNLSC struggled to improve its reputation and resorted to sending representatives around villages with loud speakers, offering gifts, such as t-shirts, glasses, sugar and soap to enlisted recruits, and then taking them in their cars to the

[82]ZNA S138/22 Chief Native Commissioner Files, 'Native Movements, 1923–26', 22 April 1925.

[83]Nyasa Africans were reported to bleach their blue *situpa* (identity certificate), so that it looked like the certificate of an indigenous African. This way, migrants could avoid some of the restrictions of the inter-territorial labour agreements, such as the system of deferred payment, and the two-year return policy.

[84]Nkhoma, 'The Competition for Malawian Labour', p. 13.

[85]MNA IDCNE 1/7/2 Correspondence—Labour—RNLSC (Ncheu) January 1956.

[86]Southern Rhodesia had revived the national recruitment agency during WW2 when they practised a policy of forced labour for a time due to extreme wartime shortages of farm workers. B. Rutherford, 'Another Side to Rural Zimbabwe: Social Constructs and the Administration of Farm Workers in Urungwe District, 1940s', *Journal of Southern African Studies*, 23, 1 (1997), pp. 107–126.

registration centres.[87] Recruitment agents even entered schools in search of young boys to sign up for contracts. Workers were offered money to go home for short holidays, in order to see their families and to recruit their friends and relatives, returning with them to Southern Rhodesia.[88] Recruitment was made more attractive in the 1950s when the WNLA introduced flights from Chileka Airport in Blantyre because of the prestige associated with air travel. It was not until a tragic plane crash in Francistown, Botswana in 1974, carrying 74 Malawian migrant workers, that labour recruitment was eventually banned in independent Malawi.[89]

With the new era of inter-territorial regulation of migrant labour, Nyasa men and women had to be more creative in finding ways to evade restrictions on their movement. In addition to the threat of fines and repatriation if caught outside the colony without a pass, people were vulnerable to being picked up by illegal or private recruiters who continued to target migrants along the way to labour centres either by force or through bribery. Shady figures waited at ports of entry in Sipolilo, Umtali, Darwin, Shamva, Mtoko and Mrewa and deliberately wore uniforms resembling native police and messengers to give a look of authority and authenticity.[90] Migrants who left Nyasaland without permission often did so with the help of figures known as *madobadoba*. Jenny Blande went to Southern Rhodesia in the 1950s to follow her husband recalled her journey to meet him on a tobacco farm in Darwendale in Mashonaland:

> There were people called *madobidobi* and they would come to Malawi looking for people to work for them. They came to my village and me and my friend and my three children went with them. We travelled in their truck and we sometimes slept along by streams. We passed through Mozambique, then Nyamapanda, then Mtoko. After Mtoko we met with other *adobidobi* and I volunteered to go to the farm.[91]

Although people were wary of the *madobadoba* they were critical in enabling some people to move without the required documentation.

[87] Bryson Nkoma, 'The Competition for Malawian Labour', pp. 19–20.

[88] Ibid., p. 19.

[89] See Wiseman C. Chirwa, 'The Malawi Government and South African Labour Recruiters, 1974–92', *Journal of Modern African Studies*, 34, 4 (1996), pp. 623–642.

[90] MNA Report of the Nyasaland Labour Department, 1937.

[91] Interview with Jenny Blande, Harare, June 2008.

Daniel Likhobwe left Nyasaland for Southern Rhodesia with the plan to find work in Salisbury. Daniel was from Cholo District in the south where his Lomwe family had settled after fleeing Mozambique in the early 1900s. Daniel left school in 1941 and went to join his friends who had written to him from Salisbury where there was 'lots of money to be earned'. Aware of the dangers that could be encountered on the journey, Daniel travelled with several companions. On their way they were caught by recruiters:

> When I went there, it was me and my two friends...we were caught by the *adobadobi* (*Anandidoba madobadoba*). They duped us. They took us somewhere and made us work for them, it was *chibalo*. We worked for them for a year. They just take people and they make you work for them for a period of time, after that I went to work at the hotel in Salisbury.[92]

Daniel had been warned about the *madobadoba* but struggled to avoid them, especially when they needed help with transport or finding work. Johani Jobson claimed that the *Madobdoba* were 'white Rhodesians who tricked Malawians' by offering them food and promises of employment, before taking people to exploitative farms where they might not be paid for six months or more. 'We were warned of this when we were still in Malawi, so we were careful'.[93] Fully aware of the risks they faced in travelling across borders to find work, Nyasa men and women continued to leave independently of labour recruiters.

Migrant Journeys

Travel to the labour markets could be hazardous due to dangerous wildlife and there were significant risks in passing through Tete Province in Mozambique. It was safest for migrants to travel together in groups known as *ulendos* which helped to safeguard against attacks by 'highwaymen' or coercion into labour by Portuguese *capitãos*.[94] Village headman

[92] Interview with Daniel Likhobwe, Thyolo District, February 2008.

[93] Interview with Johani Jobson, Harare, May 2008.

[94] *Ulendo* translates from Chichewa as 'journey'. For more on *Ulendos* and early encounters with the Portuguese, see E. P. Makambe, 'The Nyasaland African Labour *Ulendos* to Southern Rhodesia and the Problem of the African "Highwaymen", 1903–1923: A Study in the Limitations of Early Independent Labour Migration', *African*

would occasionally accompany larger groups of labour migrants. Those who made it safely as far as northern Mashonaland could easily find employment on white settler farms. Better resourced *ulendos* with good supplies of food and blankets would travel further on to Salisbury, Bulawayo, or even Johannesburg. The arrival of one large *ulendo* was noted in the local Southern Rhodesian press: 'A further gang of about fifty native labourers from Nyasaland arrived in town on Friday morning, as usual chanting their weird songs and brandishing sundry sticks and knobkerries…'[95] Migrant men and women worked on farms in Mashonaland *en route* to towns and cities or farms and mines in South Africa. It was common to work several different jobs, saving up money and provisions along the way, before continuing the journey further south. Certain routes were more frequently travelled than others: migrants from the north and north eastern districts of Nyasaland took the train from Salima to the south, via Balaka and Blantyre (see Map 1.1). A few went on foot to cross the border at Fort Jameson and from there they could find transport to Sinoia in Southern Rhodesia. Others went via Chirmunda, taking the Nsusa ferry crossing over the Zambezi and entering through Mozambique. Free motor transport—the *Ulere* service—was provided by the Southern Rhodesian government and Africans from north and western districts, including Lilongwe and Dedza, made good use of the service once in Southern Rhodesia. Migrants from other parts of Nyasaland took the *Ulere* trucks all the way from Blantyre to Salisbury, via Tete. *Ulere* was often viewed with suspicion, as the government officer explained:

> Nyasaland natives love to be free agents and many think that if they travel by the free services provided by the Southern Rhodesian Government they will be under some obligation when they reach their destinations…so [they] prefer to make their own way down.[96]

Affairs, 79, 317 (2008), pp. 548–566. *Capitãos* refers to African 'boss-boys', or overseers of African labour. In this case, the *capitãos* were employed by the Portuguese authorities as recruiters of labour. See glossary.

[95] *Rhodesia Herald*, 2 September 1910—Quoted in Charles Van Onselen, *Chibaro*, p. 120.

[96] MNA Transmittal files, LAB 9/4 'Revised Tripartite Labour Agreement', The Labour Commissioner, Zomba, 3 July 1942.

By the 1930s, more than half of the migrants leaving Nyasaland were thought to travel to Southern Rhodesia on foot. The majority could not afford the railway while others distrusted the transport provisions provided by territorial governments.[97] Migrants from the Lower Shire, Blantyre, Chiradzulu and Chikwawa went on foot to either the Katsanya or the Msenangwa ferry crossings of the Zambezi and some joined the *Ulere* at Changara in Tete province. From the southern districts many walked across the Zambezi Bridge and south through Mozambique to Messina.[98] 'Foot travellers' preferred the old village pathways to the 'modern highways' under construction.[99] Varying routes was strategic; it helped to avoid thieves waiting for returnees carrying money and goods back home. Covering such large distances on foot was intense and people often arrived in Southern Rhodesia and South Africa in extremely poor health. The Nyasaland Labour Commissioner described a scene as he drove from Salisbury to Zomba in the early 1940s, 'I met gang after gang of natives, carrying with them a little food, some of them very foot-sore and doing long marches without water' (Image 2.1).[100]

The Nyasaland government worked closely with the Portuguese and the Southern Rhodesian governments, providing shelters and facilities, in an attempt to improve the health of migrant workers when they arrived at their destinations.[101] In the 1920s, Southern Rhodesia had established a sub-department under the Chief Native Commissioner to supervise facilities for the passage of 'northern natives'. Shelters and rest camps were constructed along frequently travelled routes, where migrants could find food, water, latrines and basic medical facilities. In 1927, around seventy shelters were constructed along the established labour routes and fifty more were built in the 1940s, following recommendations from the Emigrant Labour Committee. Chiefs and headmen sometimes took a

[97] U. Weyl, *Labour Migration and Underdevelopment*, p. 52.

[98] MNA Transmittal files, LAB 9/4 'Labour Agreements', Memorandum by Acting Labour Commissioner, 15 January 1942.

[99] MNA Transmittal files, LAB 9/4 'Revised Tripartite Labour Agreement', 15 January 1942.

[100] MNA Transmittal files, LAB 9/4 Misc. files. Labour Commissioner to the Chief Secretary, Zomba, 25 June 1942.

[101] MNA Transmittal files, LAB 9/4 Labour Commissioner to the Chief Secretary, Zomba, 25 June 1942.

Image 2.1 'Travellers' from the Margaret Read Collection (MR/F/42/01, 'Travellers', Margaret Read Collection, Institute of Education Archives, UCL. Used with permission)

hand in providing for travellers to the south, but often only when it was in their interests to do so.[102]

Migration patterns from Nyasaland changed in the 1940s. While previously, migrants had mostly originated from the north, several factors gradually combined to push more men from the south of Nyasaland to look for work beyond the borders (see Table 2.4). The population of the Southern Province grew at an astonishing rate in the early twentieth century. Lomwe migrants from Mozambique were accused of causing 'incalculable harm' to the land and replacing local labour on the estates.[103] However, it was not so much the scale of Lomwe immigration that forced Nyasaland Africans to leave. Real pressures were created by the European plantations and the colonial regime. People were simply in search of a better deal elsewhere. The Lomwe were the immigrant scapegoats of the time, held to blame for the structural inadequacies of the Nyasaland economy. Lomwe men like Daniel Likhobwe, whose families had barely settled in Nyasaland for a generation, began to look to the economies of the south for better opportunities.

Conclusion

This chapter has provided an overview of early labour migration from colonial Malawi and the transformation of migration patterns and labour controls from the early 1900s to the mid-1930s. Migration from the northern region of Nyasaland was much greater than the rest of the colony, until the 1940s when larger numbers came from the southern and central regions. Many of the earliest migrants to leave Nyasaland were mission-educated and able to secure better paid employment outside of the colony. Remittances and money earned through labour migration was often reinvested in home villages and the consequences were not always as dire as the missionaries and European settlers suggested. This will be explored in the next chapter. Migrants from Nyasaland were often absent from home for longer periods than other labour migrants around the region, in part because of the longer distances they travelled. Importantly, not all Nyasaland labour migration was circular. A significant number of

[102] MNA Transmittal files, LAB 9/4 Labour Commissioner to the Chief Secretary, Zomba, 15 January 1942.

[103] MNA S1/174Ai/35 Native Welfare Committee Minutes, 11 May 1936.

people remained in Southern Rhodesia and became *machona*. Some men migrated with their wives and others were later joined by their families, or they married and raised new families away from Nyasaland.

The circular system that characterised migration elsewhere in the region came to account for more Nyasa migration after the 1930s. Prior to this, and subsequently still, independent migrants left the territory of their own free will without contracts, registration certificates or passes, and with no intentions of working in the mines of South Africa and Southern Rhodesia. These migrant experiences will be explored in more detail in the subsequent chapters.

CHAPTER 3

Gender, Class and Migration

Bishop Guilleme was an experienced Catholic missionary from the order of the White Fathers (established in Nyasaland from 1889) who spent more than thirty years living and working in the protectorate. He described the perceived effects of emigration on Nyasa women in the 1930s:

> With rare exceptions the emigrants go alone without wives or children... It thus happens that young households break up almost as soon as formed. The separation which, except for two or three intervals of a few months, lasts for six, eight, or ten years, begins in the first years of marriage. What happens to the woman who is left behind? She has much difficulty in carrying on the necessary cultivation without help; she is unable to keep up her hut or to repair it, still less to rebuild it. She is also unable to earn the money required for her maintenance and that demanded each year by the tax collector. If she has children they are a burden to her strength. Very few Europeans seem to realise to what depths of poverty a Native woman without her husband will fall.[1]

[1] Bishop Guilleme, *Africa*, 5, 1 (January 1932), quoted in 'Reports and Enquiries: Recruiting and Native Welfare in Nyasaland', *International Labour Review*, 33 (1936), p. 856.

Z. R. Groves, *Malawian Migration to Zimbabwe, 1900–1965*, Cambridge Imperial and Post-Colonial Studies Series,
https://doi.org/10.1007/978-3-030-54104-0_3

Guilleme was right that some women struggled to sustain themselves and their children in the absence of their husbands, but this was not consistent throughout every village. Women were able to find new opportunities in the absence of their husbands, within the changing social and economic systems of rural life. Pottery, beer brewing, growing and selling crops, and prostitution were all means of economic survival for women left behind without support, although these occupations were also part of the concern.[2] The increasing independence of women was a problem as far as missionaries and rural patriarchs were concerned.

This chapter explores migration and social change in Nyasaland and Southern Rhodesia with a focus on marriage, divorce and the effects of mission-education, as well as the experience of returned migrants. Gender and class played a crucial role in shaping the migration experience, but these dynamics have often been overlooked in studies of Malawian migration. Women migrated as wives and as single women making decisions about their lives, just like their male counterparts. However, women from Nyasaland have remained relatively absent from scholarship, in part, due to their absence from historical records, which concentrate almost exclusively on the migration of single men. Historians have rarely examined Nyasa women beyond concerns about the family and their behaviour and morality in the absence of men. Yet, Nyasa women were not simply passive victims of the migrant labour system. Labour migration could mean a boost to the family's economic status and for this reason some women pressured their husbands to search for work outside of the colony. Nyasa women migrated and started new lives outside of the colony with their husbands and alone in increasing numbers following the inter-territorial labour agreements between colonies in the late 1930s. Women's experiences of migration were as diverse as their male counterparts. This chapter shows how migrant men and women sought to transform their lives and sometimes their wider communities on their return, through education, and the spread of new religious groups and political ideas. It also challenges dominant stereotypes of Nyasa migrant men as poor, uneducated and unskilled, and Nyasa women as poor deserted wives.

[2] Precious Gawanani, 'Coping with the Absence of Men: The Experiences of Migrants' Wives in Madisi, Dowa District, 1936–1987', BEd Thesis, University of Livingstonia (2007), p. 26.

Social Change Among Men, Women and Children

By the 1930s there was a marked absence of men from many Nyasaland districts. Following the depression of the 1920s and the crash of the tobacco market towards the end of the decade, the Nyasaland government came to embrace the recommendations of the Emigrant Labour Committee report (hereafter referred to as the Lacey Report) in 1935 and to resume labour recruitment in order to control labour migration. In the early 1940s, British anthropologist Margaret Read remarked how 'the chief export of Nyasaland in the past fifty years has been men'.[3] African women were said to make up less than ten per cent of those leaving Nyasaland in the 1930s, although the number of single women leaving was thought to be increasing.[4] One of the consequences of widespread male migration was fear about the breakdown of 'traditional tribal society'. The Lacey report painted a 'consistently gloomy picture of deserted wives, undisciplined children, [and] uncultivated fields'.[5] 'Clandestine' or independent labour continued to leave Nyasaland at an increasing rate, despite pass laws and the reintroduction of labour recruitment intended to control the levels of migration.

The Nyasaland Northern Province Association, a group composed of European missionaries, viewed with 'great alarm, the huge exodus of natives from the productive areas of the Northern Province'.[6] Missionaries disliked migration as there were fewer men left behind to evangelise and town-life was thought to 'spoil natives', corrupting them and giving them 'ideas above their station'.[7] Missionaries feared that migration left women unsupervised and therefore undermined the stability of 'tribal life'. They warned about the bleak future of Nyasaland's rural areas if migration was left unchecked:

[3] Margaret Read, 'Migrant Labour in Africa and Its Effects on Tribal Life', *International Labour Review*, 45, 6 (1942), p. 606.

[4] Report of the Committee appointed by His Excellency the Governor to Enquire into Emigrant Labour, 1935 (Zomba, 1936), p. 16. Hereafter, the Lacey Report.

[5] Read, 'Migrant Labour in Africa', p. 611.

[6] MNA LB 2/2/1 'Northern Province Association, Lilongwe' Letter to the Chief Secretary, Zomba, 22nd March 1939.

[7] Rev W. Y. Turner, 'Some Aspects of the Native Labour Problem in Africa', *Central Africa: News and Views*, 1, 2 (1935), p. 5. Similar views are expressed in colonial district reports.

> In the northern half of the Protectorate the moral, social and physical life of our Native population will be so affected that any attempts by Missions, Government or other agencies to maintain, let alone improve upon the present low standards of health and happiness will be abortive. Home life will cease to exist; all belief in the sanctity of marriage will disappear. Immorality will be the rule. In consequence, venereal disease will affect one hundred percent of our native population. The birth rate will fall.[8]

This alarmist prediction was clearly an overreaction although there was cause for concern in some parts of the protectorate. Migrants were said to 'become lost to their families at home' with village life 'seriously affected'.[9] Growing numbers of *machona* were noted with concern by missionaries and district officials.[10] Initially, the percentages of absent males were only really considerable in the northern districts.[11] Yet, by the late 1930s more people were leaving the central and southern districts to the extent that '...in some areas of the territory no less than fifty percent of the able bodied men are absent from their villages at labour centres, chiefly in Southern Rhodesia'.[12] Nyasa migrants were said to go 'uncontrolled and either never return or stay away for long periods'.[13] The average duration of service for Nyasaland migrants in Southern Rhodesia was between three to five years, but there was considerable variation across the colony. The district commissioner for Central Shire reported that African men could be away 'between 4 months and 30 years and more'.[14] In West Nyasa and Mzimba districts in the north, durations of up to 20 and 28 years were recorded, respectively while Fort Manning, Chiradzulu and Mzimba district commissioners estimated that most of

[8] Extracts from the Report of the Committee appointed by His Excellency the Governor to enquire into Emigrant Labour, 1935, published in, 'Emigrant Labour', *Central Africa: News and Views*, 1, 4 (April 1936), p. 16.

[9] Report of the Labour Branch for the year 1938, p. 5.

[10] The increasing number of *machona* was highlighted in the Lacey Report, see Chapter 2 for table of statistics and an account of the highest migrant sending districts in the 1930s.

[11] MNA S1/1550/25 'Provisional Agreement', 1936.

[12] MNA S1/174Ai/35 Letter from Governor to Ormsby-Gore accompanied by Provisional Agreement on Labour, Salisbury 1936.

[13] Ibid.

[14] The Lacey Report, p. 99.

the African men who left their districts for work failed to return.[15] In response to the concerns raised by the Lacey Report and the newly established Labour Bureau in 1938, the Nyasaland government commissioned the British anthropologist Margaret Read to investigate the effects of emigrant labour on village and 'tribal life' in the colony.[16] In her correspondence with the Chief Secretary in 1939, Read outlined the multiple issues at stake:

> Are we chiefly concerned with matters like the birth rate, the country's food supplies, the necessary reserve of labour to supply public works, European estates and the semi-skilled jobs? Or about matters slightly less concrete, that is less easily computable in figures, such as the effective working of the Native Authorities Ordinance; the maintenance of family life and of tribal moral standards; and the raising of the general standards of living in education, nutrition, housing, sanitation etc....?[17]

In Salisbury, migrants would experience urban living and modern amenities that were scarcely available in Nyasaland. Men would return for short periods before leaving home again in search of the higher standards of living and freedom of urban life to which they had become accustomed. Returned migrants complained about the limitations of rural life and chose, where possible, to reside in more developed locations.[18] According to Read, young men on their return to Nyasaland found village life 'intolerably dull and stagnant, the houses dirty, the women slovenly, and the food inadequate and badly cooked'.[19]

[15] Ibid., p. 100.

[16] Read, 'Migrant Labour in Africa', p. 611. Like the anthropologist Audrey Richards whose work is critically re-examined by Henrietta Moore and Megan Vaughan, *Cutting Down Trees: Gender, Nutrition and Agricultural Change in the Northern Province of Zambia, 1890–1990* (London, 1994), Margaret Read was commissioned to work in Nyasaland prior to the establishment of the famous Rhodes-Livingstone Institute. On the history of colonial anthropologists and researchers in central Africa, see Lyn Schumaker, *Africanizing Anthropology: Fieldwork, Networks and the Making of Cultural Knowledge in Central Africa* (London, 2001).

[17] MNA LB 3/10/1 'Emigration from Nyasaland: Its effects on village life. Preliminary report' From Margaret Read to the Chief Secretary, June 1939.

[18] Interview with Ibrahim, Dedza District, February 2008.

[19] MNA LB (Labour Board) 3/10/1 Preliminary report by Margaret Read, presented to a meeting held on the 2nd August 1939.

Ibrahim was a labour migrant from Dedza who lived in Salisbury for nearly forty years. When he returned to Malawi in the 1990s he missed the city so much that he eventually decided to buy a small property in Blantyre.[20] In and around the slowly industrialising city of Blantyre, returned migrants became involved in nationalist movements and urban politics during the late 1940s and 1950s, most notably the Blantyre branch of the Nyasaland African Congress. Economic differentiation became a greater feature of Blantyre in the 1940s, where a class of returned migrants, teachers and clerks had retired to become maize mill owners, builders and traders.[21]

Women sometimes left to go in search of their husbands and many arrived in Salisbury to find them living with other women; they would then make their way to the Nyasaland Government Representatives' office, 'penniless and destitute', asking for help.[22] The 1936 Salisbury Agreement signed by the governments of Northern and Southern Rhodesia and Nyasaland sought to provide additional support for abandoned wives and children by introducing a system of deferred payment and compulsory family remittances for all contract workers. The system of payment would boost the revenue of the protectorate and encourage migrants to spend more time at home than outside of Nyasaland, although workers in the north (outside of Mzimba District) rarely signed labour contracts. Some officials became convinced of the merits of allowing wives and families to migrate while others remained opposed.[23] It was not until the 1950s that rules surrounding the migration of women and families began to be relaxed.

The Nyasaland government introduced further measures in the late 1930s to prevent women being left destitute. Men were required to apply for passes with a note from their group headman naming their nearest male relative who would be responsible for the wife and hut they left in the village.[24] It was already standard practice among migrant men from

[20] Ibid.

[21] See Joey Power, 'Building Relevance: The Blantyre Congress, 1953–1956', *Journal of Southern African Studies*, 28, 1 (2002), pp. 45–65; Megan Vaughan, *The Story of an African Famine: Gender and Famine in Twentieth Century Malawi* (Cambridge, 1987), pp. 104–105.

[22] MNA LB (Labour Board) 3/10/1 Preliminary report by Margaret Read.

[23] McCracken, *A History of Malawi*, p. 184.

[24] MNA NNC 3/1/4 Annual Reports – Chinteche, 1929–1935.

Tonga and Tumbuka villages to arrange for a brother or eldest son to watch over their wives and families in their absence. Some men were absent for such long periods that complaints were made to the Native Affairs office in Nyasaland by relatives left behind to deal with abandoned children. One letter to the Chief Native Commissioner in Salisbury noted:

> A native of this village by name of Saidi of Nkagula village, Chief Ntumanji, Zomba District, has complained to me that his brother, Jailos Bitoni, employed at the Cam and Motor Mine has been absent from his home for many years without supporting his child.[25]

It was suggested that Jailos' attention be drawn to his brother's complaint, to impress upon him 'his obligation to provide sustenance for his child'.[26] Enquiries were frequently made on behalf of families to ascertain whether their relatives were alive, where they were now living, and what their intentions were as to 'paying a visit to their homes, or at least communicating with their relatives'.[27]

Local chiefs and headmen in Nyasaland put pressure on district officials to search out *machona* and persuade them to return. Headman Makanjira from a village in Dowa District requested that he send his son to Southern Rhodesia, 'to visit people there' and 'to try to induce his people to come back to Nyasaland'.[28] Major Burden, the Nyasaland Government Representative in Salisbury, was said to have 'more to do with actual *machona* than any District Commissioner'. He found and interviewed young migrant men who claimed they could not afford to return or did not want to leave because of the higher wages in Southern Rhodesia. Native Authorities and parents asked him to trace and return lost ones:

> In fifty per cent of the cases the addresses given were so inadequate that men could not be traced. At least seventy five per cent of those who were found and interviewed, at first stated that they had no money with which

[25] ZNA CNC S138/22 'Native Complaints' Letter from the Chief Secretary's Office, Zomba, to the Chief Native commissioner, Salisbury, 15th February 1924.

[26] Ibid.

[27] ZNA CNC S138/22 'Native Complaints' Letter from the Chief Secretary's Office, Zomba, to the Chief Native Commissioner, Salisbury, 7th January 1925.

[28] The government discussed awarding a small grant for the purpose of the visit. MNA NC 1/8/1 Correspondence between Resident by the 'Strodgson' and the Provincial Commissioner for the Central Province, 26th March 1927–12th April 1927.

> to return, but when pressed they admitted that they did not wish to go home either because they had lucrative employment which they did not want to lose, or they had married local women and reared families, or that they had no desire to leave the towns and mines and return to the restrictions of tribal life.[29]

Missionaries and colonial officers portrayed women whose husbands had migrated as victims, abandoned and dependent on the government and a burden to their families.[30] However, women could choose to end a marriage if a husband had been absent for a long period, and in some cases they would migrate themselves in search of a more attractive lifestyle in the towns and cities, in place of a life confined to rural poverty. Women travelled to Southern Rhodesia independently of male companions, although this was strongly frowned upon by rural patriarchs, district commissioners and missionaries who expressed concerns about immoral 'runaway girls' taking up prostitution in the industrial centres of the south.[31]

The effects of labour migration were experienced in different ways by men, women and children, chiefs and village headmen, mission-educated Christian elites and uneducated peasants in remote rural areas. Ethnicity also shaped experiences of migration, to some extent, although Nyasaland's villages and districts were often mixed and not organised exclusively by ethnic group. The Lacey report speculated that: 'The Tonga, Tumbuka and Ngoni resident in these districts [in the northern region] are perhaps the very tribes on whom communal obligations press most heavily'.[32] Such obligations could include the payment of *lobola* or bride price, school fees, or the purchase of cloth, blankets and imported goods that came to seen as necessities. Cultural traditions and practices associated with ethnicity were often more flexible and less uniform than was suggested by missionaries and colonial anthropologists. Margaret Read worked among Ngoni and Chewa villages in the Northern Province, but

[29] MNA LB 3/10/2 Native Welfare Committee, Nyasaland, 1940.

[30] A newspaper article on the 31st January 1947 read: 'Those who wonder into the territory, working here and there, making no provision for their families, and returning when they see fit, perhaps after many years with nothing to show for their labour but a bundle of cheapjack goods…In the meantime wife and family have probably been a charge on their government. It is this type of migration that Nyasaland is determined to stop.' *Rhodesia Herald*, 31st January 1947.

[31] See, for example, the Lacey Report, p. 16, p. 32.

[32] The Lacey Report, p. 21.

she had also spent time in Blantyre and its surrounding areas: 'I was for the first two years concentrating on the Ngoni, but the mixture of tribes made it impossible to study one exclusively. This year in the work with the nutrition survey and in the emigration inquiry, I have been in contact with a number of tribes'.[33] In a study of 110 villages she learned about the aspirations of young migrant men from different backgrounds and the impact of migration on women and customs in different social systems.[34] In the area where Read conducted her research, migrant men were absent from Nyasaland from between three and seven years.[35] Longer periods of absence did not necessarily mean they lost contact with their families and rural homes. The Nyasaland Northern Province Association complained that, 'many of the women fall into immoral living if the husbands stay longer than two years. The Government and the missions do not want the men to be away for any longer than this period'.[36] It was also suggested that most husbands stopped remitting money after two years, which was a crucial factor in the government's desire for greater control of migration. Money remitted meant more money spent in the colony.

Native Authorities and headmen complained that divorce had become more common as a result of labour migration, most notably in marriages where no bride price was paid (for example among the matrilineal ethnic groups, including the Chewa). According to A.G.O. Hodgson, a colonial administrator who spent time 'observing' the Chewa and Ngoni: 'A [Chewa] wife may divorce her husband if he is impotent; or if he fails to maintain a habitable house, or to do his share of the work; or if he fails to pay her tax, feed and clothe her properly; or on account of desertion or ill-treatment'.[37] It was assumed that Nyasa women could more easily challenge family heads, or elders who had facilitated their marriage, in

[33] MNA LB 3/10/1 Minutes of the Native Welfare Committee meeting, 7th September 1938.

[34] When examining Read's work it is important to keep in the mind the way evidence was collected and the underlying assumptions about labour migration which sometimes obscured the real picture. See Moore and Vaughan, *Cutting Down Trees*, p. 147; Schumaker, *Africanizing Anthropology*, pp. 80–85.

[35] RHL MSS Afr. S. 997 (8) Memorandum on Labour Migration, 1948.

[36] MNA LB 2/2/1 Letter to the Nyasaland Northern Province Association, 23rd March 1939.

[37] A. G. O. Hodgson, 'Notes on the Achewa and Angoni of the Dowa District of the Nyasaland Protectorate', *The Journal of the Royal Anthropological Institute of Great Britain and Ireland*, 63 (1933), p. 140.

the absence of their husbands. Among the Ngoni and other groups that traditionally paid *lobola*, there were also occasions when divorce was filed on grounds of desertion by wives abandoned in Nyasaland and Southern Rhodesia. Samuel Ndhlovu's wife Agata approached the District Commissioner in Dowa in the early 1950s after her husband had been absent for more than four years. Writing to the Nyasaland Labour Representative in Salisbury, the Dowa DC explained: 'The woman is asking for a divorce on the grounds of desertion. I would be grateful if enquiries could be made at his home and he be asked his intentions'.[38] In Dowa, the rate of divorce had increased but more often in cases where migrant's returned rather than due to desertion.[39] Migrant men would sometimes deliberately return home without warning so they could check on their wife's fidelity and if she had been unfaithful he would claim damages. Wives would also have to deal with the consequences of their husband's unfaithfulness abroad: 'When he returns she runs the risk of contracting venereal disease'.[40] Family marriage counsellors, or *Ankhoswe*, were involved in efforts to restore relationships when migrants returned, particularly if men were absent for many years, or when accusations of adultery had been made. In more extreme cases, village headmen, or officials from traditional courts would intervene in marriage disputes.[41]

Women from matrilineal Chewa delineations were considered more at liberty to leave their villages, partly due to the absence of a binding payment of *lobola*. The matrilocal patterns of settlement, which several Chewa lineages still followed, meant that husbands moved to join new wives in their homesteads. Wives remained in their home villages and were provided with support from direct kin when husbands were absent for lengthy periods of time. In patrilocal kinship groups, women moved to their husbands' homesteads away from their direct family. Read suggested that patriarchal groups among the Ngoni generally showed greater stability in family and village life. However, 'sexual liberties' could

[38] MNA Transmittal Files: Dowa District Commissioner IDCDAI 1/2/1 Letter from the Nyasaland Government Representative in Salisbury to the District Commissioner at Dowa, Nyasaland. 14th July 1954.

[39] Gawanani, 'Coping with the Absence of Men', p. 38.

[40] The Lacey Report, p. 34.

[41] Gawanani, 'Coping with the Absence of Men', p. 38.

be taken by brothers-in-law when husbands were away.[42] Matrilineal groups were also thought to show better care for women and children. In contrast, the binding contract of bride price sometimes made it more difficult for women to divorce their husbands (even though they may have been absent for many years without contact). It was common to hear wives 'bemoan the fact that their husbands' families do not want to return the bride price...'[43] In addition to working the land so that it was in a satisfactory state for her husband on his return, there was also pressure to keep the house to a high standard. Most important would be to ensure plenty of food, which meant finding help to work in the fields.[44] It was less common for women from the Northern Province districts and areas of central Nyasaland where *lobola* was paid, to leave their villages alone.

Labour migration was an option to accumulate wealth and money for *lobola* more quickly. Evidence presented to the emigrant labour committee described how 'young men who wished to get married went out almost automatically to earn the bride-price'.[45] These 'young men' were sometimes Tonga and Ngoni youths between the ages of 10 and 18.[46] Single male migrants on their return from a period of labour migration were more desirable as husbands, and their accumulation of wealth and experience of travel gave them a higher status in the community. Tumbuka women were remarked on for pushing their husbands to migrate, as it brought greater prestige as well as the much-desired luxuries and commodities available in the more developed market economies of the south.[47] Women would tease their husbands through the songs they sang while working. The lyrics in one case suggested that their husbands feared the white man if they did not migrate to work in the white settler colonies of the south. In one Tumbuka song, husbands were (light heartedly) threatened with divorce if they did not follow the example of other men in the village:

[42] Ibid.

[43] MNA LB 3/10/1 Preliminary Report by Margaret Read, 1939.

[44] Ibid.

[45] The Lacey Report, p. 21.

[46] Ibid., p. 16.

[47] Gawanani, 'Coping with the Absence of Men', p. 41.

'Wanalume wali pano ku Harari wakopa koci?
Wali kukoma Mzungu? Kuwaleka ndiko'

('Why don't our husbands go to Harare/Rhodesia?
Because they have killed a European there?
Divorce them')[48]

Besides increased poverty, villages with high numbers of absent men were concerned over the moral consequences of abandoned wives. It was feared that women would resort to 'immoral activities', in order to support themselves and their children, in the absence of so many men from the villages. Among the Chewa, it had become more common for women to migrate by the late 1930s: 'Some go to Southern Rhodesia, others to Blantyre, Lilongwe, Kota Kota, Mponela, to any place in fact where money is plentiful, and a prostitute's trade can be a paying one'.[49] Colonial anthropologists like Read argued that matrilocal forms of marriage gradually gave way to patrilocal systems because, 'the wife's morals can be better watched over by his relatives...'[50] However, this assumption was later revisited.[51] Not only was there a more unidirectional relationship between matrilocal and patrilocal forces, patrilineal and matrilineal social patterns were over-simplified and depicted as closed and complete.[52] In reality, the Ngoni patrilocal system was shaped as much by interactions with matrilocal villages as vice versa. Furthermore, the establishment of colonial rule, which saw new restrictions on people's movements and reorganisation of political units, also influenced the transformation of patrilineal and matrilineal practices, making it hard to attribute these changes specifically to migration.

The difficulty of preventing women from leaving their homes, and sometimes their husbands, led to the consolidation of a political alliance

[48] Robert Boeder, 'Malawians Abroad: The History of Labour Emigration from Malawi to Its Neighbours', PhD Thesis, Michigan State University, Ann Arbour (1974), pp. 202–203.

[49] MNA LB 3/10/1 'Emigration from Nyasaland: Its effects on village life. Preliminary report' From Margaret Read to the Chief Secretary, June 1939.

[50] Ibid.

[51] Cynthia Brantley, 'Through Ngoni Eyes: Margaret Read's Matrilineal Interpretations from Nyasaland', *Critique of Anthropology*, 17, 2 (1997), pp. 147–169.

[52] Brantley, p. 149.

between African male elites and the Native Administration in Southern Rhodesia, and the same was true in Nyasaland. Moral discourse on gender roles and the breakdown of family life was used to manipulate the Tonga and other educated migrant men into accepting the restrictions placed on the movements of migrant labourers. The District Commissioner for Chinteche reported:

> A large number of women have been in the habit of emigrating to Rhodesia where they become harlots in the townships and in the vicinity of the mines. The Council of Chiefs have done their best by prohibiting the emigration of women who cannot prove that they have been called by their husbands. This is a praiseworthy effort, for the Chiefs fully realise that venereal disease is bought back by these women.[53]

Women and their 'promiscuous behaviour', and migrant men who fell outside of the control of the colonial government, were blamed for the spread of sexually transmitted diseases:

> The natives who are not under control in Southern Rhodesia and elsewhere, spread venereal diseases in this country. It is sad to see how formerly happy and healthy families are simply ruined in this way. Such men, who have lost their balance are generally immoral and a curse to their environment.[54]

The government used the issue of control over women, or the threat posed by abandoned women, to justify imposing tougher regulations on labour migration: '...women are left deserted by their husbands, many of them cannot find husbands at all and they have nothing to do. The remedy is to see that their husbands return to them and that too many young men are not allowed to leave the country at one time'.[55] However, Read found that adultery was not necessarily more common in areas of great out-migration: 'it is not on the whole true to say that emigration is the chief cause for increased adultery and greater laxity in observing the tribal moral codes. In some areas irregular sex relations have increased,

[53] MNA NNC 3/1/4 Annual Report, Chinteche District, 1935.

[54] MNA LB 2/2/1 Letter to the president of the Nyasaland Northern Province Association, 23rd March 1939.

[55] MNA NNC 3/1/4 Annual Report, Chinteche District, 1935.

but not, by any means, only among women whose husbands are away'.[56] Labour migration worked with other economic forces to reshape the lives of individuals and families in rural communities. These changes were also a continual process.[57]

'Matrimonial Troubles of Native Foreigners'

Migrant complaints were regularly conveyed to the Native Administration in Nyasaland through the Nyasaland Labour officers stationed in Salisbury and Johannesburg. Grievances often related to marital issues and concerned wives who had 'gone missing' while living in Southern Rhodesia or were written on behalf of women who had been abandoned and left without provision back in Nyasaland. In 1924, Swaleyi Wadi Mharuko, based in Que Que, Southern Rhodesia, wrote to the Nyasaland Native Superintendent because his wife was refusing to return to Nyasaland with him. He had left his home district together with his wife after gaining permission from his local traditional authority. When the time came for them to return to Nyasaland, his wife refused to go. Mharuko explained:

> When I left Nyasa [sic] I had my wife from Kota Kota and the Magistrate from Kota Kota knows all about this and when I came in this country called Rhodesia with my wife… and now the woman don't like to come back with me to Nyasaland, she wants to stay here and now she is just going about…[58]

Swaleyi asked the Native Department to help him, insisting that his wife, Pachikwanu, be forced to return:

> I am not working. I have nothing on me now. If the Government is going to assist me to this matter I will be much oblige [sic]…the first time we went to the Native Commissioner for the same case, and the NC said take

[56] MNA LB 3/10/1 Preliminary Report by Margaret Read.

[57] Moore and Vaughan, 'Married Men and Abandoned Women', *Cutting Down Trees*, pp. 164–172.

[58] ZNA Chief Native Commissioner (CNC) S138/22 'Native Movements', Letter from Nyasa Swaleyi Wadi Mharuko, to the Native Superintendent, Zomba, Nyasaland, 4th March 1924.

> your wife and the woman run away from me till today, but I don't want to leave her here...[59]

Nyasa women found opportunities to escape marriages when they went to Southern Rhodesia. Marriages contracted by Native Law and Custom were not registered outside of Nyasaland, which meant Nyasa women could desert their husbands and marry other men in Southern Rhodesia without consequences under the 1916 Native Adultery Punishment Ordinance. For an African marriage to be recognised in Southern Rhodesia, either *lobola* had to be paid, or the marriage had to take place according to Christian rites and a certificate issued.[60] Accompanying a husband and migrating to Southern Rhodesia therefore held new possibilities for Nyasa women, just as migration did for Nyasa men.

Marriages between partners of mixed territorial origin were most common with Shona women and Nyasa men. The majority of African women employed and living in Salisbury were classified as indigenous (or Shona), and at least half of the male labour force was known to originate from Nyasaland.[61] A small percentage of Nyasa women were formally employed in Southern Rhodesia, but a much larger number lived in the settler colony with their husbands than the census data accounted for. Figures collected by the Southern Rhodesian and South African authorities were often in respect of men only.[62] Nyasaland's Provincial Commissioner, J. C. Abraham who investigated the working and living conditions of Nyasaland migrants abroad in the late 1930s, found that women's employment was relatively negligible; there was at least one Nyasaland woman for every one thousand Nyasaland men.[63]

[59] ZNA CNC S138/22 'Native Movements'.

[60] ZNA CNC S138/47 'Native Marriages'.

[61] In 1936, 107,581 Southern Rhodesian men were in employment, compared with 70,362 men from Nyasaland. In 1942 the numbers had risen to 131,399 and 72,069 respectively. MNA S21/2/1/3 Minutes from an informal discussion on matters relating to native labour in the office of the Nyasaland, Northern and Southern Rhodesia, Inter-territorial Conference Secretariat, 5th September 1941.

[62] J. C. Abraham, *Nyasaland Natives in the Union of South Africa and in Southern Rhodesia* (Zomba, 1937), p. 3.

[63] In 1931 only 55 Nyasaland women were recorded as living in Southern Rhodesia. By 1936 it had increased to 87. These figures were according to the number of passes issued but it is likely that far greater numbers of women were there without authorisation. Ibid.

Women were not issued with passes in Southern Rhodesia which made it difficult to estimate their numbers, but they were found working in domestic service, more than any other formal -urban occupation. Most single women worked informally, making money brewing beer, selling crops or through prostitution. By the early 1950s the number of African women in the urban areas had increased significantly and for the first time they were included in labour regulations concerning conditions of employment.[64] The increased number of women working in the city was not without continued opposition from African men, missionaries and the local authorities.

Native Commissioners and government labour officers in Salisbury continued to receive complaints around marriage and the payment of *lobola*. One Nyasa man from Dowa district called Jack worked at the Globe and Phoenix Mine in Southern Rhodesia. He wrote to complain that his wife had run away from him and stolen his money. After looking into the case, the Native Commissioner found that Jack's wife was 'a prostitute who had appeared at his hut and said, "I want to be your wife", and he had accepted her'. The Native Commissioner complained that people were 'building up their own morality and they must live with it…Cases of this nature are brought into this office nearly every day'.[65]

Daniel Likhobwe from Cholo (whose experience of being tricked by the *madobadoba* was briefly discussed in the last chapter) had travelled to Southern Rhodesia in the 1940s. After a year or so working on a farm he finally managed to get to Salisbury where he met up with some friends from his village who helped him get a job at one of the city centre hotels.[66] Daniel was only eighteen when he left Nyasaland. He returned to get married once he had earned enough money and he and his wife went back to Salisbury together. As was often the case, Daniel already

[64] 'The regulations apply to all Africans employed within ten miles of the Municipal Areas of Salisbury, Bulawayo, Umtali, Gatooma and Que Que or within the jurisdiction of the Town Management Board.' MNA S36/1/1/5 'National Native Labour Board'—The regulations included an increase in the minimum wage, compulsory increments for three years continuous service, improved leave and overtime benefits and an improved scale of gratuities after long service with the same employer. However, the regulations did not apply to the farming and mining industries, government service, domestic servants and juveniles.

[65] ZNA CNC S1542/C16/5 'Complaints by natives, 1938–39.' This complaint was made in April 1936.

[66] Interview with Daniel Likhobwe, Thyolo District, February 2008.

had another wife in Southern Rhodesia, a Manyika woman who worked as a domestic servant for a white family in the city. When the time came for him to permanently move back to Nyasaland (on hearing that his father had passed away), his Manyika wife did not accompany him. He explained, 'I only had one child and they told me that if I wanted to get the child I had to pay £27. I didn't have the money'.[67] Having two families and leaving one behind in Southern Rhodesia was a common story among Nyasa men.

Motivated by the poverty in his village, Geoffrey Mpinganjira left Ncheu in the central region of Nyasaland in 1941. Geoffrey married a Shona woman during his seventeen-year stay in a township in Gatooma. When he returned to Nyasaland, his wife's family would not allow her to accompany him, as they claimed he had not finished paying *lobola*.[68] Shona women rarely returned to Nyasaland with their husbands, and only in cases where *lobola* had been paid. Alfred Zingwa, another migrant from Ncheu, described how his Ndebele wife refused to return with him to Nyasaland because of the poverty and the well-known hardships of rural life in Nyasaland. Southern Rhodesian wives complained to the Labour Officers in Mlanje and Cholo of ill treatment from their husbands and husbands' relatives on coming to Nyasaland. One district report reflected on the 'sociological aspects' of migration and issues arising from migrant men bringing Southern Rhodesian women back with them:

> It is suggested that the trouble is partly due to the different cultural standards of Nyasa women compared with the Mashona and Ndebele women, and also because the diet is so different. In some cases conciliation has been achieved, but where this is not possible, the husband is usually persuaded to send his wife back to Southern Rhodesia – in these cases, he is often anxious to obtain a refund of the bride price from her family.[69]

The issue of South African wives relocating to Nyasaland with their husbands was discussed at a Northern Provincial Meeting in 1945. One chief suggested they should demand a deposit from such women to

[67] Ibid.

[68] Interview with Geoffrey Mpinganjira, Ntcheu District, February 2008.

[69] MNA S36/1/1/4 'Sociological Aspects', Migration Abroad, 1945.

cover the costs of their repatriation as these relationships so often broke down.[70]

When migrants from Nyasaland had not paid *lobola* and the marriage was not recognised as legitimate, the colonial authorities did little to help with marriage complaints. Yet even when Nyasa migrant men attempted to pay a bride price they could still encounter problems in Southern Rhodesia, often in the form of opposition from Shona fathers. An application to the Governor of Southern Rhodesia to authorise a 'native marriage' in 1930, illustrates how one woman's father refused permission for them to marry:

> Mindirireyi declines to consent to the marriage even though Martin [the Nyasa] undertakes to remain in Southern Rhodesia. "I do not want them to register a marriage. I know the Blantyre as Martin. I do not want Martin as a son-in-law as he is a man who comes from a long way off."[71]

Marriages between Nyasa men and Shona women caused resentment among Shona men -Nyasa migrant men were perceived by other migrant men as a threat.

Living away from Nyasaland for many years, some migrants inevitably established themselves more permanently in Southern Rhodesia. In these cases, Nyasa men often sent for their wives to join them. From 1936 it was possible for recruited labourers to arrange for their wives to travel from Nyasaland free of charge, organised by the official recruitment agencies. Women were only given travel permits to leave Nyasaland provided husbands could guarantee 'married quarters' had been arranged.[72] During the famine in Nyasaland in 1949, migrants worried about the welfare of their families back at home. That year the Nyasaland Government Representative in Salisbury helped arrange for more

[70] Records of the Northern Provincial Council Meeting, 1945 cited in Boeder, 'Malawians Abroad', pp. 206–207.

[71] ZNA CNC S138/47 'Native Marriages', Refusal of Parents' Consent in Native Marriage, 26th April 1929.

[72] In the Union of South Africa accommodation was not generally provided for African workers to bring their wives. Nyasaland women were not permitted entry to the Union. Nonetheless, there were at least three hundred Nyasaland women known to be living there. ZNA MS 844/7 An Appeal for the Control of Native Labour, 1945.

women than usual to join their husbands.[73] Chiefs and parents were unhappy about wives and families leaving their villages, but it was encouraged more often from the 1950s. The new Migrant Labour Agreement in 1948, which aimed to better control independent labour, relaxed the rules around compulsory return after two years and the deduction of wages for deferred pay, if workers were accompanied by their families.

From the early 1950s more migrant men were taking their wives with them to Southern Rhodesia but accommodation to house them was not always adequate.[74] Litness Huwa left for Salisbury in 1952 to join her husband on a farm just outside of Salisbury. She left with her two children and many other women looking to be reunited with their husbands: 'I travelled with a group of women all following their husbands. Everyone was following their husbands at that time'.[75] She was able to stay with her husband in Salisbury in accommodation provided by her husband's domestic employer. Married accommodation remained limited in Salisbury and was not something which either the government or the municipality went to great lengths to improve until the mid-1950s. Even where married accommodation was available, lower paid migrant workers in Southern Rhodesia struggled to provide for their families on such meagre wages. Workers' grievances over their poor wages which prevented them from living with their families were voiced strongly during the industrial action of the 1940s (see Chapter 5).[76] More and more migrants wanted to build a life in the city with their families. Yet many obstacles

[73] MNA Secretariat General Registry (Transmittal files) 12710. I Labour Department, Annual Report, 1949–1950. For more on the famine including an examination of the most widely affected areas, and the different experiences of men and women throughout the crisis, see Vaughan, *The Story of an African Famine*.

[74] MNA 14239.II Nyasaland Government Representative, Salisbury: Labour Inspections, 1953.

[75] Interview with Litness Huwa, Sharpvale, Ntcheu District, February 2008.

[76] In 1944 the Howman Committee produced a benchmark study of African urban poverty. This is discussed in, Kenneth P. Vickery, 'The Rhodesia Railways African Strike of 1945, Part I: A Narrative Account', *Journal of Southern African Studies*, 23, 4 (1998), pp. 545–560; Kenneth P. Vickery, 'The Rhodesia Railways Strike of 1945, Part II: Cause, Consequence, Significance', *Journal of Southern African Studies*, 21, 1 (1999), pp. 49–71. Also, Teresa Barnes, '"So That a Labourer Could Live with His Family": Overlooked Factors in Social and Economic Strife in Urban Colonial Zimbabwe, 1945–1952', *Journal of Southern African Studies*, 21, 1 (1995), p. 95.

stood in their way: poor living conditions and a lack of married accommodation meant that married men were often forced to leave their wives and children in Nyasaland.

Doris Marikwa's story illustrates the experience of a Nyasaland couple who chose to live together in Southern Rhodesia and to raise their family outside of Nyasaland.[77] Doris' husband first went to Southern Rhodesia alone before he was married. He worked in a mine for several years and later returned to Nyasaland to find a wife. He married Doris, a Ngoni woman from Mulanje, and returned to Southern Rhodesia until the birth of their first child. Doris explained:

> When the child was born, he [the husband] stayed with me for a while, but then he went back again after I was pregnant. He came back once more when our second child was born, and at this point we decided to move to Southern Rhodesia to live together. I had seven more children after we came here.[78]

Doris and her husband waited several years before they were able to move permanently to Southern Rhodesia. They lived for many years on a farm just outside of Salisbury. Doris brewed beer to sell to the other farm workers at weekends to make some extra cash. Later they moved to a house in Dzivarasekwa, a suburb to the west of the city centre built in the 1960s to accommodate the city's expanding African population. Doris' son-in-law bought them the house and they settled there for the remaining years of her husband's life. Doris and her husband retained links with Nyasaland after leaving but they were determined to stay in Southern Rhodesia and had no intention of returning once they had secured a house. A report from 1957 outlined the ongoing problem of Nyasa migrants finding married accommodation in Salisbury and securing better jobs because they were hampered by the 1948 Migrant Worker's Act:

> Migrant workers in urban areas are handicapped, whenever a selection has to be made for a position of real responsibility, by virtue of the need for them to return home every two years unless accommodation can be found for the man's wife. The same state of affairs does not apply to the same

[77] Interview with Doris Marikwa, Harare, June 2008.

[78] Ibid.

> degree in rural areas where accommodation for families presents a less formidable problem.[79]

Despite the difficulty in finding suitable accommodation in town, migrant workers still found ways to settle and sometimes to build permanent homesteads in the reserves in Southern Rhodesia. The Lacey Report noted that:

> Marriage with women resident in the countries to which our labourers migrate is doubtless responsible for keeping many permanently abroad. There must be thousands of Nyasaland-born men who have become absorbed in life in the reserves in Southern Rhodesia. It is possible, in certain circumstances, for an immigrant Native to change his "foreigner's" pass for a local inhabitant's pass in Southern Rhodesia.[80]

Among the successful applicants for the Native Purchase Areas were retired British South Africa Policemen (BSAP), and mission teachers and evangelists, many of whom were from Nyasaland, Mozambique or South Africa.[81] A significant number of Nyasas were employed by the BSAP and their monthly publication for the African Regiment—*Mapolisa*—included articles published in Chinyanja and English aimed at a Nyasa audience. Features included stories from workers who had returned home while on periods of leave and were enjoying a break 'on the banks of Lake Nyasa'.[82] Writing from Nyasaland, NC. Yacobe explained, 'It was after twelve years of absence from my country Nyasaland, that I happened to visit home this year for my holidays'.[83] Yacobe spent three weeks at the Bembeke White Fathers Mission and praised the schools run by the government and the missionaries: '…there is a great change in the territory today…the people who come from Nyasaland should rejoice and be

[79] MNA Secretariat Dept. (Transmittal files) 14239.II Nyasaland Government Representative, Salisbury, Report, April 1957.

[80] The Lacey Report, p. 29.

[81] Terence Ranger, 'African Politics in Twentieth Century Southern Rhodesia', in T. O. Ranger (ed.), *Aspects of Central African History* (Portsmouth, NH, 1968), p. 227.

[82] 'N.C. Thydon Kamwendo has now arrived in Nyasaland and according to latest reports is thoroughly enjoying a well-earned leave on the banks of Lake Nyasa.' *Mapolisa*, 1, 18 (June 1938).

[83] *Mapolisa*, 1, 21 (September 1938).

glad that the Government of our country has done something very important for the improvement of our people'.[84] A later edition of *Mapolisa* told the story of Yohane who was retiring after forty years' service with the African Police. Yohane had joined the Kings African Rifles in 1916 and was returning to Nyasaland with his family, after his long-standing employment with the BSAP *Askari* platoon.[85]

Independent Churches and 'Native Associations'

Besides concerns over labour shortages and the spread of venereal disease, another concern shared by European missionaries and the colonial government was the spread of 'Ethiopian style' African independent churches, emanating from South Africa with returned migrants. Reverend Rens, a Catholic missionary from the Central Region warned:

> The natives not under direct European control in Southern Rhodesia and the Union, come into contact with agitators and undesirable sects. There are now already too many of them in Nyasaland, spreading wrong literature, poisoning the minds of natives…we can expect trouble in the future.[86]

It is unclear which 'sects' the Reverend referred to here, although it may have been the Watchtower movement, which had recently resurfaced in Ncheu District under the control of Willie Kabvala in the early 1940s.[87] Young mission-educated men were among those who left the northern province of Nyasaland in large numbers in the first few decades of British control. Villages exposed to the early presence of Scottish missionaries had access to an education system seen as 'superior' to any other in British Central Africa at that time.[88] Educated and skilled migrant men with high aspirations, predominantly Tonga, Tumbuka and Ngoni, travelled outside of the territory to seek employment in Southern Rhodesia *en route* to

[84] Ibid.

[85] *Mapolisa*, 19, 2 (February 1956).

[86] MNA LB2/2/1 Letter from Rev Rens.

[87] MNA PCC1/23/4 Watch Tower—Ncheu District (Political), 25th August 1941.

[88] John McCracken, *Politics and Christianity in Malawi 1875–1940: The Impact of the Livingstonia Mission in the Northern Province* (Blantyre, 2000), especially 'Chapter Six: The Overtoun Institution', pp. 171–196.

the higher-earning mining and industrial centres of the Union of South Africa.

New African associations, such as the West Nyasa Native Association, had already begun to appear in areas close to mission stations, prior to World War One. After the war these organisations became a more prominent feature of the political landscape in Nyasaland. Membership of the groups often included returned migrants and ex-soldiers, seeking to carve out new roles for themselves in the village. This new class of young migrant men was fully committed to Christianity and a modern economy; they possessed literacy and technical skills, and were influenced by their contact with early African political associations in Southern Rhodesia, such as the Union Native Vigilance Organisation.[89] The Native Associations of Nyasaland were essentially elite organisations led by Tumbuka and Tonga teachers, many of whom were educated at the Livingstonia Mission.[90] The North Nyasa Native Association was the first African organisation of its kind and dated back to 1912 when they were recorded to have held their first meeting.[91] European missionaries encouraged the formation of these groups for a number of reasons. Elliot Kamwana's Watch Tower movement had grown rapidly in 1908 and left missionaries feeling uneasy about independent African organisations.[92] These feelings were further exacerbated by the violence of the Chilembwe Rising in

[89] See 'The South Africa Antecedents', in Michael West (ed.), *The Rise of an African Middle Class: Colonial Zimbabwe, 1898–1965* (Bloomington, 2002), pp. 121–123; and 'The South African Influence', in Terence Ranger (ed.), *The African Voice in Southern Rhodesia, 1898–1930* (London, 1970), pp. 45–63.

[90] McCracken *Politics and Christianity*, pp. 304–308.

[91] Ibid., p. 305; Andrew Ross, *Colonialism to Cabinet Crisis: A Political History of Malawi* (Zomba, 2009), p. 22.

[92] Elliot Kamwana was a Tonga man from the Northern Province of Nyasaland and became the first Watch Tower prophet in the territory. The Watch Tower was an American religious group which spread to South Africa, where it was picked up by Kamwana and carried back to Nyasaland. He was credited with transforming its ideology into an anti-colonial movement which spread rapidly throughout the Protectorate in 1908. That year Kamwana claimed to have baptised over nine thousand people causing alarm to European missionaries and the colonial State. See Karen Fields, *Revival and Rebellion in Colonial Central Africa* (Princeton, NJ, 1985), p. 125; Markku Hokkanen, *Medicine, Mobility and the Empire: Nyasaland Networks, 1859–1960*, pp. 23–24.

1915, which demonstrated the potentially 'disturbing effects' of education on 'the native mind'.[93] European missionaries kept a watchful eye on the activities of these associations in order to extend a degree of influence over their nature. They provided facilities, such as meeting places and books, and were 'anxious to channel, rather than suppress, the aspirations of the new intelligentsia'.[94] Listening to the voice of these emerging elites was seen as vital to the development of the territory and the administration hoped this would avert any further clashes with a potentially 'dangerous class' of educated African men.

By the 1920s these kinds of African organisation had become more numerous. Later, some of the groups amalgamated to form the Nyasaland African Congress in 1944 (see Chapter 6). The North Nyasa Native Association concerned itself mainly with issues of personal improvement. They lobbied the government for increased opportunities within Nyasaland, regarding higher paid employment and greater participation within local government, and they voiced concerns for 'unchaste women', particularly in light of the increasing migration of women. Morality, education, sanitation and village reconstruction were fundamental issues on their agenda.[95] These were largely conservative associations and their politics contrasted with the mass participation and excitement surrounding the Watchtower movement of 1908, which had instructed its followers to desist from involvement in political organisations. The Watchtower also advocated beer drinking and traditional dance practices, which most Christian missionaries sought to eradicate or distance themselves from.

As the new educated class grew, their role in the future of the Protectorate was ambiguous. On the one hand the associations were welcomed by the authorities, but they were also representative of a growing class of 'detribalised' Africans who were no longer satisfied by 'tribal society'. The Provincial Commissioner for Zomba explained:

> It would be a great misfortune if the more enlightened natives instead of setting an example to the more primitive natives in the reserves cut

[93] West, *The Rise of an African Middle Class*, p. 125. For a detailed account of the Chilembwe Rising see, George Shepperson and Thomas Price, *Independent African: John Chilembwe and the Nyasaland Rising of 1915* (Blantyre, 2000).

[94] McCracken, *Politics and Christianity*, p. 305.

[95] MNA S1/1481/19 Letter from the District Commissioner, Karonga, 27th January 1931—concerning the activities of the 'North Nyasa Native Association'.

> themselves entirely adrift from them and attempted to fit into a civilisation for which they were not fitted by education or upbringing and which was not prepared to accept them on equal terms.[96]

Colonial administrators referred uncomfortably to Africans adopting 'European standards' and political and economic views. Frustrations inevitably grew among educated elites who were denied access to the rights and institutions which they felt their new status entitled them. The Provincial Commissioner for Zomba explained, '...there are natives for whom the tribal system as it exists does not provide opportunities and who seek for temporary or permanent escape from it...'[97]

Returned Migrants and 'Detribalised Natives'

The Nyasaland government wanted to create new political channels for educated African men that would reduce the influence of independent mission teachers and, at the same time, implement more vigorously the policy of indirect rule.[98] The process, however, was not always straightforward. In Chinteche District, the government was especially wary of 'politically minded natives, who are utterly detribalised in their outlook and ever ready to seize any opportunity of obtaining notoriety for themselves...'[99] Labour migration and 'contact with South Africa where normal native outlook is warped by agitators'[100] lead to a disregard for 'tribal traditions'. The government saw migrants who spent long periods of time outside of the colony as a threat to the system of indirect rule that was implemented in Nyasaland in the early 1930s. From this point, the colonial administration became more dependent upon the 'traditional' authority of chiefs and village headmen to exercise control over their locales. However, returned migrants responded less to the direction and authority of traditional leaders, and district officials felt that they needed to be brought into line. As one government official insisted: 'Some organisation must be provided into which these natives [returned migrants] will

[96] MNA S2/23/25 Provincial Commissioner, Zomba, 16th April 1927.

[97] MNA S2/23/25 Memorandum from the Provincial Commissioner, Zomba, 16th April 1927.

[98] McCracken, *Politics and Christianity*, p. 334.

[99] MNA NNC 3/1/4 Annual Report, Chinteche District, 1932.

[100] MNA NNC 3/1/4 Annual Report, Chinteche District, 1930.

fit and which will provide them with an outlet for their ambitions as well as the disciplinary effect that communal village life and interests have hitherto supplied'.[101] He continued: 'Our aim is to devise a system which will provide a place for these chiefs who show themselves capable of assimilating more modern ideas as well as to the progressive natives who might otherwise find no sphere for their activities'.[102]

In 1932 the Atonga Tribal Council of Chiefs was established to provide a channel of communication between the 'outspoken' Tonga people and the Nyasaland government.[103] The council consisted of 32 chiefs from the lakeshore area representing the heads of family groups involved. It was an executive authority used by the colonial government to control what was considered a 'potentially troublesome area' and 'an independently minded people'.[104] The Tonga Tribal Council was one of several local administrative councils, intended to help forge an alliance between the more progressive chiefs and young migrant men, and to strengthen the systems of traditional authority and indirect rule. Tonga and Tumbuka people had quickly embraced education and Christianity. As a result, the Lakeshore Tonga and surrounding northern Tumbuka became the focus of studies by missionaries and anthropologists, including Thomas Cullen Young, a Scot who worked in the area between 1904 and 1931. Later in the 1950s, anthropologist Jarp Van Velsen challenged some of the 'conventional wisdoms' about the detrimental effects of labour migrancy and the weakening of village kinship systems.[105] As a general rule, Tonga men would leave behind their families in Nyasaland when they migrated for work outside of the territory. Yet the large absence of Tonga men from the northern region of Nyasaland did not always affect the levels of food production, as was sometimes the case in other parts of the territory,

[101] MNA S2/23/25 Provincial Commissioner, Zomba, 1927.

[102] Ibid.

[103] McCracken, *Politics and Christianity*, p. 335.

[104] MNA S1/123/36 Memorandum describing the organisation of the 'native tribes' of the West Nyasa District.

[105] T. Cullen Young, *Notes on the History of the Tumbuka-Kamanga People's in the Northern Province of Nyasaland* (London, 1932); J. Van Velsen, *The Politics of Kinship: A Study in Social Manipulation Among the Lakeside Tonga of Nyasaland* (Manchester, 1964).

where widespread out-migration was seen to be a problem.[106] The Tonga diet was based on fish and cassava, the cultivation of which was minimal and performed by women rather men.[107] Tonga labour migrants organised themselves in their villages so that at least one man would remain per hamlet. The remaining man would then be expected to represent the interests of the hamlet. The system was said to work well, except (according to Van Velsen) there was always one man who complained that his brothers were better dressed than him as they worked away earning the money and were able to buy better clothes in the south.[108]

The Tonga were closely monitored by European missionaries and colonial officials because of their outstanding independence. In addition to their staunch economic independence and political outspokenness, they were also strongly associated with the formation of independent African churches. Chinteche was renowned for its high number of 'native controlled' missions.[109] In 1932, six independent missions were listed in the district, including The Watch Tower Bible and Tract Society, which was recorded to have more than 3000 members.[110] The Messenger of the Covenant Church attracted a large membership of more than a thousand African men and women. By 1937, eight native controlled missions were recorded in the West Nyasa District alone (see Map 2.2) and the most popular was the *Mpingo wa Afipa wa Africa* with nearly 2500 members. The Last Church of God and his Christ also had over a thousand followers.[111]

[106] In the areas where Margaret Read conducted her study, she observed impoverished villages where women and families struggled to maintain the land and their homes. Anthropological research sites were sometimes chosen by the government as places that in their estimation would be the most useful to investigate. Schumaker, *Africanizing Anthropology*, p. 80.

[107] J. Van Velsen, *The Politics of Kinship*, pp. 12–13.

[108] Ibid., p. 72.

[109] MNA NNC 3/1/4 Annual Report, Chinteche District, 1932: Native Missions.

[110] This was due to the legacy of Elliot Kenan Kamwana, leader of the Watch Tower 'Revival' in 1908. Chinteche was Kamwana's home district and the area to experience the largest number of conversions and baptisms.

[111] MNA NNC 3/1/5 Annual Report, West Nyasa District, 1937, 'Native Controlled Missions.' All statistics of native controlled mission churches were derived from this source.

Compared to the north, there was greater diversity within Ngoni and Chewa communities in the central region, according to levels of education and standards of living. In part this reflected the uneven influence of nearby Christian missions. Catholic missions were more prevalent in the central region and their later arrival in the area (compared with the Scottish missionaries in the north and south), as well as their approach to evangelising and African education, had a different impact on the established social systems of the Chewa.[112] In districts where educational standards were high, migration was strongly associated with upward mobility. Margaret Read noted the correlation between education and migrant labour: 'Where ever men have been to school they want, sooner or later, these goods which denote to them a higher standard of living, and they tend on the whole to seek employment where wages are highest'.[113] Higher levels of education and exposure to missionary teachings created stronger tendencies to migrate. Spending money outside of Nyasaland on European style imported goods was not new to the Tonga who had been leaving the protectorate since the 1890s, but the District Commissioner (quoting from a resident's report in 1907) again noted its importance in the late 1930s:

> '[T]he Atonga love money not so much for itself as for what it brings, and will save up for years to enable them to come back to their villages, scatter money left and right, and play the rich man. I met one of those individuals the other day and asked him why he did not work. His reply was rather characteristic, "We Atonga are gentlemen, we do not work here."'[114]

A sense of pride developed among the Tonga in seeking work *only* outside of the colony. Certain types of work and employment within Nyasaland were seen to be beneath Tonga men. Ownership of modern goods and commodities indicated to the wider community that you had a relative working in Southern Rhodesia or the Union. Read observed, '…the old headman who tells you of his exploits in past tribal fights may proudly

[112] Chief Gomani in Ncheu had more than 80,000 Africans of mixed tribes, religions, educational standards and points of view to consider in his district: MNA LB 3/10/1 Native Welfare Committee, Letter from Margaret Read to Mr Mackenzie Kennedy, 4th May 1939.

[113] Margaret Read, 'Migrant Labour in Africa', p. 626.

[114] MNA NNC 3/1/5 West Nyasa District Annual Report, 1937.

display two khaki shirts sent him by a son in South Africa; bicycles, sewing machines, books and oil lamps may be found in the huts in varying numbers according to the degree of education reached'.[115] It would be clear from a glance which households had a migrant worker sending home remittances, or which families had benefitted from a long-term migrant worker's return. In some villages, migration evoked a great deal of prestige.

Men and women in more marginalised areas in central Nyasaland and further from the mission centres also sought to change their fortunes by seeking employment outside of Nyasaland. This was the case with Malauzi Chikoya from Ntcheu who went to work in Southern Rhodesia because of the financial benefits, but also 'to develop himself'.[116] Those with little or no education found employment with lower wages, such as farm work, or if they were more fortunate, domestic service in the urban centres. Money that was sent home was sometimes shared out among the community. Chikoya was only educated up to standard four. He left school because his family were poor and went to Southern Rhodesia during his late teens in the 1950s. At that time, work opportunities were plentiful and although things became harder later in the decade with rising unemployment and political unrest in the 1960s, Chikoya continued to send money home to his mother for the duration of his absence. At first Chikoya worked at Mazowe Mine and later in Harare although his final years in Zimbabwe were spent happily living with his wife in Bulawayo. When he returned to Malawi in the mid-1990s he was warmly welcomed back to his village. In some villages migrant remittances were invested in long-term reconstruction projects or peasant farming. In poorer villages, migrants on return would see 'no result from it [remittances] except a number of stretching hands'.[117]

Native Improvement Associations

Migrants who had spent time outside of the colony were naturally more aware of wider regional and often global events. Read recalled how 'an ex-sergeant of the King's African Rifles who served in Somaliland may ask

[115] Margaret Read, 'Migrant Labour in Africa', pp. 612–613.

[116] Interview with Malauzi Chikoya, Ntcheu District, February 2008.

[117] Margaret Read, 'Migrant Labour in Africa', p. 616.

you about the war in Abyssinia and compare Italian and British colonial rule; a cook on leave from Johannesburg may discuss the relation of wages to hours of work…'[118] A broader awareness and experience of the world was gained through travel, military recruitment and labour migrancy. For many these experiences came to inform their political careers, as was the case with John Chilembwe and Hastings Kamuzu Banda, among others. Clements Kadalie left Nyasaland as a young educated migrant with high aspirations, and soon developed a critical attitude towards the colonial regime. Kadalie founded the first African Trade Union organisation in southern Africa in 1919, which became the most remarkable political movement in South Africa of its time.[119] Born at Chifira, a Tonga village near Bandawe in Chinteche District (later Nkhata Bay District), like other labour migrants originating in the area, Kadalie attended the Overtoun Institution at Livingstonia Mission, from 1907 until 1912. After teaching for a year he left Nyasaland in 1915 with high aspirations, in search of employment in the south. Kadalie made his way through several jobs, working first in an office on a cotton estate in Mozambique, before leaving for Southern Rhodesia. Trekking for a week with several travel companions, they reached Shamva Mine where Kadalie secured further clerical work. He later recalled that it was at Shamva where he first experienced the colour bar.[120] After a year, he left Shamva and having failed to find suitable employment in Salisbury, he continued his journey further south where he was to encounter discrimination on a whole new level.

Kadalie arrived in the Cape in 1918, where his brother had been living for some years. Meetings were organised among the dockworkers forming the basis of the Industrial and Commercial Workers Union (ICU).[121] Following the First World War, a shortage of essential commodities and a fall in real wages aggravated tensions among the poorly paid black and coloured workers who were struggling to survive the economic climate. Strike action was arranged by Kadalie as leader of the ICU, and wage increases were eventually awarded in response to their actions. News of the organisation's success spread throughout the Union of South Africa

[118] Ibid.

[119] Ranger, *The African Voice*, p. 149.

[120] Clements Kadalie, *My Life and the ICU: The Autobiography of a Black Trade Unionist in South Africa* (London, 1970), p. 34.

[121] D. D. Phiri, *I See You. Life of Clements Kadalie, the Man South Africa, Malawi, Zimbabwe and Namibia Should Not Forget* (Blantyre, 2000).

and new branches began to organise themselves. In 1926 the colonial authorities suspected an attempt to establish a branch of the ICU in Nyasaland; Tonga migrant, Isa Lawrence, was arrested on his arrival from Beira in Portuguese East Africa and sent to Zomba Central Prison for importing prohibited literature into the colony. Letters from Kadalie found on Lawrence, suggested he should return to Nyasaland and extend the organisation there.[122] Having worked for a period at Shamva and the Falcon Mines Kadalie had connections in Southern Rhodesia. Wages were especially poor in Southern Rhodesia at the time and unrest over the rising cost of living reached a crisis point in 1927.[123] Under the direction of Nyasa migrant Robert Sambo, who was based in Bulawayo in the 1920s, a workers' organisation was established in Southern Rhodesia with the assistance of another Nyasa, John Mphamba. Through the association African grievances could be heard by the government, as well as their employers.[124] Sambo was later deported to Nyasaland by the Southern Rhodesian government and the activities of the ICU were revived shortly afterwards by 'Sergeant' Masotsha Ndhlovu.[125] Having spent the past ten years working in South Africa, Ndhlovu had closely observed Kadalie's organisation in the Cape. Other than its limited success in Southern Rhodesia, the ICU did not achieve widespread support outside of South Africa as was envisaged. The limited scale of urban development and fragmented nature of the urban centres in Nyasaland partly explains the failure of any trade union style movement to establish roots in the Protectorate at this time.[126] However, these organisations illustrated the ability of African migrant workers to coordinate significant protests, even during the difficult years of the 1920s and early 1930s. They also demonstrate Nyasa

[122] MNA S2/68/23 Letter from Government House, Zomba to the Secretary for the Colonies, 20th June 1928.

[123] A series of strikes took place on the mines in Southern Rhodesia in 1927, most notably at Shamva Mine. See Ian Phimister and Charles Van Onselen, 'The Labour Movement in Zimbabwe, 1900–1945', in Brian Raftopoulos and Ian Phimister (eds.), *Keep on Knocking: A History of the Labour Movement in Zimbabwe, 1900–1997* (Harare, 1997), pp. 17–18.

[124] On Robert Sambo, John Mphamba, and the establishment of the ICU in Bulawayo, see West, *The Rise of an African Middle Class*, pp. 140–147.

[125] Phimister and Van Onselen, 'The Labour Movement in Zimbabwe', p. 18.

[126] John McCracken, 'Blantyre Transformed: Class, Conflict and Nationalism in Urban Malawi', *Journal of African History*, 39, 2 (1998), pp. 247–269.

migrant involvement in politics away from home, a theme to be explored in further detail in Chapter 6.

The Nyasaland administration and European missionaries had encouraged migrant labour in the early colonial period. Engagement with the capitalist wage economy was an essential aspect of missionary education. However, by the 1930s frustration with the lack of opportunities at home was increasingly obvious. The Provincial Commissioner for Zomba had expressed his concerns on the issue some years beforehand: 'Too great a stress can be laid on production and mere material advantage and there is a very great danger of the deliberate creation of the class of natives who are now proving such a problem in South Africa and of whom we shall have some experience'.[127]

Kadalie's uncle, Isaac Clements Muwamba, and his cousin, Alexander E. Muwamba, both worked in Northern Rhodesia. With their level of education, they easily obtained clerical jobs at Lusaka and Ndola, respectively. The Muwamba family came from a strong line of influential men in their home village Chifira, in Chinteche District. During the 1920s correspondence between the three men was monitored by the Nyasaland and Northern Rhodesian authorities. It was noted when Kadalie's uncle received from his nephew a copy of *The Negro World*, the American publication associated with Marcus Garvey's 'Universal Negro Improvement Association' (the journal had received a small yet significant readership in South Africa). The magazine raised suspicion over Muwamba's character and intentions, although he was hitherto regarded as a man of 'good reputation'.[128] In 1923, Muwamba requested the formation of a 'Native Improvement Association' in Lusaka, to combat what he described as, 'the weekend quarrels, differences and disrespectfulness' among the African workers of many different tribes. The proposed scheme was not in connection with any other organisation and Muwamba's main aim, along with a couple of fellow Nyasas, was to educate and instil in migrant workers 'respect for civilised law and order'.[129] When writing to the Native Commissioner at Chilanga, Muwamba referred to the 'secrecy

[127] MNA S2/23/25 Provincial Commissioner, Zomba, 1927.

[128] MNA S2/71/23 Letter from the Secretary's Office, Livingstone, Northern Rhodesia to the Chief Secretary, Zomba, Nyasaland Protectorate, 26th June 1923.

[129] MNA S2/71/23 Letter from D. Mackenzie-Kennedy, Chilanga, to the Secretary, Livingstone, 31st May 1923. The letter contains references to communication from Isaac Muwamba.

and foolishness' of Elliot Kenan from Bandawe (meaning Elliot Kenan Kamwana of the Watch Tower movement). Similar to the South African migrants in Southern Rhodesia discussed above, Muwamba proclaimed his allegiance to Britain, 'I am a British subject; I have no desire to be anything else, but I wish to help my own people towards civilisation'.[130]

The Native Administration in Northern Rhodesia was also cautious about men like Muwamba who sought 'to advance' beyond a certain level. Kadalie and Muwamba emphasised the importance of education and the civilising mission, which reflected their distinctive social class. Kadalie boastfully described his ambitions from an early age, 'When we were both boys you [Alexander Muwamba] and I had a burning desire to ascend to the loftiest pinnacle – hence my adventure when I chose not to take up clerical situation there but to proceed southwards'.[131] His ambition was to go to Europe and the United States, and in his letters to Alexander he referred to a planned excursion which his uncle had helped to finance. Kadalie and his relatives emphasised the need to lead their fellow Africans away from 'the barbarism fashion' and to take up their rightful place in their country. They strongly believed that once they had adopted 'the modern system' civilised Africans would be recognised by the colonial State and 'equal opportunities for all civilised men' would be achieved.[132] The following passage in correspondence between Muwamba and Kadalie illustrates these ideas:

> It is the white man that is ruling Nyasaland and not any black Chief. The white man is determined to turn [sic] the country his own and it behoves to us to be up and doing to culture ourselves in the white man's government. To do this our beloved Chifira [the village in the Northern Province where Kadalie's family originated] must produce most cultured and educated men who will participate to agitate for the modern government alongside the white man. What we require is that we should send men to sit as legislators at Zomba where laws are made to govern Nyasaland.[133]

[130] MNA S2/71/23 Chilanga, 31st May 1923.

[131] MNA S2/71/23 Letter from Clements Kadalie to Mr. E. Alexander Muwamba, 29th April 1923.

[132] The slogan of the ICU was 'Equal opportunities for all civilised men'.

[133] MNA S2/71/23 Kadalie and the ICU.

Muwamba's attitudes were representative of the period of polite politics which preceded the more confrontational tactics employed by the nationalists in the late 1950s (see Chapter 6). But the letters between Muwamba and his cousin also reveal the ethnic ideologies of the inter-war period. Labour migrants wanted stricter social controls and strong traditional leaders to exercise control over women and land in their absence. African intellectuals wanted to shape these controls by encouraging progress, education and training for the betterment of their people.[134]

Conclusion

By the 1920s a distinct class of educated Africans had emerged, many of whom were involved in the Native Associations in Nyasaland, or early political groups outside of the territory. The emergence of this new social group should be understood within the context of the early and pervasive missionary presence in Nyasaland, together with increased mobility due to labour migrancy and African involvement in the First World War. Carl F. Hallencreutz noted the inaccuracy of the 'northern' stereotype in his exploration of the early church scene in Harare:

> The discussion about the role of the northerners in the social and religious history of Zimbabwe has been inspired by one stereotype and one simplification. The stereotype is that the migrants from Nyasaland were heavy womanisers, who made many Shona women from neighbouring chiefdoms hesitant to move into the city. The simplification is that they brought the Watch Tower movement from Nyasaland to Zimbabwe.[135]

A more accurate depiction of Nyasaland migrants would recognise their contribution to the establishment of new denominational churches in Salisbury's townships, a topic which will be explored in the next chapter. These churches were led by the young mission-educated Africans, like those discussed in this chapter. Class and gendered experiences of migration in Malawi were far more varied than accounts have hitherto described. Nyasa men brought their wives from Nyasaland to the

[134] Leroy Vail and Landeg White, 'Tribalism in the Political History of Malawi', in Leroy Vail (ed.), *The Creation of Tribalism in Southern Africa* (Berkeley, 1989), p. 163.

[135] Carl Fredrik Hallencreutz, *Religion and Politics in Harare, 1890–1980* (Uppsala, 1998), p. 53.

city, in some cases on a permanent basis. Other migrant men married local women, sometimes women with ancestral links to Nyasaland.[136] Informal attachments and temporary unions with Shona women were also common. Some Nyasa women travelled to Southern Rhodesia independently of husbands or male guardians.

Social change was not necessarily more prominent in the areas that experienced the highest levels of migration. The effects of migration could be permanent or short-term, positive and negative throughout the territory. Money received in remittances was invested in individuals' homes, small businesses, and land purchases and spent on school fees. Migrants living away from Nyasaland for many years at a time often retained homesteads for their retirement. In their absence this would be maintained by a wife or a male relative. Claims to a rural home, despite living in poor quality accommodation in Salisbury, further attested to the relative status and wealth of labour migrants in rural societies. Village reconstruction and improvement on a broader level sometimes occurred as a result of the wealth distributed by returned migrants, but as Read's report indicated, this was not always the case. Changes were easier to implement when living under a progressive chief.

The spending capacity of Africans increased through widespread labour migrancy. New commodities including bicycles, gramophones (*gumbagumba*) sewing machines and milk separators appeared in remote villages throughout the territory.[137] These commodities became indicators of class and status in rural Nyasaland. Some families were hit hard by the economic depression during the inter-war years, which combined with increasingly restrictive labour legislation and made it harder to save money. Native associations proliferated during this period and new independent 'native controlled missions' also acted as an outlet for African grievances. The World War Two economic boom later helped to change fortunes again for many African men, providing the opportunity for personal improvement among a growing African middle class, which will be explored further in Chapter 5. The African middle classes became

[136] Several men interviewed recalled how Shona wives often had a father, or sometimes both parents, from Nyasaland. Many had settled in Southern Rhodesia a generation before.

[137] 'Some people would go to Rhodesia if they wanted to buy a bicycle and some wanted to buy gramophones. Some would buy big radios that you don't get these days, called *gumbagumba*', Interview with David Ngowe, Sharpvale, Ntcheu District, February 2008.

increasingly important in Nyasaland from the late 1940s into the 1950s in a variety of capacities, including their economic importance to the developing urban centres of the protectorate (notwithstanding the future political significance of this social class during the Federation period).

Like other colonial-era anthropologists across the region, Margaret Read, was chiefly concerned with the impact of migration on family life in her study of the late 1930s. Increased migration did not always equate to a rising standard of living, but it did alter the activities of men and women, and relations between husbands and wives and their families. It had an effect on the stability of marriage, and what Read described as 'respect for moral codes'. Read crucially recognised that there were two very clear influences in the rural areas of Nyasaland at the time of her study: labour migration and the missionary presence. Each carried a potential ideological impact upon the formation of new codes of behaviour and ideas of morality: 'It seemed to me that frequently the main emphasis in [church] teaching about the home and family life was limited to the sexual behaviour of husband and wife, and gave far too little attention to building up the 'externals' of home life and to providing some guiding principles for social behaviour under changing conditions'.[138] Yet the single process creating the most significant changes in social conditions, at least in some parts of Nyasaland, was migration.

[138] Margaret Read, 'Migrant Labour in Africa Today', *The Frontier: A Christian Commentary on the Common Life*, 1, 7 (1950), p. 259.

CHAPTER 4

Nyasa Migrant Identities

This chapter is concerned with cultural identity and associational life in Salisbury from the early 1900s to the 1960s. Salisbury's African Townships were diverse spaces, with mixed populations, rich associational life, and vibrant urban cultures. So-called 'foreign' migrants dominated the townships and defined 'the moral, linguistic and social tone'[1] of the urban locations. Workers were drawn to the city from across central and southern Africa. Townships were densely populated, ethnically heterogeneous, and characterised by increasing social and economic differentiation and a strong degree of occupational and residential mobility in the 1940s and 1950s. Studies of migration in southern Africa have often focused on specific ethnic groups.[2] However, ethnicity did not always dominate social relations in multi-ethnic urban situations. Labour migrants could be influenced by aspects of ethnic construction at home and migrant

[1] Enocent Msindo, 'Ethnicity Not Class? The 1929 Bulawayo Faction Fights Reconsidered', *Journal of Southern African Studies*, 32, 3 (2006), p. 433.

[2] David Coplan, *In the Time of Cannibals: The Word Music of South Africa's Basotho Migrants* (Chicago, 1994); Peter Delius, *A Lion Amongst the Cattle: Reconstruction and Resistance in the Northern Transvaal* (Portsmouth, 1996); Terence Ranger, 'Missionaries, "Migrants and the Manyika": The Invention of Ethnicity in Zimbabwe', in Leroy Vail (ed.), *The Creation of Tribalism in Southern Africa* (Berkeley, 1991). Deborah James, *Songs of the Women Migrants: Performance and Identity in South Africa* (Edinburgh, 1999).

Z. R. Groves, *Malawian Migration to Zimbabwe, 1900–1965*, Cambridge Imperial and Post-Colonial Studies Series,
https://doi.org/10.1007/978-3-030-54104-0_4

anxieties were sometimes minimised by the strength of ethnic ideologies, which were important in the control and surveillance of women and land in the absence of men.[3] This was seen to some extent with the Atonga Tribal Council in the last chapter. Nonetheless, many migrants were away from home for especially long periods, during which they built up vested interests in Salisbury, in the form of marriages to local women, new families and newly acquired urban (and rural) homes. For some migrants, ethnicity took on new meanings or became less important as a defining feature of their identity.

This chapter expands our understanding of ethnicity and cultural identity among migrants in Salisbury. Different types of migrant associations, such as burial societies, religious expressions, and 'traditional' dance groups are explored. These organisations were assumed by the colonial authorities to operate along ethnic lines, yet they were often indicative of broader cultural identities. The cultural identity of (Nyasa) migrants in Salisbury cannot be reduced to ethnicity. Nor can Nyasa labour migrants be considered a coherent class.[4] This chapter breaks down the identity label 'Nyasa' in order to explore the cultural roots of different ethnic groups encompassed within the term and the ways in which people came to identify themselves alongside other Africans in the townships.

Mutual Aid and Burial Societies

Like the compounds and townships of the Witwatersrand in South Africa, rural-based patterns of association were reproduced in modified form in the African urban areas of Southern Rhodesia.[5] Religious and cultural practices from Nyasaland were established in the townships alongside new kinds of urban associations, like mutual aid societies. Mutual aid groups often took the form of burial societies. These groups were open

[3] Vail, *The Creation of Tribalism*, pp. 9–10.

[4] Ian Phimister and Charles Van Onselen described class as the major organising principle behind the 1929 'faction fights' in Bulawayo, in 'The Political Economy of Tribal Animosity: A Case Study of the 1929 Bulawayo Location "Faction Fight"', *Journal of Southern African Studies*, 6, 1 (1979), pp. 1–43. Their interpretation of the violence was later challenged by Enocent Msindo who argued that class identities alone obscure the complexities of other interests, besides that of production: 'Ethnicity, not Class?', p. 433.

[5] Peter Delius, 'Sebatakgomo; Migrant Organisation, the ANC and the Sekhukhuneland Revolt', *Journal of Southern African Studies*, 15, 4 (1989), p. 588.

to members from different ethnic groups. Monthly fees were paid in return for financial support and food if sick or help with purchase of the coffin and funeral arrangements, in the event of a death. Agnes Galatiya was born and raised in Salisbury. Her mother was Shona but her father was from Mwanza in the southern region of Nyasaland. Agnes married a Nyasa man from Ncheu in the central region. They met in Salisbury where they later married and lived for many years before moving to Malawi in the mid-1990s. Agnes described the burial societies as a Nyasa/Malawian innovation in Salisbury where they replaced a function usually provided by village communities:

> Some of them [burial societies] were for everyone but there were some specifically for Malawians. These organisations were started by Malawians. Because they were not originally from there, they did not have the villages or places to go for funerals and burials, so that is why they came up with the societies. They used to collect money weekly or monthly as a contribution towards these societies, so they could buy food and coffins for the burial ceremony. The Shona later joined these societies because they were impressed by the organisation.[6]

Mutual aid and social welfare societies date back to the earliest days of migration to the city but they became more prominent during the years of economic depression in the 1920s and 1930s. Nyasaland experienced an employment slump at this time due to mine closures in Southern Rhodesia and the Union.[7] Unemployment and depression hit hard in certain areas, and mutual aid groups helped to provide security for those who suddenly found themselves destitute and without work. The first Nyasaland Burial Society formed at the Cam and Motor mine in Kadoma in 1930; others soon appeared in Salisbury.[8] The Atonga Society and the Loyal Mandabele Patriotic Society also functioned like burial societies and held branches in the mining compounds and African townships. These groups provided support structures to substitute traditional kinship networks and enabled migrants to maintain ties with rural homes.

[6] Interview with Agnes Galatiya, Ntcheu District, February 2008.

[7] MNA S2/4ii/31 Recruitment of Labour: General Applications Government Policy—Letter to Native Commissioner, Blantyre from Ebden Estates in Southern Rhodesia, 8th August 1934.

[8] Robert Boeder, 'Malawi Burial Societies and Social Change in Zimbabwe', *Journal of Contemporary African Studies*, 1 (1982), p. 340.

The activities and structures of the burial societies became more highly organised over time. They were not exclusive to specific ethnic groups, despite what the names of the groups implied. Members often originated from the same village or area, but groups also formed among those who worked in the same occupation or lived in the same residential area. Shared ethnicity was not an essential qualification to join. Workers from the 'Zambezi' region, for instance, formed the Northern Rhodesia Burial Society, and elected a Sotho man as president.[9] Associations were established by urban residents who had been in the towns for the longest periods. Leaders of the groups were known among residents as 'chiefs' or 'headmen' making deliberate use of traditional designations as they would be used in rural settings to add a sense of authenticity. Ibrahim had moved to Salisbury in the 1950s. His neighbours were ethnically diverse, and included people who identified as Yao, Shona, Ndebele, Senga and Sena.[10] African residents from all backgrounds resided in the city and became involved with these groups. Ibrahim described his experience of the burial societies:

> When a Malawian passed away we [the members of the burial society] would come together and discuss how we would organise things. We used to go and buy the coffin, food and a cloth, and anything else that was needed for the funeral. We would have some kind of a chief. These societies were organised according to where you came from and in a group of about fifteen people we would choose a chief. Tambala, Kachindamoto, many... If there were very few people from your home district you could come together with another group to make it bigger. They were not just for when people died. They would be used for when people were sick as well.[11]

Emulating rural political structures allowed these support groups to receive greater recognition from the municipality. Tradition in this sense was welcomed by the settler colonial authorities who approved of any mechanisms to help keep the village as home in the minds of migrant

[9] Tsuneo Yoshikuni, *African Urban Experiences in Colonial Zimbabwe: A Social History of Harare Before 1925* (Harare, 2007), p. 125.

[10] Interview with Ibrahim, Dedza District, February 2008.

[11] Ibid.

workers. Mutual aid societies could register with the location superintendent or appropriate authority under the Friendly Societies Act.[12] Burial societies developed different organisational guises over the years. In June 1951, the Nyasaland Government Representative attended a meeting of the Combined Nyasaland Burial Societies in the Harare Recreation Hall.[13] Some burial societies later organised according to religious affiliation, for example, a group of Muslim Yaos in Salisbury created the Mpondo Yao Burial Society, and in 1969 the Malawi Catholic Burial Society was registered in the city.[14] Providing kin with a proper burial was a traditional obligation maintained by most urban migrants, regardless of religion or ethnicity. Sometimes it was possible for bodies of the deceased to be returned to Nyasaland. When this was too expensive, funerals were held on the edge of the city, or in rural areas of Southern Rhodesia, where access to land had been granted.[15] If bodies of the deceased could not be taken back to Nyasaland, some migrants feared that the spirits could remain restless. Felistas Ngowe was less concerned about this. She lived in Zimbabwe for 35 years, having left Ncheu in 1960 to go and join her husband who had been working away in Bulawayo for six years. She talked about the importance of the burial societies in supporting Malawians away from home:

> The burial societies were there. They used to collect money for when there was a funeral. There were a number of them, including the Chapita and Ntcheu Club. If a member died they would write letters back to their district to inform people that they had died. There were different branches, and they would collect money for all of the funeral costs. It was possible to arrange for the body to be sent back, but the people from the group wouldn't necessarily go too. It was much easier when this person was going

[12] ZNA S138/10 and N3/21/2 cited in Boeder, 'Malawi Burial Societies and Social Change in Zimbabwe', p. 341.

[13] MNA Transmittal File: Secretariat Dept. 14239 Nyasaland Government Representatives—Salisbury Reports Vol. 1 (3.3.7F/1295) 'Nyasaland Burial Societies', June 1951.

[14] Boeder, 'Malawians Abroad', pp. 231–234.

[15] Interview with Felistas Ngowe, Ntcheu District, February 2008. Maskito and Tsabtsaba take a visit to the cemetery on the edge of Harare in Saidi, *Old Brick Lives*, pp. 97–98.

> to be buried in one of the villages in Zimbabwe. Then many people would go.[16]

The costs of joining these societies were prohibitive for some. Educated migrants criticised the groups for being parochial as they were seen to organise along ethnic lines. Yet, burial societies were versatile organisations that differed from one to the next in their organisation and structure and could promote various interest groups. By the 1940s, burial societies even formed under the political umbrella of organisations like the Reformed Industrial and Commercial Workers' Union.[17] Another was organised specifically for African women: the Daughters of Africa Burial Society, which formed in 1944 among a group of women working at Salisbury hospital.[18] Burial societies were dismissed by some urban residents as corrupt money making schemes, or simply opportunities for the leaders to gain status and recognition in the city. Nonetheless, they remained a prominent feature of urban life throughout and beyond the colonial period; and it was rare for Nyasa migrants not to be involved with them at some point during their stay in the city.

Tea Parties and Dance Associations

Salisbury's townships also saw the development of sub-cultures with more cosmopolitan styles. A big trend in the 1920s was the 'tea party', which earned a reputation extending as far as Cape Town.[19] The tea party was an all-night dance held at township beer halls. These events attracted a younger generation of urban workers who popularised new styles of music and dance, such as the *Tsaba Tsaba*, which soon spread back to the rural areas.[20] Later, in the 1950s and 1960s, they were associated with the

[16] Interview with Felistas Ngowe, 2008.

[17] Scarnecchia, 'The Politics of Gender and Class in the Creation of African Communities, Salisbury, Rhodesia, 1937–1957', PhD Thesis, University of Michigan (1993), p. 170.

[18] Boeder, 'Malawi Burial Societies', p. 347.

[19] Yoshikuni, *African Urban Experiences*, p. 123.

[20] ZNA S235/392-3 'Night Dances'. Yoshikuni, *African Urban Experiences*, p. 123; Terence Ranger, *Bulawayo Burning: The Social History of a Southern African City* (Woodbridge, 2010), pp. 138–140 and pp. 178–181.

emerging African urban elite in Harare Township, and attended by influential Africans of the time, such as the journalist Lawrence Vambe, and mission-educated pioneer of homecraft clubs for township women, Mai Musodzi. Tea party meetings and concerts were modern forms of entertainment.[21] The growth of tea parties as a popular pastime illustrated the development of new cultural forms in the colonial city. Participation at these events was pan-ethnic.[22]

The social organisation of dances and gatherings in the townships was of concern to colonial officials. According to the Native Commissioner at Wankie in North-western Matabeleland, tea-meetings were 'an innovation introduced by non-indigenous natives and copied by indigenous natives'.[23] He suspected they were brought to cities and mining towns by returning migrants or those with origins in South Africa. Similarly, Mozambican migrants were thought to have introduced the *Butwa* dance to Salisbury, and Nyasas the masked 'secret society' and associated dance, the *Gule Wamkulu* (discussed below).[24] Shona cultural practices and dances were slower to arrive in the city, reflecting the fact that longer distance migrants invested more heavily in the cultural life of the townships, at least before the 1950s. By the 1960s, *Jerusarema* and *Mbende*

[21] Mhoze Chikowero discusses tea parties and the *Tsaba Tsaba* in a chapter on criminalised leisure, exploring different interpretations and perceptions. He explains how some felt the tea parties were mimicking white settler culture ('real tea parties' were hosted by mission-educated elites who did not drink alcohol). In contrast, the *Tsaba Tsaba* was a syncretic underclass cultural form. Mhoze Chikowero, *African Music, Power and Being in Colonial Zimbabwe* (Indiana, 2015), pp. 187–212. Richard Parry also suggested that tea parties were the product of mission educated Africans and espoused the cultural values of Christianity as imported via the mission schools of Nyasaland and the Cape: 'Culture, Organisation and Class: The African Experience in Salisbury 1892–1935', in Brian Raftopoulos and Tsuneo Yoshikuni (eds.), *Sites of Struggle: Essays in Zimbabwe's Urban History* (Harare, 1999), pp. 58–61.

[22] Maurice Vambe, '*Aya Mahobo*': Migrant Labour and the Cultural Semiotics of Harare (Mbare) African Township, 1930–1970', *African Identities*, 5, 3 (2007), p. 362.

[23] ZNA S235/392-3 'Night Dances', Native Commissioner, Wankie to the Native Commissioner at Bulawayo, 29th September 1930.

[24] Vambe, '*Aya Mahobo*', p. 357. Richard Parry offers an alternative view of the origins of the *Butwa*, suggesting it was carried south with migrant workers from Katanga. Parry, 'Culture, Organisation and Class', pp. 66–70. Bruce Fetter describes the *Butwa* as a 'powerful organisation' in Elisabethville, prior to World War One. He suggested that Malawian migrants were one of the groups who avoided association with the *Butwa*. 'Malawians were Elisabethville's first African elite and represented a distinct minority among migrants in the city.' *The Creation of Elisabethville, 1910–1940* (Stanford, 1976), p. 38.

were more commonly performed, having been brought to the city by migrant workers from Mashonaland East.[25]

Some of the dances in Salisbury did have strong associations with specific ethnic groups. Stephen Tsinambuto from Ntcheu District lived in Bulawayo in the 1950s. Stephen recalled how he and others would meet and dance 'the Ngoni dances' and sing traditional songs on special occasions and festivals.[26] Gilidala Galatiya Kathyole (married to Agnes Galatiya, mentioned above) recalled frequent performances of *Ingoma*—Ngoni dances—in Salisbury, in the 1950s and 1960s.[27] Both men spent long periods away from Nyasaland and helped to set up new associations with individuals and groups on the basis of common interest in the urban locations where they resided. New connections were forged at many different levels, sometimes drawing from familiar cultural resources, at other times finding new ones. Gilidala Galatiya and Stephen Tsinambuto were also members of the Church of Central Africa, Presbyterian (CCAP)—a church often associated with Nyasas—during their time in Southern Rhodesia, although neither had attended this church before they migrated.

The Native Affairs Department in Southern Rhodesia observed the growing popularity of so-called 'tribal dances' in the city. Missionaries in Southern Rhodesia expressed disapproval of excessive beer drinking at meetings which they thought were 'harmless in nature' but enabled the meeting of young people 'without adequate tribal or parental control.'[28] A letter from the office of the Southern Rhodesian Missionary Conference to the Native Commissioner's office explained, '…it would not be too much to say that illicit sexual indulgence is generally speaking one of their objects.'[29] In the 1920s and 1930s, patriarchal control of African women and youth was an especially important concern for European settlers in Southern Rhodesia. 'Black Peril' fears (white settler anxieties about African men sexually assaulting white women) were used to justify

[25] Vambe, '*Aya Mahobo*', p. 357.

[26] Interview with Stephen Tsinambuto, Ntcheu District, February 2008.

[27] Interview with Mr Galatiya, Ntcheu District, February 2008.

[28] ZNA S235/392-3 'Night Dances'.

[29] ZNA S235/392-3 'Native Dances', Letter to the Secretary of the Southern Rhodesia Missionary Conference, 24th December 1930.

attempts by the administration to bolster chiefly authority in controlling the mobility of African men and women.[30] Urbanisation created new opportunities for men and women, and urban culture was also a draw to young African men and women looking to escape rural life and constraints.

Beni was another imported style of dance which became popular in the townships and mining compounds of Southern Rhodesia from the 1920s.[31] Originating from German East Africa in the late 1890s, the dance was initially picked up by the Kings African Rifles (KAR) who had served there during the First World War, and brought back to central and southern Africa by returning Nyasaland soldiers. Disbanded from the KAR, ex-soldiers continued to perform the dances in villages and bomas around Nyasaland, later making an appearance in parts of Southern Rhodesia, like Salisbury, where high numbers of Nyasas resided.[32] In Nyasaland, the authorities had noted that the *Beni* dance could be performed by anyone, 'irrespective of tribe or religion.'[33] Suspicious of any association which they did not understand, the dancers were treated cautiously by the Nyasaland government. An advisor to the governor concluded that, 'It [the Beni dance] is without doubt a strong weapon ready to be used for anyone who can gain control over it'.[34] To further fuel their doubts about the motives or purpose of the dance in Nyasaland, in a number of cases *Beni* groups were linked with cases of larceny, and in particular, theft of clothing. The dance involved practising European style military drills to the accompaniment of a brass band, while wearing smart uniforms.[35] Correspondence with British Governors in Nairobi and

[30] See Jock McCulloch, *Black Peril, White Virtue: Sexual Crime in Southern Rhodesia, 1902–1935* (Bloomington, 2000).

[31] Terence Ranger, *Dance and Society in Eastern Africa 1890–1970: The Beni Ngoma* (Berkeley, 1975).

[32] John E. A. Mandambwe was recruited to the Kings Africa Rifles in 1939. After the war he finished his education in Southern Rhodesia and during the 1950s spent several years working in Salisbury at his uncle's butchery. M. Kolk (ed.), *Can You Tell Me Why I Went to War?* (Zomba, 2000), pp. 69–70.

[33] MNA S2/11/21 Activities and Significance of the *Beni* Dance—notes by Captain Sydney Fairbairn.

[34] Ibid.

[35] For more detail on the *Beni* dance see J. Clyde Mitchell, *The Kalela Dance: Aspects of Social Relationships Among Urban Africans in Northern Rhodesia* (Manchester, 1956) and Ranger, *Dance and Society in Eastern Africa.*

Dar es Salaam informed the Nyasaland Administration, 'It is not considered that the *Beni* dances have any political significance.'[36] Nonetheless, the dance was viewed by administration as immoral and continued to be regarded with suspicion:

> I understand the dance is not popular among the more sober-minded natives as it is said to lead to adultery. Where practised it forms an irresistible attraction to the women of the neighbourhood, some of whom are tempted to become unduly intimate with the gaudily dressed dancers.[37]

Beni dances became a popular form of entertainment across central Africa in the 1930s, 1940s and 1950s. Participants from different ethnic groups engaged in dance competitions and displays in towns and mining compounds throughout Southern Rhodesia. Like many other Nyasas in the city, Ibrahim, used to enjoy the competitions and festivals that took place in the compounds and townships: 'There was the *Gule Wamkulu*, the *Beni* practised by Yao, Mang'anja and Chewa, *Chintali* and *Mganda* they were both Chewa dances, and the *Malipenga* which was danced by the Tonga'.[38] J. Clyde Mitchell's famous study of the *Kalela* dance on the Copperbelt in the 1950s suggested that the dance was 'essentially a tribal dance…its songs emphasise the unity of the Bisa against all other tribes on the Copperbelt'.[39] The objective of Mitchell's ethnographic study was to resolve the apparent paradox of tribalism in a modern urban setting. 'Tribal' dances, like the burial societies, could also be linked to regional identity or ethnicity. But very often they served a practical function and were less about maintaining cultural rituals. These associations were important for distinguishing new class identities and were sometimes closely aligned with religious beliefs. In some ways, they became a symbol of common migrant solidarity. Migrants in urban areas formed

[36] MNA S2/11/21 Activities and Significance of the *Beni* Dance.

[37] MNA S2/1/21 The Bene [sic] Dance—Theft of clothing by natives in connection with the Beni Dance, from the government offices, Ncheu to the Chief Secretary Zomba,1921.

[38] Interview with Ibrahim, Dedza District, February 2008.

[39] Mitchell, *The Kalela Dance*, pp. 8–9. It is thought that the *Beni* dance was later reinvented as the *Kalela* when organisers of the *Beni* were suspected by the authorities to have incited riots. See, pp. 9–12.

new allegiances across ethnic, religious and territorial lines that were still compatible with 'traditional' identities.

The *Nyau* Societies

Another cultural association brought to Southern Rhodesia by Nyasa and Northern Rhodesian migrants and popularised in Salisbury during the colonial period was the *Nyau* societies or *gule wamkulu* (the great dance).[40] *Nyau* societies were male associations formed among the matrilineal Chewa and involved the invocation of spirits through performance and dance in order to teach moral and social values and to connect with the ancestors. In Southern Rhodesia, the societies became an example of a proclaimed 'traditional' cultural practice, associated with a specific ethnic group from Nyasaland and Northern Rhodesia (the Chewa or Nyanja) and which over time came to hold a much wider appeal. Some background of the societies is provided in order to better contextualise the nature and practice of the society in the two locations—rural Nyasaland and urban Salisbury.

As described in Chapter 2, the establishment of British colonial rule in Central Africa in the late nineteenth century coincided with a series of dramatic upheavals in the region. The Chewa and Mang'anja people in the central and southern parts of the territory had recently undergone invasions from Ngoni groups entering from the south, and both ethnic groups had been subjected to slave raids by Yao newcomers from the east. Chewa communities were displaced, chiefdoms were weakened, and traditional village authorities broken up. These events, combined with the introduction of a new colonial economy, land alienations and the onset of labour migration, brought great disruption and change to the territorial landscape. Chewa and Mang'anja *Nyau* societies and rain shrine cults were maintained despite these changes, but only through the adaptation and transformation of ritual practices.[41] The *Nyau* societies coped

[40] The dance societies are sometimes referred to in Harare and elsewhere in Zimbabwe as *Zvigure*, *Chinyau* or *Zinyao*.

[41] An explanation of the impact of Christianity and colonialism on the *Nyau* societies and the *Chisumphi* rain shrine at Bunda is provided in Peter Probst, 'Expansion and Enclosure: Ritual Landscapes and the Politics of Space in Central Malawi', *Journal of Southern African Studies*, 28, 1 (2002), pp. 179–198. On interactions between the *M'Bona* cult and Christianity, see M. Schoffeleers, 'The Interaction between the M'Bona Cult and

with the effects of widespread change brought by colonial rule more convincingly than other cultural practices in Nyasaland.

The *Nyau* was a precolonial association of Chewa speaking people from the north of the Shire highlands, stretching into North-Eastern Rhodesia (see Map 2.2). According to Chewa traditions, the *Nyau* dated back to the arrival of the Maravi (Malawi) royal family (Phiri clan) who migrated to the territory from the area which later became the Belgian Congo.[42] *Nyau* was continued by the Mang'anja (Chewa speaking people in the southern parts of the territory) and the Chewa (Nyanja and Chipeta) although there were slight variations between practices and rituals observed from one society to another.[43] Performance of the *gule wamkulu* would take place at funerals, the installation of chiefs and at the carrying through of important transition or initiation rites.[44] Life size animal guises made of grass and bamboo enclosed the dancers and formed an essential part of the rituals of the *Nyau*. Other dancers would wear masks in order to disguise themselves from the audience. The identity of the dancers, disguised as spirits and animals (*zilombo*) would remain hidden behind the elaborate masks and structures.[45] A combination of singing, dancing and drumming would accompany ritualistic ceremonies.

Christianity, 1859–1963', in T. O. Ranger and J. Weller (eds.), *Themes in the Christian History of Central Africa* (California, 1975), pp. 14–29. On the clash between the *Nyau* societies and the Catholic Missions, see Ian Linden with Jane Linden, *Catholics, Peasants and Chewa Resistance in Nyasaland, 1889–1939* (California, 1974). On the transformation of *Nyau* societies in Nyasaland, see Deborah Kaspin, 'Chewa Visions and Revisions of Power: Transformations of the Nyau Dance in Central Malawi', in J. Comaroff and J. L. Comaroff (eds.), *Modernity and its Malcontents: Ritual and Power in Postcolonial Africa* (Chicago, 1993), pp. 34–57.

[42] J. M. Schoffeleers, 'The Meaning and Use of the Name *Malawi* in Oral Traditions and Pre-colonial Documents', in B. Pachai (ed.), *The Early History of Malawi* (London, 1972), pp. 91–103.

[43] See M. Schoffeleers and I. Linden, 'The Resistance of the Nyau Societies to the Roman Catholic Missions in Colonial Malawi', in T. O. Ranger and I. Kimambo (eds.), *The Historical Study of African Religion*, p. 257.

[44] J. W. M. Van Breugel, *Chewa Traditional Religion* (Blantyre, Kachere Press, 2001), p. 126. In Malawi after independence, the *Nyau* would perform at national political events and in more recent times at weddings and on the request of chiefs or important officials offering a fee. Leroy Vail and Landeg White, 'Tribalism in the Political History of Malawi', Malawi' in Vail, *The Creation of Tribalism in Southern Africa*, pp. 151–192.

[45] The animal structures are based on Chewa folklore, including the lion (*Mkango*), the Cow (*Ng'ombe*) and the mythical beast (*Kasiya Maliro*).

Dances and ancestor veneration were performed at the chief's invitation in his village. The chief was significant in the control of *Nyau* societies, although the society was more strongly associated with the village level rather than broader ranging political structures.[46] Although the *Nyau* was a male association, a version of the *gule wamkulu* was performed at initiation ceremonies for girls, known as *Chinamwali*, where senior Chewa women would lead the ceremony. Chewa boys were initiated into the *Nyau* with the performance of a ceremony to mark his rites of passage into full manhood. Women sometimes held another position in the performance, as vocalists accompanying the dancers. Their songs could be expressions of public opinion, personal comments on village life or relationships, or moral teachings reminding the people of the ancestral customs concerning conjugal relations.[47]

Catholic missionaries, rather than colonial administrators or Scottish Presbyterians, came to have the most pervasive influence on Chewa communities in Nyasaland in the early twentieth century. The White Fathers and the Montfort Fathers expanded throughout Chewa and Ngoni dominated areas, aiming to introduce widespread elementary education throughout the territory. Newly converted members were forbidden from continuing ties or forging associations with the *Nyau* or any other 'heathen practices' including witchcraft.[48] During the 1920s and 1930s, Catholic missionaries, particularly the White Fathers, repeatedly came into conflict with villagers who withheld their children from attendance at Catholic schools. Chewa chiefs, in defiance of the Catholic missionaries, prevented the building of new schools in their areas and attendance at schools plummeted during this period. In retaliation, a concerted campaign was launched by Catholic missionaries against the *Nyau* societies. Missionaries lobbied the colonial government to have *Nyau* banned on the grounds that they were immoral 'secret societies' posing a political threat to the colonial system.[49]

The *Nyau* societies were established by migrants in the urban areas of Southern Rhodesia from the earliest days of Chewa migration to the city.

[46] Kaspin, 'Chewa Visions and Revisions of Power', p. 35.

[47] Van Breugel, *Chewa Traditional Religion*, pp. 152–153.

[48] See Linden, *Catholics, Peasants and Chewa Resistance*, pp. 117–137.

[49] On the political significance of so-called 'secret societies' see D. H. Johnson, 'Criminal Secrecy: The Case of the Zande Secret Societies', *Past and Present* 130, 1 (1991), pp. 170–200.

As early as 1922, the Native Location department noted: 'The Chipeta [Chewa] are the people who indulge in the *Chinyao* moonlight dances with effigies, and are a bad lot'.[50] As a 'secret society', they would meet to perform 'night dances' in discrete locations on the edge of the commonage and in graveyards. The activities of the *Nyau* raised the suspicions of the local authorities and other urban migrants. The 1920s and 1930s was a period of heightened concern over the control of Africans in Southern Rhodesia and the spread of African Independent Churches and 'Ethiopianism'.[51] In 1926, Africans associated with the Watch Tower were dealt with by the CID under immigration laws, and deported.[52] The Southern Rhodesian government announced in 1932 that it would refuse entry to any further members or representatives of the Watch Tower Bible and Tract Society who were known to emanate from Nyasaland.[53] Native Commissioners were encouraged to report back on the circulation of 'dangerous propaganda' and even 'native choirs' were to be closely monitored. The Native Commissioner of Sinoia reported in 1926 the arrest of two Africans—one of whom claimed to have been taught by a 'John Chirenga of Nyasaland who conducted military operations in Blantyre in 1915.'[54]

African police were sent to spy on *Nyau* meetings after CID reported masks were found near Brickfields in Salisbury Location.[55] One mounted Constable stationed at Salisbury, Trevor Alfred Wright, provided the following account of a dance which he had attended near the Location:

[50] ZNA LG52/6/4 Native Location Department Report, 30th May 1922.

[51] See Parry, 'Culture, Organisation and Class', p. 61.

[52] ZNA S1219 Police CID Headquarters—Circulars, 17th February 1926—'Watch Tower Church'.

[53] ZNA S1219 Police CID Headquarters—Circulars, 1932.

[54] ZNA S138/106 Chief Native Commissioner files, 'Control of Unrecognised Religious Denominations', 1923–28. The African teacher referred to here would have been John Chilembwe founder of the Providence Industrial Mission and responsible for the African uprising in 1915, see George Shepperson and Thomas Price, *Independent African: John Chilembwe and the Origins, Setting and Significance of the Nyasaland Native Rising of 1915* (Edinburgh, 1958). There were no proven connections between the Watch Tower Movement and Chilembwe's church, the Providence Industrial Mission (PIM). Anyone found preaching anything of a subversive or seditious nature was threatened with deportation.

[55] ZNA S1219 Police CID Headquarters—Zvinyao Dance: Salisbury Location, 12th May 1926. *Zvinyau* or *Zinyao* are more variations on the spelling of *Nyau*.

> A large open space had apparently been selected for the dance, a number of natives wearing grass frills around their waists and carrying rattles, commenced to dance and were surrounded by a crowd, around the outskirts of the crowd three natives armed with battle axes and assagais kept running, suddenly one would enter the circle and shout out that he had sighted game, and he would be followed by a large mask representing some sort of animal, the natives in the circle would then pretend to attack the animal…during the dance dust was continually thrown over the dummy animals, I was informed that this was to disguise the fact that there were human beings inside the masks. There was nothing obscene about the dancing and the crowd appeared to be ruled by a rod of iron by the older natives who were acting as police for the occasion.[56]

Another case was brought to court after a meeting was disturbed by a local Shona man who was reportedly beaten by two Nyasa men. The court heard how, '…persons straying into the vicinity of the dance were tied up and threatened with physical violence.' The magistrate remarked, 'what is done in Nyasaland must not be done in this country.'[57] The dance had been banned from the location in the 1920s because of the violence that often resulted during the events. 'They work themselves into such a pitch of excitement that they attack other natives who are unlucky enough to get caught in their way when they are escorting their effigies to and from the dancing ground…'[58]

The *Nyau* was vilified in the Rhodesian press in much the same way as they had been by the Catholic missionaries in Nyasaland. Emphasis was almost always on the immorality of the naked dancers and stories of theft by young *Nyau* men running riot through villages.[59] Police reports from the 1920s connected members of the society with 'malicious injury to property':

[56] ZNA S715/1 Police CID Headquarters, 'Native Dances', Report by Trevor Alfred Wright, Salisbury, 20th September 1926.

[57] ZNA S715/1 Reported in the *Rhodesia Herald*, 11th October 1927.

[58] ZNA LG52/6/4 Native Location Department Report, 1922.

[59] One of the first actions by a *Nyau* initiate was to run through his wife's village and steal his mother-in-law's chickens. This act was significant as part of the male association within a matrilineal society. When a *Nyau* member is wearing a mask, Kaspin argues that this presents a reversal of the order of things in society. For further explanation of this 'logic of opposition', see Kaspin, 'Chewa Visions and Revisions of Power', p. 39.

> The fact that the accused, in this case being seen coming from the cattle kraal, naked, points towards the crime being associated with native superstition, witchcraft or the "chinyao". It is a belief amongst the natives that a person going about at night is a "takati". A person bent on crime will go naked as he believes he "cannot be seen"...The "chinyao" is danced naked. I am unable to find a reason, except that their forefathers told them to dance without clothes. Some natives maintain that the "Chinyao" is a trouble dance because it is danced naked and at night, and that always means trouble... All natives interrogated in this case were naturally reticent on the subject of "Chinyao" and little information could be obtained.[60]

Headlines such as 'Death Dancers' appeared in the *Rhodesia Herald*.[61] Little was understood about the nature of the *Nyau* in Southern Rhodesian settler society although Constable Wright's account of the dance differed from the sensationalism seen in the press and contrasted with accusations made by missionaries and government commissions regarding the lack of 'tribal control' and the immorality of the dances. A letter from the Native Commissioner to the Secretary of the Southern Rhodesia Missionary Conference in 1930 went some way in trying to understand the significance of the *nyau*:

> The old dances (which include night dances) are of an ancient origin and have long been established in the traditions and customs of the Natives. In some cases they are of religious significance, such as harvest thanksgiving or the invocation of the departed spirits...[62]

The letter concluded that they might be harmless in nature, but efforts should still be made by the authorities to prevent them. Like the tea parties, night dances and gatherings organised by Africans beyond the control of the municipality or other authorities were not to be tolerated. Location life was rigid and strict regulations governed every aspect of movement in the 'European' city. Dancing was permitted but only under the conditions and efforts were made to organise recreation along ethnic

[60] ZNA S715/1 Police Headquarters, Detective Barham Reports, Makwire R.C.A II/8/26 'Malicious Injury to Property', Gatooma, 6th September 1926.

[61] *Rhodesia Herald*, 28th August 1923. Another headline read, 'Sworn to Secrecy: Further details of the mystery dance.' *Rhodesia Herald*, 29th August 1923.

[62] ZNA S235/392-3 Chief Native Commissioner to the Secretary of the Southern Rhodesia Missionary Conference, 'Native Dances', 24th December 1930.

lines: 'Each tribe in the location has been allotted a piece of ground set aside for dancing…No native is permitted to leave the location between 9 pm and 5am, unless permission is granted by the Superintendent or employer.'[63] In the 1940s, the Nyasaland Catholic Labour Chaplain made calls for the Rhodesian authorities to take stronger action against 'the dirty *Zinyau* dances': 'when shall it be understood that we are before a real secret society binding their members with a terrible oath of hating the white man?'[64] In light of the history of the *Nyau* in Nyasaland, and their turbulent relations with the Catholic missionaries, these comments were hardly surprising. By the 1940s it was estimated that more than eight hundred members of the *Nyau* society in Salisbury practised the *gule wamkulu* ceremony once a month at full moon. Rituals involved 'nude dancers' and participants wearing masks, 'some painted red with human faces to represent spirits'.[65]

Besides the elaborate costumes and flamboyant ceremonies, the *Nyau* society functioned much like the burial and mutual aid societies. Andu Pangani, who only came to Southern Rhodesia in the early 1960s described how the groups connected migrants to a network of people which allowed them to maintain ties with home communities: 'We used to enjoy ourselves during those activities. They made us feel at home'.[66] Migrants came together to practise 'traditional' customs and built up new support networks essential for survival in the city. In the 1950s, the Urban African Affairs Commission suggested that traditional practices and tribal customs were changing and would probably disappear altogether along with extended family obligations.[67] Yet, despite disapproval from missionaries, and attempts by government officials to ban the dances, the *Nyau* society continued to flourish among a wider section of Salisbury's African community as Andu Pangani recalled:

> I remember the Chinyau Dance Group which used to entertain people from Malawi. But I remember that some Zimbabweans also used to attend

[63] ZNA S85 Native Affairs Commission, Salisbury Municipal Location, Government notices relating to the location, 3rd December 1930.

[64] ZNA S517 'Social Welfare Laws and Regulations', Nyasaland Catholic Labour Chaplain, 1946.

[65] 'The ChiNyau Ceremony of the Northern Natives', *Mapolisa* 10, 8 (1947), p. 41.

[66] Interview with Andu Pangani, Mount Pleasant, Harare, May 2008.

[67] S51/1 Urban African Affairs Commission, Oral Evidence, Salisbury, 1957.

> since they enjoyed seeing how the Nyau's used to dance and dress. Other people though used to say that Nyaus were very superstitious and bad they didn't understand why they used to dress like that with their masks.[68]

By the 1950s *Nyau* societies had established a multi-ethnic base in Salisbury. Men and women from a variety of ethnic backgrounds, including local Shona, watched for entertainment and sometimes even participated in the events.

Josphat Banda described himself as a *Gule* dancer.[69] He was from a village in Dedza where the *Nyau* societies were very popular. Josphat moved to Salisbury in 1965 after Malawian independence. He used to meet his friends at the weekends to practise their dances: 'Some *Nyau* groups would behave in different ways to others' he suggested, 'for instance, the group in Mufakose would kidnap Shona and force them to join their groups, but my friends and I who had come from Malawi did not want to throw away our culture so we used to go to the locations during the weekends to dance the *Gule* dances'. Interestingly, Josphat considered the *gule wamkulu* to be an important part of his identity as a Yao, even though the society is not generally associated with Yao ethnicity in Malawi.[70] Other urban residents were intrigued by the masks and the costumes, but they were also suspicious as they associated the *Gules* and other Nyasas with *juju* and criminal activity.[71] Over time, as the popularity of the dances increased, the society became more open to outsiders. Whereas members of the CCAP would not previously have associated themselves with the society, some did start to watch the performances that took place on special occasions, although those who practised the full rituals of the dance were not thought to be Christians.[72]

The *Nyau* society in Salisbury came to represent an expanded Nyasa or Malawian identity. Its wider membership grew beyond Chewa and Mang'anja migrants to include Nyasas (and later, Malawians) from other ethnic groups, more broadly. People could engage with the *Nyau* on

[68] Interview with Andu Pangani.

[69] In Zimbabwe the dancers are called *Gures,* in Malawi they are referred to as *Gules*. There is no 'l' sound in Chishona, and no 'r' sound in Chichewa, or these sounds are interchangeable.

[70] Interview with Josphat Banda, Dzivarasekwa, Harare, June 2008.

[71] Interview with Andu Pangani, Harare, June 2008.

[72] Interview with members of the CCAP headquarters in Harare, August 2009.

different levels. For Chewa and Mang'anja migrants it remained an important part of tradition that was continued as part of their new urban lifestyle. In this sense it also took on new meaning for Nyasa migrants. Andu Pangani, viewed the society as a means of retaining ties with Nyasaland; he described it as an important part of his cultural heritage. *Nyau* meetings could be an important source of solidarity. For some Nyasa migrants interested in routes to greater social mobility, religious associations such as the CCAP provided more practical benefits and allowed them to maintain ties with rural kin, through a modern Christian and 'respectable' institution (the church is discussed in more detail in the following chapter). *Nyau* was depicted as primordial and backward looking, whereas the CCAP and other churches were indicative of aspiration among urban residents, especially for more educated elites.

The *Nyau* evolved among the Nyasa and later, Malawian diaspora without the same nationalistic political association which it later came to hold back in Malawi. Instead of representing a hallmark of Chewa culture, it was adopted in Zimbabwe as a marker of broader 'Nyasa' (or later Malawian) identity. Following independence in Malawi in 1964, the *Nyau* societies and Chewa identity were transformed once again. Malawi's first president Hastings Kamuzu Banda redefined the *Nyau* societies as a part of the national culture. Chewa ethnicity was expanded and elevated in status as Banda sought to establish stronger alliances across the ethnically diverse southern region.[73] The rise of Chewa ethnicity was intimately bound up within the political process of nation-building and the regional and ethnic dimensions of the 1964 Cabinet Crisis which brought the newly independent country to a state of emergency in its infancy.[74] Banda acted as a culture broker, redefining the *Nyau* as an historic symbol of anti-colonial resistance and authenticity. Cultural practices and symbols could be shaped by their environments, as well as a kind of ethnic consciousness.

[73] Vail and White, 'Tribalism in the Political History of Malawi', p. 180.

[74] On the events surrounding the Cabinet Crisis, see Andrew Ross, *Colonialism to Cabinet Crisis: A Political History of Malawi* (Zomba, 2009); Colin Baker, *The Revolt of the Ministers* (London, 2001).

Nyasa Cultural Markers

In the process of migration, Nyasas developed contacts with migrants from other areas, primarily Mozambicans and Northern Rhodesians, but also Shona, Ndebele, Sotho and others.[75] Migrants from Nyasaland, Portuguese East Africa and Northern Rhodesia, who formed the majority of the population in the townships, shared Chinyanja as a common language and it soon became the African lingua franca of Salisbury rather than the local language Chishona, at least until the 1950s. One manager of the Witwatersrand Native Labour Association (WNLA) described in 1908 how 'the whole of the town [of Salisbury] was overrun by Nyasaland natives. In the public offices, in the shops, in the factories, in private houses and hotels the lesser services were invariably performed by these natives. The common language in the streets was Chinyanja.'[76] Labour officers working in Salisbury were encouraged to learn Chinyanja.[77] African newspapers, such as *Nkhani Za Nyasaland* and *Bwalo La Nyasaland* were printed and widely circulated in Salisbury, as was *The Nyasaland Times*. Radio broadcasts were made in Chishona and Chinyanja.[78] Many migrants recalled how important it was to be able to listen to the radio so they could keep up with events back home.[79]

African migrants learned to speak different languages through contact with one another in the beer halls, at work, and in other common areas of the townships. Most learned to speak Chishona very quickly. Gilidala Galatiya stayed in Salisbury for so many years, he felt that he 'became like a Shona. It reached a point where we used to communicate a lot more in

[75] For information on the African population of Salisbury by nationality from 1911–1969, see Yoshikuni, *African Urban Experiences*, p. 160. Breakdown by ethnicity is not available for this period.

[76] C. Knipe, District Manager, WNLA to Major Pearce, Zomba, 11 January 1908 in Correspondence Relating to the Recruitment of Labour in the Nyasaland Protectorate, cited in E. P. Makambe, 'The African Immigrant Factor in Southern Rhodesia, 1890–1930: The Origin and Influence of External Elements in a Colonial Setting', PhD Thesis, University of York (1979), p. 614.

[77] MNA S1/6/38 Southern Rhodesia: Reports by Itinerant Labour Officers, Note to Chief Secretary, 27th March 1939.

[78] MNA S21/2/1/5 Broadcasts in Chinyanja of war news, 7th May 1941.

[79] Interview with Ibrahim from Dedza District, February 2008. On the potential for radio to create new communities and transcend boundaries, see Liz Gunner, Dina Ligaga, and Dumisani Moyo (eds.), *Radio in Africa: Publics, Cultures, Communities* (Woodbridge, 2012).

Shona than in Chichewa [Chinyanja]'.[80] Similarly, Ibrahim and his family lived in Salisbury for so long they communicated in Chishona more often than Chinyanja, and this continued to be the case when they returned to Malawi in the 1990s. Marriages between Nyasa men and Shona women were especially common in Salisbury (as was discussed in the previous chapter) so it was not unusual for migrant households to communicate in two or more languages. Agnes Galatiya, whose mother was Shona, and father a Nyasa, described the shared solidarity between those people from mixed marriages:

> There are so many who had a mother from Zimbabwe or South Africa and a father who was Malawian. I used to spend my time with those people. And when you heard that someone's father was from Malawi you could even stay in that person's house as if they were your relative.[81]

Northern migrants in Salisbury were from a variety of ethnic and territorial backgrounds but speaking a common language provided a degree of unity.[82] Dzoole Bello, a Lomwe man from Thyolo District, described his encounters with other Nyasas in Southern Rhodesia:

> I met other people there. You could get to know them because of the language, we spoke the same language, but most of them I didn't know before I went…Just by the language I could tell that this person was a fellow Nyasa, and you would ask each other where you were from…I also used to speak Zezuru [one of the six dialects among those which make up the Shona group]. There were so many languages, because there were so many different tribes there. For example, Makolekole [Makorekore]…and Chilapalapa was like our English.[83]

Chilapalapa (sometimes referred to as Fanagolo) was a language commonly used in communications between different racial and ethnic groups, especially in the mines and other workplaces across southern Africa. It is often described as a pidgin or hybrid of Zulu, English and

[80] Interview with Mr Galatiya, Ntcheu District, February 2008.

[81] Interview with Agnes Galatiya, Ntcheu District, February 2008.

[82] Msindo describes language as an important 'identifier' in colonial Bulawayo: Msindo, 'Ethnicity, not Class?', pp. 446–447.

[83] Interview with Dzoole Bello, Thyolo District, February 2008. Makorekore is another ethnicity falling within the Shona group.

Afrikaans, although it is likely to have included words from many more southern African dialects, including Chewa/Nyanja and Shona.[84]

The strength of ties between Northern Rhodesian and Nyasaland Africans was also highlighted through shared language as well as certain cultural practices. Ibrahim's wife was born in Southern Rhodesia, and her father was from Northern Rhodesia. For Ibrahim this was an advantage in gaining his father-in-law's approval of their marriage: 'I used to run some errands for him. Malawians and Zambians get along very well. Zambians and Malawians are like cousins of some sort, the Senga from Zambia, and the Yao from Malawi.'[85] Stephen Lungu told a similar story about his parents:

> My mother comes from the eastern part of Zambia, which is called Chipata and they had a similar culture [to Malawians]. My father comes from Salima. Their culture was more or less similar in the Central Region and Chipata, and so they used to have these arranged marriages. My mother was 'given' to my father when she was only thirteen. My father was about fifty and so the gap between a thirteen-year-old and a fifty-year-old was just too wide.[86]

Religious institutions provided another valuable means for men and women to forge new networks in the city. Several African churches in Salisbury conducted services in Chinyanja in the 1920s, and for a while Chinyanja was the language of instruction in the Presbyterian schools in the city.[87] Already, from 1911, census figures showed that next to the Anglican Church, Presbyterians from Nyasaland were the largest denominational community in Salisbury. The Presbyterian Church later incorporated Chishona into its sermons as the number of Southern Rhodesian African migrants entering the city and joining the congregation increased. Long-term Nyasa migrants used Chishona for professional

[84] Ireen Mudeka, 'Gendered Exclusion and Contestation: Malawian Women's Migration and Work in Colonial Harare, Zimbabwe, 1930s–1963', *African Economic History*, 44 (2016), p. 32.

[85] Interview with Ibrahim, Dedza District.

[86] Interview with Stephen Lungu, Chatham, Kent, November 2006. Stephen did not approve of his parents' marriage which was always a tense relationship and broke down when he was still very young.

[87] Carl Fredrik Hallencreutz, *Religion and Politics in Harare, 1890–1980* (Uppsala, 1999), p. 53.

or business matters, while Chinyanja was more widely spoken at home, or at church, and around fellow 'northern' migrants. Nyasa men recalled learning to speak Chishona in beer halls whereas women often learnt languages from each other in church guild groups. Stephen Tsinambuto's wife went to women's meetings in Bulawayo with other Nyasa women. They used to go to the choir and church meetings together and lent each other money when someone needed help.[88] Litness Huwa also recalled how the women's groups in Salisbury involved people from different ethnic groups, 'there were Shona and others from Malawi'.[89] The group used to help organise weddings, she added, 'cultural dances would always accompany weddings. Singing and dancing was very important. When we had weddings, we would sing and dance like we do here in a village in Malawi. All of the people at a wedding would do dances from their own countries'.[90] New urban vernaculars evolved as a result of mixed marriages and the multi-ethnic urban population. One example of this noted in post-independence Zimbabwe, is an amalgamation of Chishona and English, referred to as 'ChiHarare'. When spoken by people of Malawian descent it draws upon elements of Chinyanja.[91]

Fanagolo or Chilapalapa was used in communications between Africans, Europeans and Indians in Salisbury, and more widely throughout central and southern Africa. The African-based pidgin dialect varied from one place to another. Stephen Lungu suggested that the dialect spoken in Salisbury in the 1960s was greatly influenced by migrants from Nyasaland:

> Some of the Chichewa language used was a mixture. They [Malawians] also spoke a language which they called 'Fanagolo', it's a 'Lapa' a mixture of Zulu, English, Chewa...It's a Zulu word. It is mixed, like slang but it was adopted as a mine language, those who couldn't speak English that's the language they spoke, in Zimbabwe it used to be called 'Chilapalapa.'

[88] Interview with Stephen Tsinambuti and Mrs Tsinambuto, Ntcheu District, February 2008.

[89] Interview with Litness Huwa, Sharpvale, Ntcheu District, February 2008.

[90] Ibid.

[91] Sinfree Makoni, Janina Brutt-Griffler and Pedzisai Mashiri, 'The Use of 'Indigenous' and Urban Vernaculars in Zimbabwe', *Language in Society* 36, 1 (2007), p. 38.

> All those that worked in the mines, the farms, or the white suburbs, garden boys and cooks and so on, they talk Chilapalapa.[92]

Urban migrants moved with ease across language boundaries and were equally adaptive in their displays of ethnic or cultural identity through dance, dress and other kinds of customs. Nyasas were able to move between social contexts drawing from various cultural options available to them. This process expanded identities beyond ethnicity. Ethnic identities in African townships remained salient in some contexts but moved into the private or domestic sphere as new cultural identities became more prominent. Membership of religious institutions, linguistic unity and other common aspects of urban labour migration became symbols of Nyasa culture. Migrants identifying with the *Nyau* or burial societies were not identifying with ethnicity per se although this was often implied. Anthropologists from the Rhodes-Livingstone Institute who wrote at length about African cities in the region painted a picture of African urban worlds, divided between the fading micro-loyalties of 'the tribe' and the emerging cosmopolitan culture of a more permanently urbanised African class.[93] This interpretation failed to account for the multi-dimensional aspects of ethnicity and expanded cultural identities displayed in Salisbury, which incorporated rural ethnic origins, ancestry, language, customs and religion.

Cultural labels such as 'Nyasa', *MaBlantyre*, *MaNyasarande* or 'Blantyre Boy' were used in a generic and popular way to define Nyasa migrants in the city. Similarly, the term 'Shangaan' was used to describe Tsonga-speaking peoples of south east Africa, on the Witwatersrand. More generally, it became all-embracing and referred to all Mozambicans employed in the mines in South Africa.[94] At times African labelling

[92] Interview with Stephen Lungu, Chatham, Kent, November 2006.

[93] A summary of the research conducted by the Rhodes-Livingstone Institute is provided in M. Gluckman, 'Tribalism in Modern British Central Africa', *Cahiers d'Etudes Africaines*, 1, 1 (1960), pp. 55–70.

[94] Patrick Harries, 'Exclusion, Classification and Internal Colonialism: The Emergence of Ethnicity Among the Tsonga-Speakers of South Africa', in Vail, *The Creation of Tribalism in Southern Africa*, p. 86.

could be 'as crude and arbitrary' as that of the missionaries and colonial authorities.[95] Names such as *Mabhurandaya* also applied to those of mixed Shona-Nyasa/Malawian parentage, and to people who had never been to Nyasaland. Agnes Galatiya explained:

> Sometimes the Shona weren't treating us nicely. They used to call us *Mablantyre*, even though my mother was Zimbabwean, because she belonged more to her father's side. I used to feel insulted when they called us *Mablantyre*, or *mabwidi* or *obwera*. These were names for foreigners.

While these labels were derogatory from some, for others they were simply a marker of a shared cultural heritage.[96]

Conclusion

Historians and anthropologists have previously noted the ways in which migrants drew upon their rural origins to arrange their lives in the city.[97] Charles Van Onselen described the 'social and conceptual baggage of the countryside',[98] which made its way to the mines and colonial cities. This chapter has developed these ideas by illustrating how traditional rural identities sat alongside new 'modern' ones, forming multiple layers of migrant identity. In the case of Nyasa migrants, identity expanded beyond ethnicity. Local stereotypes and ideas of difference informed the process of identity formation. Being Nyasa meant being bound by territorial and linguistic unity, speaking the language of 'northern migrants'—Chinyanja, but it also involved grasping new identities which others had devised. In this case the *Nyau* and the CCAP provide examples of new cultural markers. This chapter has begun to explore the religious lives of migrants in the city and the following chapter will examine church and religious affiliations in more detail. In the 1950s colonial officials suggested that 'tribal' mixtures were responsible for the lack of cohesive community spirit

[95] Jocelyn Alexander and JoAnn McGregor 'Modernity and Ethnicity in a Frontier Society: Understanding Difference in Northwestern Zimbabwe', *Journal of Southern African Studies*, 23, 2 (1997), pp. 187–203.

[96] Interview with Agnes Galatiya, Ntcheu District, February 2008.

[97] James, *Songs of the Women Migrants*, p. 23.

[98] Van Onselen, *Chibaro*, p. 195.

within the urban areas.[99] Yet, migrants used various 'traditional' customs to create new networks to help ease the pressures of the urban environment. With the rise of nationalist politics many of these identities were contested once again as we shall see in Chapter 6.

[99] ZNA S51/8 Urban African Affairs Commission, 1957.

CHAPTER 5

Community, Leisure and Urban Life

This chapter situates Nyasa migrants in Salisbury during the industrial and urban expansion of the 1930s to the 1950s. As the Depression hit the regional economy, flows of migrant labour from Nyasaland to Southern Rhodesia slowed as fewer employment opportunities were available. A period of economic recovery followed in the 1940s, and migration to and within the colony increased once again. White settlers viewed an African urban influx as a threat to the economic and political hegemony of white Southern Rhodesia and made stronger demands for 'total' racial segregation between Europeans and Africans. The result was a series of new laws designed to more tightly regulate labour and mobility, pushing indigenous Africans into 'Native Reserves' and the urban wage labour market where they would live in townships on a temporary basis only entering European areas of the city for work purposes or with permission. The full impact of this legislation was felt in the 1950s as greater numbers of Africans from within Southern Rhodesia moved into Salisbury on a more permanent basis. Salisbury underwent enormous expansion during these decades. As the city increased in size and population, new townships were built leading to the creation of new African urban communities. At the same time, municipal control tightened over every aspect of African urban life.

Labour from the northern colonies of Nyasaland and Northern Rhodesia had long been welcomed into Salisbury. Yet, in the late 1950s,

Z. R. Groves, *Malawian Migration to Zimbabwe, 1900–1965*, Cambridge Imperial and Post-Colonial Studies Series,
https://doi.org/10.1007/978-3-030-54104-0_5

when the growth of the federal economy began to slow and competition for jobs intensified once again, policy shifted towards the creation of a more permanent African labour force. Local government favoured Africans from within the settler colony when allocating new township housing and attempts were made to marginalise 'alien' labour from the urban economy. Despite the challenges of urban life, Nyasa migrants still found and created a sense of community in Salisbury's townships. Entire families from Nyasaland settled in the city, laying down roots and paving the way for successive generations of migration from Malawi. New churches were established in the city to cater to the spiritual needs of migrant workers and urban residents re-ordered their social lives around church meetings, leisure pursuits and the local beer hall.

African Urban Areas Before 1950

Salisbury Native Location (later known as Harare African Township and from 1980 as Mbare) was the first official residence for Africans in the city. It was created in 1907 under the Native Urban Locations Ordinance (1906)—a law which formally divided the city according to race, with separate living areas for Africans and Europeans.[1] The location was situated only 5 km to the south of the city centre, and bordered the industrial area to the south west. Urban housing provision was inadequate from the start and the location was characterised by overcrowding, high rents, and a lack of amenities and facilities. During an investigation into working and living conditions for Nyasaland Africans in Salisbury in the mid-1930s, Nyasaland's Senior Provincial Commissioner, J. C. Abraham noted the inadequate provision of housing:

> ...any room falling vacant is immediately filled. In fact there is a waiting list. A single room is rented for 11s. per month and usually houses three or four or even more natives; for a double roomed hut the rent is 17s. and 6d. per month. Food for a man, wife and two children costs not less than 6d. per day; firewood is 5s. a load; beer costs 6d. a pint...The pay of a domestic servant averages 30s., and a labourer 15s. to 17s. 6d. per month...Regarding sanitation...little had been done to improve the

[1] Tsuneo Yoshikuni, *African Urban Experiences in Colonial Zimbabwe: A Social History of Harare Before 1925* (Harare, 2007), p. 9.

> sanitary conveniences of the Location, and the latrines were far too few in number.[2]

By 1936, accommodation in the Salisbury Native Location (hereafter, referred to as 'the location') consisted of 71 cottages, 124 huts and 1012 brick rooms.[3] On average, houses accommodated more than three people per room. Because of overcrowding, the location was considered unfit for 'decent natives' and a 'spoiler of families'.[4] African women were strongly discouraged from living there by officials and more conservative African men and missionaries, and were not permitted to occupy housing without their husbands.[5] Two more compounds belonging to the Native Affairs Department and the Police were built for African occupation in central Salisbury, both near the railway station.[6] After 1907, workers exercised limited choice over their place of residence, which was usually tied to employment, although some chose to reside in unofficial areas further outside of the city. Others lived on European owned farms or in accommodation provided by European domestic employers, usually the back room attached to the house or in the garden, known as the *kia*.

Like all cities, the African urban population was in constant flux. Migrant workers from within Southern Rhodesia stayed for short periods before returning to nearby rural areas during the rainy season and at harvest. Longer distance migrants moved in and out, depending on their employment status and family commitments. Farms and settlements outside of the municipal boundary accommodated large numbers of Nyasa migrants. Epworth, Chishawasha and Waterfalls Induna were close

[2] J. C. Abraham, *Nyasaland Natives in the Union of South Africa and in Southern Rhodesia* (Zomba, 1937), p. 21.

[3] Ibid. Kaytor huts in the Old Bricks (*MaOld Brikisi*) section were the oldest houses in the location and were occupied by single migrant men and some families. Jo'burg Lines (*Majubeki*) and the New Location were seen as more respectable by township dwellers. See Yoshikuni, *African Urban Experiences*, pp. 38–65 and Maurice T. Vambe, "'*Ayo Mahoba*': Migrant Labour and the Cultural Semiotics of Harare (Mbare) African Township, 1930–1970', in Fassil Demissie (ed.), *Colonial Architecture and Urbanism in Africa: Intertwined and Contested Histories* (Abingdon, 2016).

[4] Michael West, *The Rise of an African Middle Class: Colonial Zimbabwe, 1898–1965* (Bloomington, 2002), p. 101.

[5] ZNA S85 Native Affairs Commission, Salisbury Location, 1930. Oral and written evidence.

[6] Abraham, *Nyasaland Natives*, p. 21.

to the mission schools and churches in the south and east of the city (see Map 5.2). The Wesleyan Methodist Church at Epworth was especially popular among Nyasa migrants, as were the nearby Catholic and Anglican Churches.[7] Life on the peri-urban farms (those just outside of the municipal boundary) was relatively cheap and Africans residing there enjoyed greater freedom than in the Salisbury Native Location. Residents were able to keep their own gardens and even grow enough produce to sell any surplus in the city. The drawback was the inconvenient distance from town. Agnes Galatiya, whose husband worked at Gwibi College on the outskirts of the city, was one of those fortunate to gain access to a small plot: 'although we were not allowed to have a garden at the college [Gwibi], we did have a piece of land by the railway line where we used to grow maize'.[8] Access to land provided a source of food but also an additional means of income that was not available to those in the location.

Location life was highly regulated. A curfew was in place between 9 pm and 5 am unless a letter of permission was obtained by the Location Superintendent or an employer. Accommodation was not provided for casual visitors and married and single living quarters were kept as separate as possible (although there were many instances of couples living side by side with single male workers). The inner-city location was characterised by poverty, prostitution, drunkenness, and 'immorality'. The Location Superintendent, Albert Edward Horne, insisted that there were no prostitutes living in the township, although he conceded that there may be some 'loose characters': '[When] a man has saved £20 or £30 he picks up a woman, spends money on her. They live together for months until the money is finished'.[9] Waltar Chipwayo, a representative of the Rhodesia Native Association complained that many men in the location wasted their money on 'loose women' and neglected their families back home.[10] The Rhodesian Native Association (RNA) was a moderate African organisation generally tolerated by the administration. Its membership was composed of Mashonaland-based Christian landowners who were interested in achieving greater educational opportunity for Africans, access to

[7] Tsuneo Yoshikuni, *Elizabeth Musodzi and the Birth of African Feminism in Early Colonial Zimbabwe* (Harare, 2008), pp. 4–5.

[8] Interview with Agnes Galatiya, Ntcheu District, February 2008.

[9] ZNA S85 Native Affairs Commission, Salisbury Location, 1930, Oral and written evidence.

[10] Ibid.

individual 'Purchase lands', and improved representation for Africans in government. The group was most active during the 1920s and drew much of their support from the 'progressive' farmers of Mashonaland.[11] The RNA campaigned extensively on the issue of prostitution in the city. The Native Police were often criticised for their handling of so-called 'loose women'. Township residents also complained that African police lived with 'the bad women in the location'.[12] One location resident by the name Bamingo told the Native Affairs Commission in Salisbury, 'They [the native police] should be properly married men. None of the police boys have proper wives'.[13] Migrant men and women were blamed for the existence of sex work in the city. One police CID headquarters circular in 1920 addressed the 'immoral' behaviour of 'native foreigners':

> Native foreigners who are convicted of offences defined in the ordinances of 1900 and 1903 are liable to deportation. With a view therefore to dealing with native foreigners – a large number of whom are procurers and live on the earnings of prostitution – it is urged that special attention should be given to this matter.[14]

Senior (Government) Medical Officer to Salisbury and Chairman of the Native Welfare Association insisted that 'The question of the travelling prostitute [was] a serious one and should be tackled at once'. The travelling prostitute, he claimed, was at the root of all immorality: 'She is paid well, dresses well and then creates an inducement to her sister'.[15] Conservative Nyasa men could be equally judgmental about the behaviour of migrants and 'unattached women' in the city. Daniel Ndalama frowned

[11] On the Rhodesia Native Association, see Terence Ranger, *The African Voice in Southern Rhodesia* (London, 1970), pp. 105–109. On notions of respectability among women in the township, see Marja Hinfelaar, *Respectable and Responsible Women: Methodist and Roman Catholic Women's Organisations in Harare, Zimbabwe (1919–1985)* (Zoetermeer, 2001).

[12] ZNA S85 Native Affairs Commission, Salisbury, 1930, Oral Evidence.

[13] These comments also relate to the so-called ethnic rivalry between Chewa and Ngoni in the location in the 1920s. Also, ZNA S85 Native Affairs Commission, Salisbury, 1930, Oral and written evidence.

[14] ZNA S1219 Police CID HQ Circulars, 17th May 1920 'Immorality and Indecency Ordinance 1 of 1916'.

[15] ZNA S85 Native Affairs Commission, Salisbury, 1930, Oral and written evidence.

upon the actions of African men and women in Salisbury who he regarded as *dwambale* – crooks. He explained:

> We never wanted to change to that way of life, because many of them were sleeping with prostitutes. We never wanted to be like them because if we saw young women…we never would have wanted to come back. The ones who did that were the ones who became *machona*. If you were tempted by women you would never have enough money to get back home…they became like citizens over there. I just wanted to stay where I worked and get the money to buy a bicycle.[16]

Single migrant men often entered informal marriages with women in the townships who were known as *mapoto* wives (literally, women of the pots), so-called as they would perform domestic duties in return for accommodation in the location. For Daniel, the 'evils' of the city were connected to the danger of becoming *lichona* (a lost one): 'If you were tempted by women you would never have enough money to get you back home when you wanted to return'.[17]

Respectable urban dwellers regarded beer halls as places frequented by 'aliens' and 'where children and wives were lost to the control of parents and husbands'.[18] But beer halls could be an important meeting place and a point of social exchange.[19] The beer hall was a central feature of location life and aroused mixed feelings from the urban populace, employers and local authorities. Migrants learnt local languages, exchanged stories

[16] Interview with Daniel Ndalama, Thyolo District, February 2008. Born in 1915, Daniel was the oldest Malawian man we interviewed during this research. He travelled to Southern Rhodesia for the first time in 1939.

[17] Ibid.

[18] Ian Phimister and Charles Van Onselen, 'The Political Economy of Tribal Animosity: A Case Study of the 1929 Bulawayo Location Faction Fight', *Journal of Southern African Studies,* 6, 1 (1979), p. 29.

[19] The significance of beer halls, alcohol and their connection with urban culture, nationalism and different attitudes towards drinking in urban and mining centres, have been explored by many scholars. For instance, Frederick Cooper, *Struggle for the City: Migrant Labour, Capital and the State in Urban Africa* (London, 1983), pp. 7–8; Patrick Harries, *Work Culture and Identity: Migrant Laborers in Mozambique and South Africa, c.1860–1910* (London, 1994), pp. 57–59 and pp. 120–121; Charles Van Onselen, *Chibaro: African Mine Labour in Southern Rhodesia, 1900–1933* (London, 1976), pp. 166–167. More recently on South Africa, Anne Kelk Mager, *Beer, Sociability and Masculinity in South Africa* (Bloomington, 2010).

about employers, and simply enjoyed their leisure time outside of the workplace. Situated between Old Bricks (where the earliest council brick houses were built) and New Lines, the main beer hall was, 'a large barrack-like building with only the most functional amenities'. William Saidi described in his novel set in Salisbury during the 1950s how people journeyed from New Location, National, Jo'burg Lines and the bachelor hostels on the banks of the Mukuvisi River to seek 'company, boisterous earthy company'. Even those as far as Old and New Highfield travelled to the main beer hall.[20]

Beer halls in the bigger mines and locations in Southern Rhodesia were condemned by Christian leaders. The Nyasaland Labour Chaplain visited workplaces in Southern Rhodesia in the mid-1950s and described the Wankie beer hall as 'disgraceful'. The Chaplain saw illegal brewing as 'the curse of this country' and called for much tighter regulation over the consumption of beer:

> ...I do not mean that I would like to see the beer halls disappear. The only things I regret and find disgraceful are the following: too much drinking, nearly daily, and without individual rationing. The consequence in some places is much drunkenness and always that the men have not a penny left at the end of the month...To allow a married man to drink all his money away and leave his home family in poverty is not serving the liberty of the subject but giving license to be a criminal if sound Christian sociology is still admitted.[21]

Members of the church grew frustrated with the Southern Rhodesian government who refused to abolish the beer halls because they were a major source of revenue for the maintenance of urban areas. African elites were generally in agreement with the church on the issue; the battle against 'joint drinking' persisted from the 1920s and continued into the 1950s.[22] Married men did not want their wives mixing with single male migrants, and claimed that joint drinking was against their 'native customs', as well as being financially and morally detrimental to men

[20] Saidi, *Old Bricks Lives*, pp. 12–13.

[21] MNA 14239.II Nyasaland Government Representative, Report from the Nyasaland Labour Chaplain, 1st March 1954.

[22] Michael. O. West, 'Liquor and Libido: "Joint Drinking" and the Politics of Sexual Control in Colonial Zimbabwe, 1920s–1950s', *Journal of Social History*, 30, 3 (1997), pp. 645–667.

and women in the urban and industrial areas. Although many government officials were sympathetic with the views of African urban elites, the government rejected calls made by the Southern Rhodesia Conference of Native Christians in 1932 to separate the beer halls according to sex. Missionaries and educated Africans made selective references to 'tradition'. At times African elites were keen to emphasise the importance of retaining rural traditions, as was shown in the case of the visiting Nyasaland chiefs to respectable housing areas in Southern Rhodesia, and quick to point to the 'rootless individuals' who existed in a disintegrated urban environment. These were attempts to distinguish themselves from 'the migrant ranks'. The controversy over joint drinking in beerhalls was attributable in part to the skewed gender composition of the urban areas. The Howman Committee report (produced by the commission set up to investigate urban social conditions in Southern Rhodesia) described the urban areas as having 'an abnormal structure': '...an overwhelming preponderance of men, an almost complete absence of old age...and a coming and going which cuts away the roots of every association, society and personal leadership that might crystallise out of the fluid mass of the irresponsible 18-35 age group'.[23]

But this was not a fair representation of African urban society. Even in the 1930s, when conditions were arguably at their worst, individuals and families still created a sense of community. Often this was generated by local church groups as well as participation in sports and other leisure pursuits. Boxing and football were popular among migrant workers in many southern African cities and Salisbury was no exception. The first recreation ground in the location was provided in 1923 and helped to promote football although it was not until the 1940s that it replaced boxing as the most popular sporting activity among residents. Football was seen as a more respectable sport and became a prominent feature of township life across Salisbury from the 1940s.[24] One team that played regularly in Salisbury was 'the Nyasaland Tigers'.[25] Nyasa migrant Stephen Tsinambuto used to watch matches between 'the Highlanders' and 'the Dynamos' in the 1950s when players from Nyasaland

[23] ZNA S1561/51 The Howman Committee, 1944.

[24] On football in African Townships, see O. W. Stuart, '"Good boys", Footballers and Strikers: African Social Change in Bulawayo, 1933–1953', PhD Dissertation, SOAS, University of London (1989).

[25] ZNA S2584/85/2 'Native Welfare Society', Volume II.

were on both teams.[26] As far as the authorities were concerned, sport was a preferred outlet for migrant workers over 'dances of an undesirable type'[27]—but only if regulated. Conservative thinkers of the time, such as the Native Commissioner Charles Bullock, saw organised sports as a legitimate alternative to sexual activity for single male migrant workers—he hoped that these activities would reduce the prevalence of prostitution in the locations.[28]

Boxing was much more popular than football in the townships, until it came under municipal control. Large numbers used to gather and watch the fights, bringing with them stones and other weapons, which alarmed the authorities.[29] One of Salisbury's most famous African boxers was a man named Dhuri from Nyasaland, who settled with his family in Harare African Township. Native Welfare Societies encouraged sports matches along ethnic lines and Dhuri represented 'the Nyasas' in the location.[30] However, his acceptance and fame went beyond ethnicity—he was 'a Salisbury phenomenon' rather than simply 'a Nyasa migrant hero'.[31] Generations later, Dhuri's fame is still celebrated among long-term residents in Harare. Dhuri's children and grandchildren live in Mbare on the same plot once occupied by Dhuri, and his photograph is displayed proudly on the wall of their living room.[32]

[26] Interview with Stephen Tsinambuto, Ntcheu District, February 2008.

[27] Charles Bullock, Secretary for Native Affairs to Town Clerk, 1937, quote in Scarnecchia, 'The Politics of Gender and Class in the Creation of African Communities, Salisbury, Rhodesia, 1937–1957', PhD Thesis, University of Michigan (1993), p. 78.

[28] Ibid. Charles Bullock sought advice from a trained sociologist from South Africa, in regard to control over African urban areas and the regularization of African recreation in Salisbury. Terence Ranger, 'Pugilism and Pathology: African Boxing and the Black Urban Experience in Urban Southern Rhodesia', William J. Baker and James A. Mangan (eds.), *Sport in Africa: Essays in Social History* (London, 1987), p. 201. On the links between culture, leisure and social control on South Africa's gold mines, see Cecile Badenhorst and Charles Mather, 'Tribal Recreation and Recreating Tribalism: Culture, Leisure and Social Control on South Africa's Gold Mines, 1940–1950', *Journal of Southern African Studies*, 23, 3 (1997), pp. 473–489.

[29] Ibid., p. 81. On boxing and sport in African urban areas, see Ranger, 'Pugilism and Pathology', pp. 196–213.

[30] Ibid., p. 210.

[31] Scarnecchia, 'The Politics of Gender and Class', p. 84.

[32] I met with Dhuri's children and grandchildren and visited his old house in Mbare in 2012.

Daniel Likhobwe lived in Mabvuku, a township 17 km to the east of central Harare developed in the early 1950s for African families. Mabvuku became known as a 'higher-class' African residential area and when compared to other Nyasaland migrants, Daniel was relatively wealthy.[33] He worked as a waiter in a bar at a prominent Salisbury hotel for more than ten years and later ran his own laundry business. 'I used to serve Castle [a local beer] to the *azungu* (white people) and they would always give me tips. I was happy there, that was why I spent fifteen years there'. When Daniel eventually returned to Nyasaland, he had saved up enough money to buy a car and was able to drive home: 'I was made very welcome when I came back', he explained, 'because I had lots of property. I had lots of money and two accounts: one at the post office and one at the bank'.[34] Daniel lived in Mabvuku with his Nyasa wife and their only child. He was also married to a Manyika woman who worked as a domestic servant and lived at her employer's house. He described how he used to spend his leisure time in Salisbury, going to the cinema and to see dances, and playing sports:

> Sometimes I used to go and watch football but I liked boxing… I started boxing as a sport and we used to have it on Wednesdays and Sundays, young people and then the older ones. I was really good at boxing and one day a man told me I should take some tattoos [sic] to make me good at boxing, but the next time I was defeated and then I wasn't very good after that.[35]

[33] Daniel Likhobwe, Thyolo District, February 2008.

[34] Ibid.

[35] Interview with Daniel Likhobwe, Thyolo District, February 2008.

By 'tattoos', Daniel was referring to *mangoromera*, a medicine taken to give 'strength and fearlessness' when fighting.[36] Boxing and football attracted spectators from other townships:

> ...More people came to watch the boxing matches than the football matches. People really enjoy[ed] fights, they like[d] watching the blows! The matches used to take place within the locations. The grown-ups used to fight on Sundays and the younger ones on Wednesdays...The location was big so there were usually just fights within the location. But for the older people boxing on Sundays, people used to come and go to other locations.[37]

Music was another popular feature of township life. On a visit in 1936 Abraham noted the location jazz band that performed regularly for residents in the townships: 'The band belongs to a Nyasaland native who has been away from his home in Fort Johnston for thirty years; he must be quite rich, since he had just paid £35 for a saxophone'. He also commented on the eating hall leased to a man from Northern Rhodesia for £7 per month who had a retail store selling groceries at the other end.[38] Both the eating store and the jazz band were organised by 'northerners' with long-term interests in the city.

A government commission into the development of Salisbury in 1930 recognised that the Salisbury African Location had grown into 'an important Native township', and that more resources needed to go into improving the facilities and services provided. A minute in the Salisbury Welfare Society declared: 'It is no longer, as it was twenty-three

[36] The medicine was said to be made from 'the skins of such animals as the lion, elephant, hippo, honeybear, crocodile, the head of a black mamba, two kinds of fish found in the Zambesi and various herbs.' The ingredients would be burned together and pounded into a powder that was rubbed into incisions made in the wrists of those wanting to increase their strength. 'A person wishing to be a tower of strength will go as far as to have all his joints doctored as well as his chest. Some wear wrist guards (leather or python skin) which have been soaked in the preparation. The medicine is sometimes sewn into the wrist guards.' From ZNA S998 'Mangoromera', quoted in Phimister and Van Onselen, 'The Political Economy of Tribal Animosity', p. 33. See also, Terence Ranger, 'The Meaning of Urban Violence in Africa: Bulawayo, Southern Rhodesia, 1893–1960', *Cultural and Social History*, 3, 2 (2006), pp. 193–228.

[37] Interview with Daniel Likhobwe, Thyolo District, February 2008.

[38] J. C. Abraham, *Nyasaland Natives*, p. 21.

years ago, a housing place for temporary labourers'.[39] The Reverend Holman Brown from Epworth Mission in Greater Salisbury emphasised the responsibility of the government to meet with the increasing needs of the African urban populace: 'The town is growing and therefore its needs must be supplied at the location'.[40] Despite their comments, little was done to improve the housing situation until almost twenty years later when mounting political pressure forced the government into action.

'Highfield Village Settlement' was a new official outer town African housing area and the first to be built after the original Salisbury Native Location. Captain A. C. Jennings became the superintendent at Highfield when it opened in 1936, when it consisted of just 28 cottages.[41] Jennings was housed in a three roomed cottage, which served as an office until 1954 when a purpose-built venue was constructed on the village green. A borehole was drilled to provide water to the residents and as the settlement expanded, four additional boreholes were created. Eventually, in 1955, Highfield was connected to the municipal water supply, nearly twenty years after it was built. In contrast to the original Salisbury Location, 'Old Highfield' (as it became known once 'New Highfield' was constructed in the 1950s) was intended for married couples and became a more desirable place to live than the inner-city township.

When Highfield Village was first established there were no commercial services at all. By 1940 the market area consisted of five small shops, including a butchery, a carpentry shop and three general dealers. The main businesses later moved to another area of the village and the old market became a place for light industries, such as carpentry shops and garages. The one-acre cemetery was eventually extended over a new plot and the Presbyterian church was built in 1939. The first clinic opened in the settlement in 1941 and was visited twice weekly by a government medical officer. 'The North School' was the first school to be established and by 1956 there were four large schools including one devoted to Domestic Science. There was even an 'Old Man's Home' opened in 1943, under the control of the Native Commissioner for Salisbury, using a grant donated by the Lottery Trustees. All the cottages were let on

[39] ZNA RH16/4/1/3 Salisbury African Welfare Society minutes, 1930.

[40] ZNA S85 Native Affairs Commission, Salisbury Location, 1930, Oral and written evidence.

[41] ZNA S51 Urban African Affairs Committee 'Memorandum on Urban Housing Conditions by the Director and Assistant Director of Native Education', 24th July 1957.

short-term contracts until the 1950s when it became possible to rent on a longer basis, thus providing additional security for families. The Southern Rhodesian government boasted about the quality of facilities in Highfield Village: 'Visitors came from all parts of South and Central Africa to see the improvement made in African housing – a big advance on anything done in this direction anywhere in Southern or Central Africa'.[42] Old Highfield came to be associated with more 'respectable' urban dwellers, while Salisbury Location and the municipal townships in the inner-city continued to be seen as the place for bachelors and non-indigenous migrants—where *maNyasarande* should stay.[43] Yet, the location also accommodated aspirant Nyasa migrant families. Ibrahim slept at the train station when he first arrived in the city from Dedza in the early 1950s. Once he secured regular employment that provided him with accommodation, he was able to save up enough money to eventually move into a family house in the Salisbury Location. By the time he left Harare many years later he had successfully built up his own tailoring business and paid for his children to receive a decent education. Like many others, Ibrahim knew nobody when he first arrived in Salisbury; he had travelled alone by train from Blantyre without an endorsed identity certificate. Nevertheless, he found a job in a textile factory (working for the David Whitehead Textile Company) which provided him with compound accommodation and there he remained for several years until the company packed up and moved to Northern Rhodesia. He declined the opportunity to go with the company as he still held aspirations to leave Southern Rhodesia for the more lucrative employment markets of South Africa but in the mid-1950s it became harder for Nyasas to cross into the Union, so he remained in Salisbury. Ibrahim returned to Nyasaland as a relatively wealthy man. Back in Malawi, he was a respected member of the local Muslim community in Dedza. Ibrahim reminisced fondly about his time in Salisbury and the neighbourly charity he had received and was later able to extend to others when they could not afford to buy food.[44] Ibrahim's narrative demonstrates the sense of community which was felt even in the

[42] ZNA S51/8 Information presented to the African Urban Affairs Commission, 1957.

[43] Terri Barnes and Everjoyce Win, *To Live a Better Life: An Oral History of Women in the City of Harare, 1930–70* (Harare, 1992), p. 28.

[44] Interview with Ibrahim from Dedza District, February 2008.

cramped and poorly resources African urban areas of Salisbury. His experience contrasted with the negative portrayal of African urban life found in settler government reports of the 1950s:

> The essence of a community is stability for only then can roots develop. Insecurity of tenure, migratory labour, too large a proportion of lodgers, absence of families, economic life – all these militate against or make impossible the emergence of a community.[45]

Highfield expanded and other new townships were constructed in the 1950s to accommodate the increasing urban workforce. The new developments were part of a tentative policy of 'labour stabilisation', which sought for the first time to encourage workers to settle permanently in the city with their families.[46] In addition, the Salisbury City Council opened new single migrant hostels, including Carter House, the first official hostel for single African women.[47] Some employers felt that productivity and efficiency would improve if the 'vagrant bachelor' was replaced by the fully proletarianised married man.[48] The 'labour question' (as it came to be known) was debated into the 1950s and beyond. Not all employers and government officials were in favour of abolishing the temporary migrant labour system.[49] The expansion of African urban areas alarmed European settlers who lived near to the townships. Changes in urban policy resulted in part from the Land Apportionment Act of

[45] ZNA S51/8 Urban African Affairs Commission, 'Reply to Questionnaires by the Secretary for Native Affairs'.

[46] ZNA S1906 The Howman Committee: Appointed to Investigate the Economic, Social and Health Conditions of African Employed in Urban Areas, 1943–44.

[47] The Salisbury City Council had first investigated the need for 'a Hostel and Club Room for African females employed in Salisbury' in 1943, and the Federation of Native Welfare Societies had recommended it as an urgent need. For more on the Federation of Native (later African) Welfare Societies, see: Wits Historical Papers, Collection AD1715 South African Institute of Race Relations (SAIRR), 1892–1974, Item no's: 14-6-2-7 and 14-6-1-1, available at: http://www.historicalpapers.wits.ac.za/inventories/inv_pdfo/AD1715/AD1715-14-6-2-7-001-jpeg.pdf and http://www.historicalpapers.wits.ac.za/inventories/inv_pdfo/AD1715/AD1715-14-6-1-1-001-jpeg.pdf. Accessed: 5 July 2020.

[48] West, *The Rise of an African Middle Class,* p. 110. West is referring here to the terms used in the 1944 commission on African workers.

[49] Debates in British and French colonial policy regarding 'the labour question' are well documented in Frederick Cooper, *Decolonisation and African Society: The Labour Question in French and British Africa* (Cambridge, 1996), especially, pp. 323–360.

1930, which pushed more indigenous Africans into the city once it was enforced from 1941 onwards. An article in the *Rhodesia Herald* in the mid-1940s described the aims of this Act: 'In addition to clearing the way for a class of peasant farmers in the native areas, one is also creating a class of working urban dwellers who will gradually acquire habits of steady industry, and normal social life'.[50] The reality of the rural situation in many African reserves was one of widespread land alienation, overcrowding, and poor soil. Many had little option but to move to the city.

Prior to the change of labour policy in the 1940s, long-term labourers were already established in the urban areas on a semi-permanent basis. Migrant men accumulated profit from small businesses, which they built up over time and used to acquire land around Salisbury.[51] Workers from Nyasaland were occasionally bought land or cheap houses by their employers as a reward for reliable service.[52] However, opportunities for upward social and economic mobility in Southern Rhodesia diminished in the 1940s. Amendments to the Land Apportionment Act in 1941 made it illegal for Africans to lease urban premises, whether for business or residential purposes. A small number of migrants were able to earn money in the urban areas and to buy land in the nearby Native Purchase Areas. However, the Native Reserves were intended for indigenous Africans, not 'alien natives' as the Secretary for Native Affairs outlined in 1953:

> The Native Housing problem is most acute in Salisbury and Bulawayo, and Native Reserves exist within twenty miles of these towns, but Reserves

[50] *The Rhodesia Herald*, 2 September 1946.

[51] Stephen Thornton, 'The Struggle for Profit and Participation by an Emerging petty-Bourgeoisie in Bulawayo, 1893–1993', in Brian Raftopoulos and Tsuneo Yoshikuni (eds.), *Sites of Struggle: Essays in Zimbabwe's Urban History* (Harare, 1999), p. 31.

[52] This was the case with one employee of the Bulawayo Clothing factory who was granted a plot in the Bulawayo Location in 1920 when he reached retirement age. Others in Salisbury told similar stories about their houses in Dz in the 1960s. Nyasa migrant Henry Mangesana owed a house in the Bulawayo Location, which he sold to an Asian family in order to return to Nyasaland when he retired. The family who acquired the property already owned several houses which they used to accommodate migrant workers in their employment. Thornton, 'The Struggle for Profit', pp. 30–31.

> have been set aside for the communal benefit of *indigenous* natives whereas townships must cater for a proportion of non-indigenous people.[53]

Prior to the 1950s it had been possible for non-indigenous migrants to gain access to land in the nearby rural areas. If a Nyasa migrant man was married to a Shona woman, or had been resident in the country for ten years or more, they could approach a chief in a reserve and request permission to settle. Yet, due to the pressures on land this was no longer allowed.[54] The Land Apportionment Act cemented the boundaries of the Native Urban Areas, planned and built by the municipalities. Migrants no longer had the option to buy or construct properties in the suburbs of the city. The scramble for decent accommodation became desperate and the urban population continued to expand throughout the 1950s.

Strike Action and Urban Expansion

As Salisbury's industries expanded, tensions grew in the workplace and the mid to late 1940s were characterised by worker unrest and a series of strikes. Africans were not just protesting about working conditions. Accommodation and facilities provided by the municipality in the location were inadequate for the growing numbers of migrants present in the urban areas. In addition, harassment from police over pass laws and the poor conditions in which urban residents were forced to live meant migrant men were reluctant to bring their wives to join them. Mothers, wives and daughters were 'inconvenienced and humiliated' by police raids.[55] In 1944 proposals were discussed for the establishment of a Native Labour Bureau in Salisbury to control supplies of labour for mining, farming and domestic employment. One official raised the idea of family migration from Nyasaland:

> We have to realise that the bachelor native workman can never be an efficient labour force. Arrangements have to be made for the native to live on or near his job with his family... When the natives come down here as bachelors and form local attachments it is breaking up home life, but

[53] ZNA S51/8 Urban African Affairs Commission: Report of the Secretary for Native Affairs, 1953.

[54] ZNA S51/1 Urban African Affairs Commission, Oral Evidence, Salisbury 1957.

[55] Ibid., p. 96.

> if a man could come down here, get a good employer and then bring his family down he would settle down here and be a contented labourer.[56]

The following year, African railway employees in Salisbury and Bulawayo went on strike, involving 3000 and 1200 workers, respectively. According to reports, 600 Nyasaland natives were involved in the Salisbury strike, even though they were subject to dismissal and deportation if involved in illegal strike action. The Nyasaland labour representative suggested defensively that 'they [the Nyasas] had been intimidated into stopping work and behaved quietly through the strike'.[57] Strikers protested about inadequate pay, poor rations, bad housing and a lack of sympathy for their plight on the part of the railway administration. Some government officials concluded that conditions of work must be satisfactory or else there would have been more strikes during the Second World War.[58] However, an investigator from the Mining Commission quoted in the *Rhodesia Herald* suggested, '...we cannot say that the absence of strikes indicates that the natives are satisfied, because it would be a criminal offence for them to strike'.[59] Non-indigenous migrants significantly outnumbered indigenous workers on the mines and farms but they had even less power to influence their employers.

Despite the limitations on their right to protest, workers from Nyasaland had previously been involved in industrial action and urban protest. As early as 1907, a protest movement of urban residents was organised against the Native Urban Location Ordinance, which effectively confined urban residence to the location huts. Police forced a number of Nyasaland migrants out of homes which they had constructed themselves in the Kopje area—a place migrants thought more appropriate for their families to reside.[60] Similarly, Nyasas workers, many of whom were Watch Tower adherents, were held responsible for the Shamva Mine Strike in 1927.[61] The ring leader, Kufa Williams, an Ngoni man from Nyasaland

[56] MNA S36/1/1/4 Proposals for a Labour Bureau in Southern Rhodesia, 1944.

[57] ZNA F137/186C(i) Migrant Labour Report, 1946, Nyasaland Government Report for year ending 1945.

[58] *The Rhodesia Herald*, Thursday 3rd May 1945.

[59] Ibid.

[60] Yoshikuni, *African Urban Experiences*, p. 41.

[61] ZNA S715 (2) Shamva Mine Strike, 12th–17th September 1927.

had been in Southern Rhodesia for twenty years. He worked in Salisbury for a couple of years when he first came to the colony and moved around for a while, before settling into his job in Shamva where he was employed for twelve years before the strike took place. Three hundred Nyasaland workers were employed and lived at Shamva, including Yao, Ngoni, Chewa and Tonga men and many with their wives and children.[62]

Urban workers shared the same grievances as other migrant workers regardless of territorial origins. Complaints centred around the pass laws and the Native Urban Areas and Registration Act of 1946. These were fundamental concerns for migrant workers with families to support, whether they were residing in Salisbury or other urban areas in the colony. The Reformed Industrial and Commercial workers Union (RICU) attempted to improve working conditions and wages through township advisory boards and made calls for greater levels of representation for urban workers and residents. For urban residents across lines of class, gender, and ethnicity, the Native Urban Areas Registration and Accommodation Act was one of the most contested pieces of urban legislation in this period.[63] As the leading organisation in Salisbury in the late 1940s and early 1950s, the RICU engaged in an important phase of African politics, which Chapter 6 discusses further in the context of federation and African nationalism.

In the wake of the strike action in the mid-1940s, the municipal government launched several new African housing initiatives in Salisbury. The threat of urban protest and a potential alliance between the mass of migrant workers and educated African elites spurred the government into action. New housing schemes were an attempt by the government to appease the emerging middle classes, by diffusing their frustrations at having to share the same living quarters as lower-class migrants. In the 1940s the government had begun to build the first single male hostels inspired by the example of worker hostels in Johannesburg. These hostels were intended to replace the compound style accommodation for municipal workers and were considered a cost-effective way of improving the standard and supply of accommodation, while keeping single male migrants separate from the increasing number of married couples in the

[62] Ibid.

[63] A comprehensive analysis of the impact of and opposition to the Native Urban Areas and Accommodation Act is provided in Scarnecchia, 'The Politics of Gender and Class', especially Chapters 3, 4.

townships. Dulilo Hostel, the municipal hostel, was aimed at 'casual, lower class visitors and migrants seeking employment'.[64] On occasions, African men refused to take up accommodation in the hostels paid for by employers because conditions were so bad, preferring instead to stay with friends or relatives, and legally or illegally squatting in other parts of the city. In 1955, the Nyasaland Labour Officer inspected the Municipal Hostel 'Dulilo' (known as Duriro to local Shona) following a complaint from a newly arrived migrant worker. Men were crowded several into one room and conditions were described as awful.[65]

Finally, in 1955 the municipality allocated three hundred acres of land for the Ellman-Brown Housing Scheme, a new residential area to be named 'New Highfield'. These were the first houses to be made available for purchase on ninety-nine-year leases. Prices varied according to the cottage, but all houses consisted of four rooms. Business stands were also available for purchase at varying costs.[66] Housing construction in New Highfield continued throughout the late 1950s. New Highfield had a football club, a professional boxing club, several women's groups, schools and a CCAP church. When African members of the Federal Parliament came to Salisbury in the 1950s, they were housed in a block of flats known as 'Highfield House'. Housing allocated through the home ownership scheme attracted the more affluent urban workers. However, many tenants struggled with the high payments and had to take in lodgers to meet the costs. Lodgers gave the township a bad reputation and were blamed for holding illegal beer drinks and 'tea parties'.[67] *Skokiaan* queens

[64] ZNA S51/3-6 Urban African Affairs Committee, 'Section 42', 1957.

[65] MNA 14239II Nyasaland Government Labour Representative, Salisbury, Report 1955, 'Inspection'.

[66] ZNA S51/8 'Urban African Affairs' Memorandum on Urban Housing Conditions by the Director and Assistant Director of Native Education: Highfield Native Village Settlement, 24th July 1957.

[67] *Skokiaan* was a different type of beer from the traditional sorghum (opaque) beer. It was made from a variety of ingredients including butter, yeast, mealie meal, bread and sugar. It took less time to brew and was far more potent. The state attempted to ban *skokiaan* and seized vast quantities from the townships in the 1940s and 1950s. Barnes, *"We Women Worked So Hard"*, pp. 51–54; Mhoze Chikowero, *African Music, Power and Being in Colonial Zimbabwe* (Bloomington, 2015), ch. 7.

moved in from the location and single male workers preferred to stay there rather than in the hostels.[68]

The expansion of Highfield's African housing area was viewed with concern by the adjacent European residents at Waterfalls whose fears of the township encroaching on their space were articulated by the Waterfalls Town Management Board. To ease their concerns a one hundred-foot wide Gum tree belt was planted across thirty-one acres of land along the banks of the Makabusi/Mukuvisi River, and a six foot security wall was erected on the border between Highfield and Waterfalls housing areas.[69] The municipal government built several new African townships within the city and further outside in Greater Salisbury in the late 1940s and 1950s, including: Seke African Township south of Salisbury; Mount Hampton to the north; and Rugare the Rhodesia Railways compound in Lochinvar (see Map 5.2).[70] The city created eight administratively separate suburban town councils in Salisbury in the 1950s, which allocated accommodation according to preferential status, giving priority to indigenous married men; last in line were single male migrants from outside of the colony. Length of stay could determine a migrant's employment opportunities and the same could be said of accommodation.[71] The more desirable housing areas in Salisbury had waiting lists but under the terms of the 1948 Migrant Workers Act, those from Nyasaland and Northern Rhodesia were required to return to their home territory every two years.[72]

In 1951, the Federation of Native Welfare Societies (a white-run umbrella organisation concerned with the welfare of Africans in urban

[68] '*Skokiaan* queens' were women in the townships who brewed the beer and controlled the industry.

[69] ZNA S51/8 'Urban African Affairs' Memorandum on Urban Housing Conditions by the Director and Assistant Director of Native Education: Highfield Native Village Settlement, 24th July 1957.

[70] Lovemore Zinyama and Daniel Tevera, *Harare: The Growth and Problems of the City* (Harare, 1993), p. 23.

[71] ZNA S2961 Chief Native Commissioner, Annual Report, 1951.

[72] MNA S21/2/1/4 Migrant Native Labour—Provisional Revised Agreement Between the Governments of Southern Rhodesia, Northern Rhodesia and Nyasaland (1941), Point 5: 'The governments agree that it is desirable in principle that emigrant migrant Natives should return to their homes after working for an economic period, which should not exceed two years and might well be less, and that after two years they should be repatriated and should not be allowed re-entry into the territory of employment until a further period of six months has elapsed from the date of repatriation'.

areas in Southern Rhodesia) warned of the deterioration of relations between Europeans and Africans.[73] The federation was chiefly concerned with inter-racial relations in Southern Rhodesia's urban areas, where the government had rejected repeated calls from urban African residents for a greater degree of local self-government. The government's justification was the transitory nature of location life and the suggestion that urban residents were deeply divided by 'tribal differences'. To further defend their position, the government had also cited the fact that the majority of urban residents were foreign: 'To think in terms of Local Government for the 100,000 Africans of Salisbury, for instance, where 80% are non-indigenous natives and 75% remain less than two years in a job, is unrealistic'.[74] Nyasaland Africans did in fact play a significant role in the urban advisory boards in Northern Rhodesia's urban areas, and the federation committee debated whether this should also be the case in Southern Rhodesia. The Secretary for Native Affairs regarded the African urban areas as devoid of any real sense of community: 'There is not much community spirit among the Africans in the urban areas at present. This is understandable because of the tribal mixtures and the Africans have not been resident long enough to have shed their tribal shackles'.[75] On the contrary, Nyasaland migrants in Southern Rhodesia were without doubt 'long period servants'.[76] Evidence presented to the Howman Committee in 1944 suggested that many Nyasaland employees had been at the same place of work for thirty years.[77] Nyasaland and Northern Rhodesian Africans were noted in the 1950s by the Urban African Affairs Commission to have the highest average durations of service.[78] The townships were certainly ethnically diverse and the location populations were always

[73] MNA 14238I Nyasaland Government Representative, Salisbury, 1951. For further context on the Welfare Societies in Northern and Southern Rhodesia, and the involvement of Nyasa Africans within them, see James R. Hooker, 'Welfare Associations and Other Instruments of Accommodation in the Rhodesias Between the World Wars', *Comparative Studies in Society and History*, 9, 1 (1966), pp. 51–63.

[74] ZNA S51/8 Urban African Affairs Commission, 'Annexure B', A Comment on the Report of the Secretary for Native Affairs, 1953.

[75] ZNA S51/8 Urban African Affairs Commission, 'The Department of Labour', 1957–1958.

[76] J. C. Abraham, *Nyasaland Natives*, p. 23.

[77] ZNA S1906/2 Evidence presented to the Howman Committee, 1944.

[78] ZNA S51/3-6 Urban African Affairs Commission.

in flux, but the claims from government officials about 'a lack of community spirit' and 'tribal shackles' were more indicative of their racism and ignorance than the reality on the ground.

Urban planning by the municipal and central governments in the 1950s effectively tried to separate indigenous and non-indigenous workers, temporary and permanent residents, and the single and the married urban migrants. For as long as the migrant labour system was set to continue, the Urban African Affairs Commission called for 'areas of instability [to be] kept quite separate and distinct from areas of stability'.[79] The question of rights for African workers and their families was posed directly to the Secretary for Native Affairs: 'As to the rights of Africans and their families to enter the towns and reside there; should there be any distinction in regulating between indigenous and non-indigenous Africans?'[80] In response, the Secretary for Native Affairs insisted that 'no non-indigenous native is prevented from selling his labour in the same manner as the indigenous labourer and therefore the principles governing the right of urban entry to indigenous Africans apply equally to the non-indigenous'.[81] In practice, however, Nyasa migrants often experienced discrimination when applying for certain jobs or attempting to rent better quality housing. Despite attempts by the government to neatly categorise different groups of urban workers or residents, the boundaries between migrant cohorts remained blurred as men and women from different ethnic and territorial backgrounds met in the workplace, in the townships, and in the churches.

Church and Community in Salisbury

Religious institutions were hugely important to migrants in Salisbury and they helped to create a sense of belonging and community in the African urban areas. Churches contributed to the process of identity formation, and they were a central feature of township community life for long and short-term migrants. Churches fostered a spirit of community among people from different backgrounds although specific church groups were sometimes more strongly associated with Nyasa migrants.

[79] Ibid.

[80] ZNA S51/8 Urban African Affairs Commission, 1958.

[81] Ibid.

Labour migrants played an important role in creating new branches of mission and independent churches stretching from the Cape to the northern end of Lake Malawi (Lake Nyasa). Religious groups, like political associations, were carried from one place to another through migrant labour networks. The Southern Rhodesian government's obsession with the Watch Tower movement (discussed in Chapter 3) overshadowed the wider contribution of 'northern migrants' to the religious development of Salisbury, which included a number of new churches in Salisbury from the early years of the twentieth century. The Anglican Church already had a broad base throughout Mashonaland and the Methodists established a mission in Epworth in 1890 just outside of the city. The municipality allowed for an African Church area to be carved out in the northern corner of Salisbury Location in the early 1900s and a Methodist congregation set up in the inner city. By 1911, the Catholic Church and Scottish Presbyterians were also present.[82] The Methodist Society in Harare Township saw itself as 'primarily a mission to black migrants in the city'. The aim was to provide an 'inclusive fellowship for Africans who were ready to make Salisbury their home'.[83]

Church services in Harare Township were multi-lingual in order to cater to the needs of all migrant workers in the city. Second to the Anglicans, the Presbyterian Church was numerically the strongest African denomination in the city. As early as the 1910s, migrants from Nyasaland dominated the second biggest denominational church in Salisbury.[84] There were three traditions of Presbyterian Church in Salisbury, and those from Nyasaland formed the largest group. The Livingstonia Mission in Nyasaland had begun to send preachers to Salisbury and other industrial areas of Southern Rhodesia from 1904. Their main aim was to cater for the spiritual and material needs of Nyasaland migrants far from home and in need of support. The Church of Central Africa, Presbyterian (CCAP) was formed in 1926 from the amalgamation of the Church of Scotland Mission in Blantyre and the Livingstonia Mission in the north (see Map

[82] Table showing 'Ethnic/regional background and Denominational Affiliation as given by Africans in Salisbury in the 1911 Census', Carl Fredrik Hallencreutz, *Religion and Politics*, p. 52.

[83] Ibid., p. 45.

[84] Ibid., p. 51.

2.2). In Salisbury, the CCAP came to be known as 'the Church of *Mabhurandaya*', meaning the Church of those from Blantyre (or Nyasaland). Agnes Galatiya described the CCAP in Salisbury:

> The Churches were not selective, they were not meant for one group or another, but when the Shona saw that Malawians were patronising one church over another they branded it a Church of *Mablantyre*. If you saw a Shona go to that church, maybe if it was a woman, she would usually be following her husband. But Shona didn't usually go to such churches. There were several churches for Malawians and the CCAP was predominantly a Malawian church. Malawians from farms and from the towns would all attend the CCAP.[85]

Andu Pangani described how he used to go the CCAP in Harare Township (Mbare) because 'there were many Malawians. The first time I went to that church, I never thought I would see so many Malawians outside of Malawi!'[86] Churches served as a meeting place for new arrivals in the city, where migrant men and women would find others from their village or district. Churches were an important social space and connected people to an essential urban network on arrival in the city.

The CCAP was also a source of respectability, in contrast to other Nyasa religious expressions, such as the *Nyau* societies (discussed in Chapter 4). Migrants shaped their urban lives according to Christian ideals of morality. Men and women residing in the poorest areas of the location used their association with the church to differentiate themselves from the un-Christian, the unemployed, and those the authorities described as a 'class of spiv' in African urban society.[87] The church also acted as a channel for the articulation of class aspirations. They provided material support and services, such as schools and medical care—provisions which were often severely under-resourced in the African urban areas.

Churches had an important role to play in the welfare of urban migrants. Christian missions were crucial in providing education to migrant children in Salisbury long before the government accepted a

[85] Interview with Agnes Galatiya, Ntcheu District, February 2008.

[86] Interview with Andu Pangani, Harare, June 2008.

[87] MNA 14239II Nyasaland Government Representative, Salisbury, 'Unemployment in Southern Rhodesia', July 1958.

degree of responsibility in this regard. The Church of Scotland Mission established schools in and around the city long before the government provided anything for African urban children. Calls were made by Nyasaland residents in Salisbury in 1945 for schools to be opened up for their children to attend.[88] Around this time, the Nyasaland government also began to allocate funding for chaplains (representing several of the main mission churches) to make regular visits to Southern Rhodesia to check on the 'spiritual welfare' of migrant labourers. In a letter to the Nyasaland governor, one Catholic missionary, Monsigneur Auneau, set out the case for government funding: 'There are a considerable number of Nyasaland Native Catholic Christians who are employed down south and whose religious welfare is neglected'. He stressed the moral and spiritual influences of the conditions 'to which these natives are exposed' in urban and industrial areas, and proposed that 'a chaplain with intimate knowledge of their own homes, customs, and outlook' could not fail to be of great benefit to them.[89] Representations from the Catholic Montfort Marist Mission, the Presbyterian Church and the Dutch Reformed Church were granted funding to visit migrant workers and co-ordinate the efforts of the church with the Nyasaland Government Representative in Salisbury, to repatriate destitute women and encourage *machona* to return home to their families. Missionaries often spoke out about the morality of migrants away from Nyasaland and the 'evil and corrupting' influences of urban centres. Following a nine-month visit to Southern Rhodesia and the Union of South Africa in 1946, one Labour Chaplain produced a list of recommendations relating to social welfare, 'which all well born Christians would approve of…'[90] The Catholic Mission in Nyasaland strongly recommended 'the compulsory repatriation of destitute women to stop them from becoming prostitutes, [as well as] Nyasaland women living here in illegal union, at least of those lawfully married back in Nyasaland'.[91] Later in the 1950s, £300 was made available by the Nyasaland Native Development and Welfare Fund for the purchase of a cinema unit for use by the Reverend Daneel (another Labour Chaplain in Southern

[88] ZNA F137/186c Special Committee Reports on Migrant Labour, 1945.

[89] MNA S42/2/2/1 Missions—Misc. Montfort Marist Mission: Proposals to send a Chaplain to Southern Rhodesia, 1943. Also, MKHS 1/9/34 Nyasaland Labour Chaplain in Southern Rhodesia.

[90] ZNA MS239/34 Catholic Chaplaincy Report on Nyasaland Labour, 1946.

[91] Ibid.

Rhodesia), for the purpose of showing films on his visits to compounds and farms. The films included updates on church work and education in Nyasaland.[92]

Stephen Ntsinambuto went to work in Bulawayo in the late 1950s. He left Ntcheu district in Nyasaland, in search of wage labour in the south, just like his father had done when he was young. In Bulawayo he began to attend the CCAP for the first time. This was not the church he belonged to back in Nyasaland, but the one most frequented by Nyasas in the township where he lived. Others attended the Seventh Day Adventist, Assemblies of God, and the Anglican Church. It was not uncommon for migrants to attend different denominational churches in Salisbury to the ones they had belonged to in Nyasaland, or to convert to a new religion altogether. A place of worship could be dependent upon the location of one's workplace and residence. Others were influenced by their neighbours, friends or partners. For Stephen and his wife Rhoda, life in Bulawayo was very different from their village life in Nyasaland. Rhoda was happy living in the township, and grew fond of their lifestyle there, which included a wider diet and access to commodities not so easy to find in Nyasaland. In order that she did not forget 'Malawian culture' Rhoda and other married women in the township from Nyasaland would meet to attend choir and church meetings together.[93] They supported one another with money or in-kind when they had problems, 'just like life back home'.[94] For Rhoda, her church group became a substitute for rural kinship.

Migrant stories suggest at times a plural, instrumental approach to religion. Men and women acquired literacy and marketable skills at mission schools to improve their prospects in the labour market, and later used new denominational affiliations in the city to build solidarity and replace rural kinship networks. Migrants were also able to reconcile or combine aspects of 'traditional' belief systems with world religions such as Christianity or Islam. This was illustrated with the Christian migrant

[92] MNA MKHS 1/9/34 Nyasaland Labour Chaplain in Southern Rhodesia, Reports by Nyasaland Labour Chaplain, Salisbury—Rev Daneel from the Dutch Reformed Church Mission, Mkhoma Synod 4th February 1954.

[93] The groups Rhoda described sounded similar to the Methodist and Catholic women's organisations in Harare, written about in Hinfelaar, *Respectable and Responsible Women*.

[94] Interview with Stephen Ntsinambuto and his wife Rhoda Ntsinambuto, Ntcheu District, February 2008.

experiences of the *Nyau* in Salisbury and visits to traditional healers despite adherence to Christian moral codes of conduct. Like European missionaries, African traditional healers also made special visits to the urban centres of Salisbury and elsewhere around the region, to cater to the needs of Nyasa migrants away from home. One prominent healer from Nyasaland who became famous in Southern Rhodesia and on the Rand in the 1950s and 1960s was called Chikanga; he became known as Malawi's most powerful and successful healer.[95] Yao and Chewa migrants (sometimes known in Southern Rhodesia as *Machawa*) left Nyasaland as followers of Islam and established new Muslim associations in Salisbury.[96] Some attended Christian churches in Southern Rhodesia instead of the mosque because of the difficulty finding an Islamic community in some localities (this was a more common experience among farm workers in remote locations). The first mosque was officially constructed in Salisbury in the 1950s but there was a much longer history of African Muslim communities in the city as well as on farms and in mining towns.[97] These stories attest to the importance of religion among migrants and demonstrate the adaptability of religious practices.[98]

Youth, Unemployment and 'Foreign' Migrants in the 1950s

Greater numbers of Shona workers had entered permanent employment in the urban areas by the 1940s, but many still returned to their homes in the reserves during the ploughing and planting season and employers remained dependent upon 'alien' migrant labour. By the mid- 1950s this picture had changed with Shona workers staying in the city for longer periods. At the same time, larger numbers of Nyasa migrants continued

[95] Boston Soko, *Nchimi Chikanga: The Battle Against Witchcraft in Malawi* (Zomba, 2002); Markku Hokkanen, *Medicine, Mobility and the Empire: Nyasaland Networks, 1859–1960* (Manchester, 2017), p. 45.

[96] Ephraim Mandivenga, 'The Migration of Muslims to Zimbabwe', *Journal of Muslim Minority Affairs*, 10, 2 (1989), pp. 507–519.

[97] Ibid., p. 514.

[98] Frederick Cooper, *Africa Since 1940: The Past of the Present* (Cambridge, 2002), p. 29. For a more detailed discussion of Nyasa religious groups in Salisbury, see Zoë Groves, 'Urban Migrants and Religious Networks: Malawians in Colonial Salisbury, 1920 to 1970', *Journal of Southern African Studies*, 38, 3 (2012), pp. 491–511.

to arrive.[99] The Urban Areas Commission in the 1950s noted complaints about the 'unrestricted entry of these people', which has the effect of 'depressing wages and slowing up the advancement of the indigenous African'. In 1958 the Commission emphasised that:

> …the growing number of Africans employed as wage labourers is a reflection of the general development of the economy no matter whether the individuals concerned are employed as workers on farms, in mines, or in urban areas. But we wish to emphasize the extent to which the African people of Southern Rhodesia have become concentrated in towns.[100]

Southern Rhodesian workers had begun to take up longer-term residence in the city following the Land Husbandry Act of 1951, which was partly intended to end the reliance on non-indigenous migrant labour. The settler government's new framework of land controls and discriminatory legislation forced thousands to head to Salisbury altering the demographic of the city. For the first time in the history of the city, Africans from within Southern Rhodesia outnumbered the non-indigenous migrant population.[101]

Commercial farms in Mashonaland remained short of labour, however, and the government suggested that employment of foreign migrants should be restricted to farms and major projects.[102] On a farm visit in 1951 Nyasaland government representative, Major Burden interviewed one migrant named Nyadiri along with twenty more of the forty workers from Nyasaland employed there. Some of these men had been living on the farm for up to seventeen years. Many farms like this one were dependent upon contract labour recruited in gangs, often hailing from the same few villages in Nyasaland. Nine of the men originated from the same village in Ncheu district. Through migration families and communities could be kept together, in contrast to the common view of villages being torn apart. Workers would remain on the same farm for extended periods if there was reasonable accommodation and satisfactory wages. Farms

[99] In 1952 the Nyasaland Government Representative in Salisbury confirmed that, 'the flow of labour into the colony continues at a high rate.' MNA 14239I Nyasaland Government Representative, Salisbury Report: 1952.

[100] *Report of the Urban African Affairs Commission, 1958* (Salisbury, 1958).

[101] Raftopoulos, *Sites of Struggle*, p. 10.

[102] ZNA S51/8 Memorandum from E. Chikwanda, Umtali, 1957.

that experienced acute labour shortages were the subject of rumours of ill treatment and poor wages, which spread quickly among migrant networks. Some farmers were 'driven out of business on this account'.[103]

Territorial governments had great difficulty directing labour to the places where it was needed most. A labour report from 1953 described how labour migration from Nyasaland continued unabated with over 2000 migrant workers entering the Southern Rhodesia in a single month from the Protectorate. 'Almost without exception', it was claimed, 'these new entrants continue their journey to Salisbury and seemed to be only concerned with getting there'.[104] In 1953 the railways were in urgent need of labourers, and the Nyasaland Labour Officer made it known to people at the migrant camp in Umtali, where they had crossed the border that hundreds of jobs were immediately available at a commencing rate of 47/-a month: 'Not one of the five hundred new arrivals in the camp at the time was the slightest bit interested. Salisbury was their goal and they intended to get there'.[105]

By 1958 the growth of the Federal economy had begun to slow affecting job opportunities for the thousands of migrants still arriving into the urban and industrial areas. The textile industry had started to shrink and the brick making industry had recruited to full capacity. The situation was the same for tobacco factories, roads departments and municipal and building contractors. In one instance, the Telephone Engineering Department had required twelve new labourers and received over four hundred applications in one day.[106] Building activity was also slowing down due to credit restrictions. Burden remained sceptical about the extent of the 'unemployment crisis': 'The fuss made by the press and in the Southern Rhodesian House of Assembly about African unemployment in the towns is still in my opinion exaggerated, and is part of a campaign to keep out foreign and non-indigenous workers'.[107] The Salisbury African Labour Exchange was opened in 1958 in an effort to push the surplus labour from the towns back into the farms. That same year the government passed the

[103] MNA 14239I Nyasaland Government Representative, Salisbury, Report: 1952.

[104] MNA 14239II Nyasaland Government Representative, Salisbury, 'Labour Supply' Report: October 1953 (see Map 5.1).

[105] Ibid.

[106] MNA 14239II Nyasaland Government Representative, Salisbury, July 1958.

[107] Ibid. Also, see *African Weekly*, 30 July 1958.

Foreign Migratory Labour Act, which closed Salisbury and Bulawayo to entry for all new foreign migrants. The geographical areas covered by this Act were extended in the 1960s to include the suburbs around the major cities and by 1965 the government had introduced a Closed Labour Areas Order, which intended to replace all foreign labour.[108]

Educated and skilled workers from Nyasaland experienced unemployment in the city most noticeably in the later 1950s and early 1960s. Migrants from Nyasaland were encouraged to seek employment with *Mthandizi* (the RNLSC), or risk arriving in Salisbury to find limited employment opportunities. These people had become accustomed to urban life and higher wages and refused to take up employment on nearby farms.[109] Federal Immigration officers warned of the effects of unemployment on 'those who were born and grew up in an entirely urban society and have little rural connection'.[110] The government debated what should be done about increasing unemployment in Salisbury. Migrants entering the colony had two weeks to find a job but if they failed to gain employment could apply for replacement documents in order to avoid deportation and the restrictions of the Migrant Labour Act. Officials complained that migrants abused this system:

> Many of the applicants are irresponsible vagrants who have either never had such documents or have lost or destroyed them because they are deserters. It is a matter of wonder how such denizens of the bush will ever fit into the modern world of industry...The only work which they are hoping to obtain is that of garden-boy. If on obtaining employment, any hard work is involved, they leave and begin the search again. It is difficult to know what can be done about this increasing class of "spiv".[111]

Urban employers were encouraged to employ local labour and complaints were made in the settler press that the city was 'providing shelter and sustenance for too many native loafers'.[112] In response, the Salisbury and

[108] Bill Paton, *Labour Export Policy in the Development of Southern Africa* (Harare, 1995), pp. 124–125.

[109] MNA 14239II Nyasaland Government Representative, 1955.

[110] ZNA F119 IMM/5/1/7 Labour Survey Results, June 1961.

[111] MNA 14239II 'Unemployment in Southern Rhodesia', 17th July 1958.

[112] ZNA LG191/8/68 'Convict and Native Labour', Rhodesian Federated Chamber of Commerce, 28th Annual Congress, 1950.

Bulawayo city councils opened vagrancy camps in the early 1960s in an attempt 'to cope with unemployed youths and loafers'.[113] The Southern Rhodesia Legal Aid and Welfare Society paid a visit to these camps and discovered that many of those held there were not vagrants at all, but non-indigenous youths.

By the 1950s, there was a second generation of Nyasa 'migrants' who were, in fact, children of migrants born in Southern Rhodesia who had never visited their official country of origin. The Chief Native Commissioner estimated that forty to fifty percent of migrants arriving in Southern Rhodesia now had their families with them and about ten percent of the non-indigenous African migrant population were juveniles, i.e. less than sixteen years old.[114] As early as the 1930s, Burden had expressed concerns about Nyasa youth growing up in the city:

> Numbers of those [Nyasa men] who have been in Rhodesia for more than 5 years have contracted alliances with local women, and would, if they were permitted, occupy land in the reserves. The children of these alliances, and there are thousands of them, are growing up in the mines and towns without ever experiencing village and tribal life. Education or control of these children seems to be singularly lacking and they constitute a problem which is causing grave concern to officers of the Native Department, missionaries and the better employers.[115]

The growing numbers of locally born children was discussed by the advisory boards and the Secretary for Native Affairs, who described them as '…a group of carefree, boisterous adolescents in the age group 16-25 of many tribes and uninhibited by either tradition or respect for seniority…'[116] A specific Shona term—*Bhonirukisheni*—was used (in a derogatory way) to describe mischievous children born and bred in the city.[117] Some parents working in Salisbury chose to send their children back to Nyasaland to be brought up by grandparents as they wanted to

[113] ZNA SE 6/1 Reports of the Settlers and Residents Association, 1960–1961.

[114] ZNA S2961 CNC Report of the Native Commissioner for Labour, 1951.

[115] Burden, *Nyasaland Natives in Southern Rhodesia*.

[116] ZNA S51/8 Secretary for Native Affairs, Report, 1953.

[117] Saidi, *Old Bricks Lives*, p. 164.

shield them from the township environment and they felt it was important for them to be raised in the same environment that they had grown up in, and to learn about their culture and traditions.

In the early 1960s, the Southern Rhodesian authorities detained several young men whose parents were from Nyasaland or Northern Rhodesia and threatened them with deportation to Nyasaland. In many cases, individuals no longer had direct family in Nyasaland and they had never even entered the colony before.[118] *The Daily News* published a report in 1961 on the unfair arrests of so-called 'vagrants': 'some vagrants had fathers who are prosperous farmers, vagrants who were self-employed, vagrants who were collected when they had just come into town, vagrants who were to be repatriated although their parents were working in Southern Rhodesia'.[119] Wilson Mondayi was one of those held at the vagrancy camp and threatened with deportation. His mother stayed around Salisbury Airport and Wilson had been born in Southern Rhodesia, but his father was from Nyasaland. Wilson had never been to Nyasaland himself.[120] Another man, Isayim Friday was also born in Southern Rhodesia. Both his parents were from Nyasaland and lived in Shabani, a town in south-central Southern Rhodesia where they had worked for the past twenty years (see Map 5.1). Isayim was due to be repatriated to Nyasaland despite the fact that neither of his parents resided there.[121] The Southern Rhodesia Legal Aid and Welfare Society accused the government of trying to deport migrants from the north for political reasons; tensions were high as the Federation of Rhodesia and Nyasaland was beginning to break down and Nyasas were seen as troublemakers (a theme examined in more detail in Chapter 6).[122]

Urban policy and labour legislation made access to housing and jobs in Salisbury harder for non-indigenous migrants from the late 1950s onwards, at precisely a time when Africans from Nyasaland were meant to be able to move with greater ease throughout the territories of the

[118] This was the case with Aleke Banda whose story is mentioned in Chapter 6.

[119] ZNA SO7/1/5/21/2 'Vagrants', 14th December 1960: Report by G. Muchada refers to the *Daily News* article.

[120] Ibid.

[121] ZNA SO7/1/5/21/2 Visit to Vagrancy Centre, 5 December 1960.

[122] ZNA SO7/1/5/21/1 Southern Rhodesia Legal Aid and Welfare Society, 'Vagrants', January 1961.

Map 5.1 Major Towns in mid-Twentieth Century Southern Rhodesia

Central African Federation. Instead, new labour policies created barriers for migrating families looking for the opportunities promised to them in the industrial heartland of Salisbury during the federation years. One man who worked for the Mashonaland Bricks Company in Salisbury in 1957, wrote to the District Commissioner in his home district Lilongwe (in Nyasaland), requesting that his daughter be permitted to travel to Southern Rhodesia to join him. The father felt that he could better provide for his daughter in Southern Rhodesia as in Nyasaland she had 'a very poor living' and 'is usually sick… I have received several complaints from her telling me that she had no better living in Nyasaland and that she wanted to come back to me'. The District Commissioner replied: 'Your

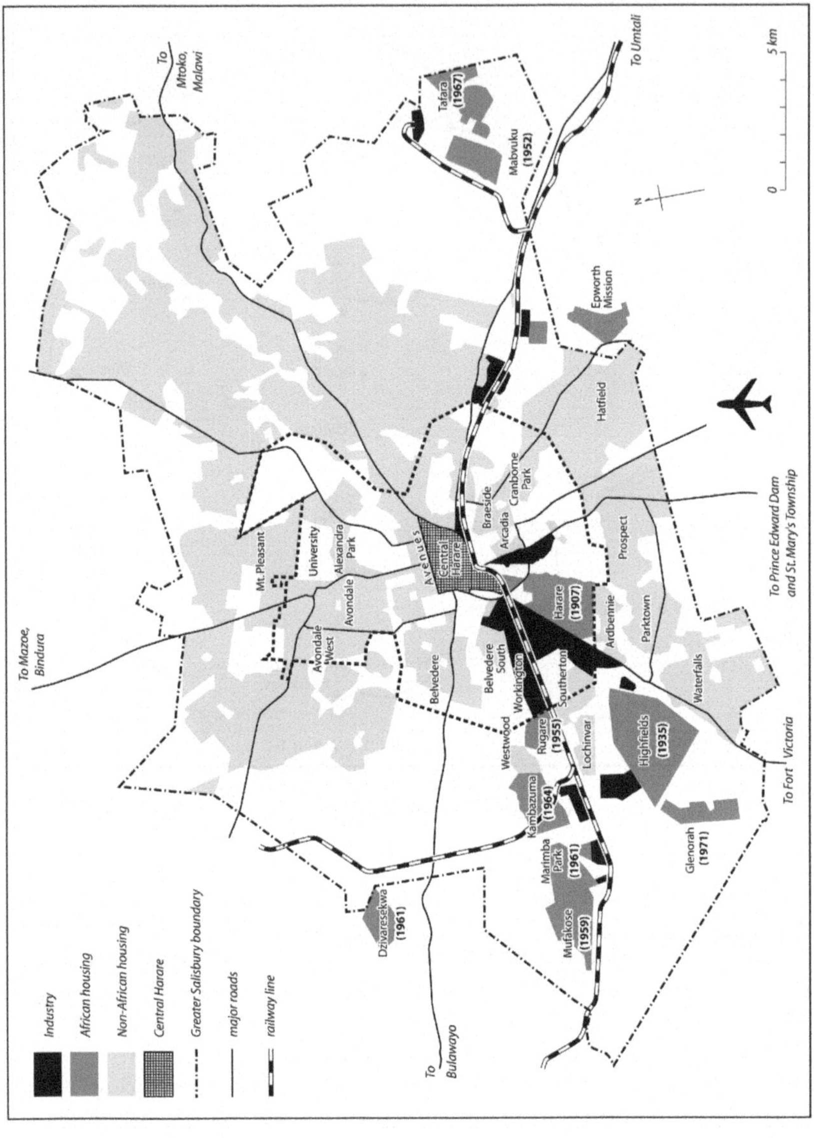

Map 5.2 Salisbury: African and European urban areas (*Source* Adapted from George Kay and Michael Smout, *Salisbury: A Geographical Survey of the Capital of Rhodesia* [Sevenoaks 1977], p. 27)

daughter Elina will be unable to go to Southern Rhodesia if she is an adult and she has no husband living there. Only married women can go to Rhodesia to join their husbands...'[123]

Conclusion

By the 1950s, Salisbury was a city of increased social stratification. Concerted efforts by the municipality to engineer the formation of a stable urbanised African middle class, through the provision of housing schemes, and representation on urban advisory boards, were only partially successful. Those able to build up small businesses worked to achieve the markers of respectability that defined their status.[124] Migrants paid fees to send their children to school, migrant women participated in church groups, and the municipality awarded prizes for the best kept urban gardens (in those areas where people were fortunate to have gardens).[125] Importantly, this social group in Salisbury included not only Africans from Southern Rhodesia, but men and women from Nyasaland, Northern Rhodesia, and Mozambique. Neither ethnicity nor territorial origin determined class status or respectability.

Migrants at the lower end of the urban class spectrum also aspired to improve their social status. Migrant men arrived in Salisbury with little more than 'a blanket, a cooking pot and the few rags in which they are clad'.[126] Over time, it was possible to transform one's status as was the case with Daniel Likhobwe and Ibrahim who both returned to Nyasaland (or later, Malawi) having acquired significant wealth. Salisbury in the 1940s and 1950s comprised a migrant population of short and long-term labourers, educated and non-educated, men and women, from a variety of ethnic groups and territorial backgrounds. African journalist and writer, Lawrence Vambe described how men and women living in the urban areas in the 1940s differentiated between those who were educated

[123] MNA (Transmittal files) NA/1/3/26 Letter to the District Commissioner, Lilongwe 2 January 1958 and Response from the DC Lilongwe, January 1958.

[124] David Maxwell describes how class formation was 'not simply defined by access to exclusive African housing.' *African Gifts of the Spirit: Pentecostalism and the Rise of a Zimbabwean Transnational Religious Movement* (Oxford, 2006), p. 63.

[125] ZNA S51/8 Memorandum on Urban Housing Conditions by the Director and Assistant Director of Native Education, 24th July 1957.

[126] MNA Nyasaland Government Representative, Salisbury, Report: 1956.

and those who were not, referring to them (in Chishona) as *va ka funda* and *vasina ku funda*, respectively.[127] The Southern Rhodesian government's policy of labour stabilisation was to ensure greater productivity and more effective control of the urban masses, echoing colonial labour policy elsewhere in Africa in the 1940s.[128] But the government's invitation to African workers to take up permanent residence in Salisbury was extended primarily towards indigenous men and their respectable wives rather than 'alien natives'. Legislation pushed aside African migrants of foreign origin and aimed to keep to a minimum the length of stay of temporary 'unskilled' workers. Municipal housing areas reflected in their design the desire to segregate temporary migrants from long-term urban residents. Labour policy in Southern Rhodesia in the 1950s and 1960s emphasised separation, a position which the municipality and central government justified with alarmist claims of growing urban unemployment and the need to establish a stable African urban community.[129]

[127] Vambe, *From Rhodesia to Zimbabwe* (London, 1976), p. 163.

[128] See Cooper, *Decolonisation and African Society*.

[129] The Foreign Migratory Labour Act of 1958 implemented in Salisbury in 1960, was the most explicit demonstration of this policy.

CHAPTER 6

Migrant Networks and Nationalist Politics—The Federation Years

In 1953 the Federation of Northern and Southern Rhodesia and Nyasaland was officially declared, linking the three territories politically and economically[1] (Map 6.1). The move went against the wishes of the African majority, particularly in Nyasaland and Northern Rhodesia where there were fewer European settlers and federation was perceived as a move away from the path towards national self-determination. African nationalist sentiment grew stronger in opposition to the federal government and from 1956 African Congress parties increased the intensity and coordination of their campaigns. Popular support for African nationalism in central and southern Africa did not become widespread until the later 1950s and early 1960s. Earlier political organisations failed to unite across rural and urban divides and to transcend class differences. By 1956 a new political force led by young frustrated intellectuals began to challenge the federal and settler governments and to demand 'secession and independence'.[2] This new generation of nationalists, many of whom had spent periods living, working and studying outside of Nyasaland, led the opposition towards federation and campaigned for independence.

[1] Officially entitled The Federation of the Rhodesias and Nyasaland but more commonly referred to as the Central African Federation.

[2] 'Secession and Independence' became the slogan of the Nyasaland African Congress in 1954. M. W. Kanyama Chiume, *Kwacha: An Autobiography* (Nairobi, 1975), p. 72.

Z. R. Groves, *Malawian Migration to Zimbabwe, 1900–1965*, Cambridge Imperial and Post-Colonial Studies Series,
https://doi.org/10.1007/978-3-030-54104-0_6

Map 6.1 The Central African Federation

African Congress parties from both northern colonies established external offices in urban and industrial centres in Southern Rhodesia to recruit Nyasa and Northern Rhodesian migrants away from home and enable collaborative efforts between territorial groups. Closer collaboration between African Congress movements created anxiety among the settler community and colonial administrators, leading the federal government to push for decisive action to be taken against African nationalists. Events reached a turning point in 1959 following the declaration of an emergency in Southern Rhodesia and soon afterwards in Nyasaland, during which the African congress parties were banned and many of their leaders and members detained. As a result of continued resistance, federation was eventually dismantled in 1963 and Malawi achieved independence soon after in 1964, quickly followed by Zambia. Southern Rhodesia took a different path as white right-wing nationalists under the banner of the Rhodesian Front Party used the opportunity to push for independence from Britain. By the mid-1960s, the interests of Malawian and Zimbabwean nationalists had begun to diverge as the two countries faced very different futures.

The history of Federation has often been told from a British imperial perspective, with emphasis on the threat presented by South Africa after 1948 and the interests of white settlers in Northern and Southern Rhodesia.[3] Nyasaland hardly features at all in some accounts of Federation, accept in as much as the colony was expected to provide 'a large pool of labour' for the industries in Southern Rhodesia.[4] Until recently, the historical literature on Malawian nationalism underplayed the contribution made by men and women whose experiences outside of Nyasaland shaped their political engagement back at home.[5] Labour migration and common experiences of travel and residence away from home were important in the efforts to build solidarity within and beyond colonial

[3] See for example Michael Collins, 'Decolonisation and the "Federal Moment"', *Diplomacy and Statecraft*, 24 (2013), pp. 21–40; Ronald Hyam, 'The Geopolitical Origins of the Central African Federation: Britain, Rhodesia and South Africa, 1948–53', *The Historical Journal*, 31, 1 (1987), pp. 145–172. In contrast, one early history of federation which explores African perspectives is Robert I. Rotberg, *The Rise of Nationalism in Central Africa: The Making of Malawi and Zambia, 1873–1964* (Cambridge, 1965).

[4] Collins, 'Decolonisation and the "Federal Moment"', p. 34.

[5] The nature of African political tradition and mass nationalism in Malawi from the mid-1950s onwards, is explored in John McCracken, 'Democracy and Nationalism in Historical Perspective: the Case of Malawi', *African Affairs*, 97, 387 (1998), pp. 231–249; Joey Power, *Political Culture and Nationalism in Malawi: Building Kwacha* (Rochester, NY, 2010); Kings M. Phiri, John McCracken, and Wapulumuka Mulwafu (eds.), *Malawi in Crisis: The 1959/60 State of Emergency and Its Legacy* (Zomba, 2013).

boundaries.[6] External branches of the Nyasaland African Congress in Southern Rhodesia (and to some extent, South Africa) were crucial to the success of the movement, both financially and as a source of inspiration, influence and solidarity from outside the colony. Through their political activities abroad, Nyasa nationalists, together with their Northern Rhodesian counterparts, radicalised the more moderate African congress members in Southern Rhodesia in the late 1950s. Strong anti-federation sentiment served to unite African political interests bringing about a moment of pan-African and regional solidarity, which coincided with major anticolonial events elsewhere on the continent, such as the 1958 All African People's Conference. This chapter looks at the background to the creation of the Central African Federation and early efforts to create effective African political movements in Nyasaland and Southern Rhodesia. It then examines the escalation of political action from 1956 in the lead up the 1959 State of Emergency. The narrative ends in 1965 when Rhodesia made a unilateral declaration of independence and the political struggles in the region appeared to diverge.

African Nationalist Politics Before 1953

The concept of 'closer association' between Northern and Southern Rhodesia and Nyasaland long predated the creation of the Central African Federation in 1953. In the early 1900s Cecil Rhodes had envisaged a unification of 'the Rhodesias'. Plans for amalgamation were later considered by the Northern and Southern Rhodesian territorial governments in 1915, and again during the 1920s and 1930s.[7] Southern Rhodesian settlers were initially hesitant over proposals to amalgamate with 'the black north'. African subjects under British Protectorate status in Nyasaland

[6] John McCracken makes this point in his review of Peter Mackay, *We Have Tomorrow: Stirrings in Africa, 1959–1967* (Norwich, 2008), see 'The Exciting Times of a Central African Don Quixote', *Journal of Southern African Studies*, 35, 2 (2009), p. 528.

[7] For a general outline of the proposals put forward by settlers from Northern and Southern Rhodesia and the colonial office, including the 1927 Hilton Young Commission, The Passfield Memorandum, 1930, and the Bledisloe Commission Report, 1939, see 'The Idea of Amalgamation 1915–1939', in Colin Leys and Cranford Pratt (eds.), *A New Deal in Central Africa* (London, 1960), pp. 1–10. For a more recent account of the imperial history of Federation, Andrew Cohen, *The Politics and Economics of Decolonisation in Africa: The Failed Experiment of the Central African Federation* (London, 2017).

and Northern Rhodesia had access to skilled occupations and a degree of political representation in the form of Provincial Councils, whereas Southern Rhodesia's African Administration was more closely aligned with the South African policy of racial segregation. In 1938 when the British sent the Bledisloe Commission to hear views from each of the territories on amalgamation, African representatives speaking on behalf of early political associations outlined reasons for their opposition to the plans. The Commission recommended that amalgamation in central Africa should not be imposed against the will of the African majority.[8]

Chiefs in Nyasaland were opposed to federation as it could mean less power and influence but also further land alienation, particularly in the Southern Province where coffee, tobacco and cotton plantations had been established in the early years of colonial rule when entire African communities had been forced from their land. There were also widespread concerns that amalgamation would lead to an increase in labour migration to the detriment of village life and the economic development of the colony. Southern Rhodesia was viewed by many Nyasaland and Northern Rhodesian Africans as, 'a conquered country, [where] the Africans have no voice'.[9] Common experiences of working and living in the settler colony shaped these attitudes. In 1944 the Southern Rhodesia Bantu Congress (SRBC) expressed their opposition to amalgamation, if it meant extending the 'native policy' of Southern Rhodesia to their brothers in the north.[10]

The Southern Rhodesia Bantu Congress was formed partly in response to the widely contested Native Registration and Sedition Bills, which were devised by the settler government in 1936 during the Huggins Administration, but the organisation was also critical of moves towards federation.[11] Membership of the SRBC included teachers, ministers and clerks from Matabeleland and Mashonaland, who protested legislation putting educated Africans at a disadvantage. They demanded greater

[8] Rotberg, *The Rise of Nationalism in Central Africa*, pp. 110–114.

[9] MNA 60/HKB/1/1/2(a) 'Federation of Nyasaland and Rhodesias: Views of Nyasaland Africans in Northern Rhodesia'.

[10] See Terence Ranger, *Are We Not Also Men? The Samkange Family and African Politics in Zimbabwe, 1920–1964* (London, 1995), especially Chapter four, 'Making Nationalism', pp. 87–124.

[11] Michael West, *The Rise of an African Middle Class: Colonial Zimbabwe, 1898–1965* (Bloomington, 2002), p. 150.

political representation, which they hoped to achieve through constitutional means.[12] However, after an initial period of activity the movement remained inactive for several years. The Reverend Thompson Samkange was elected President of the Congress in 1943 and it was hoped that his 'national outlook' would revive the organisation and bring together the grievances of rural and urban Africans. The organisation's new aim was to create the first mass-based African political movement in Southern Rhodesia.[13]

The first national African organisation in Nyasaland was established in 1944. The Nyasaland African Congress (initially the Nyasaland Native Association) was set up under the leadership of Levi Mumba, who had been secretary and a major driving force behind the North Nyasa Native Association.[14] Mumba also helped to establish the Zomba Native Association after he was posted to the Southern Province as a clerk in 1924.[15] Congress chose Mumba to lead the movement because of his experience in working across ethnically based associations. The idea was to bring together individual African associations from each district and unite them underneath one banner. The Nyasaland Congress was envisaged to become 'the mouth piece of the Africans' and founding member James Frederick Sangala invited all Africans resident in Nyasaland to join the movement.[16] Mumba and Sangala's vision for Congress was in line with Samkange's aims for the SRBC. Sangala welcomed into the organisation 'Africans who resided in, but had not been born in Nyasaland'.[17] Both congress movements were keen to establish a broad and inclusive membership base. They were inspired by the South African Native National Congress (later the African National Congress), which combined

[12] Richard Gray, *The Two Nations: Aspects of the Development of Race Relations in the Rhodesias and Nyasaland* (Oxford, 1960), pp. 162–164.

[13] Ranger, 'Thompson's Election to Presidency', *'Are We Not Also Men?* pp. 90–94.

[14] McCracken, *Politics and Christianity*, p. 303.

[15] Gray, *The Two Nations*, p. 174.

[16] Rotberg, *The Rise of Nationalism*, p. 184.

[17] Ibid.

local organisations and vigilance societies that emerged in the early twentieth century and were run by mission-educated Africans seeking the extension of civil rights and, most importantly, the franchise.[18]

The formation of a national organisation in Nyasaland was welcomed by the Bantu Congress in Southern Rhodesia. Politically active Southern Rhodesian Africans worked closely alongside their Nyasaland colleagues in voicing their opposition to amalgamation. Aaron Jacha (Secretary of the SRBC) and the Reverend Thompson Samkange discussed with Sangala in 1944 the idea of creating a Central African Congress. Jacha urged Thompson, 'that Africans ought now seek to federate, linking the Bantu Congress with the emergent Congress movement in Nyasaland'.[19] Samkange and Jacha congratulated Sangala for establishing a national movement in Nyasaland and suggested that the next step should be to join their efforts in achieving full rights for Africans throughout central Africa.[20] Following Jacha's departure in 1945, Jaspar Savanhu (Secretary of the SRBC and editor of the Bulawayo-based African newspaper *The Bantu Mirror*) insisted that, 'Tribal differences, petty jealousies, minor differences of opinion must be swept aside'.[21] Broad and inclusive membership of both Congress parties was stressed, in their efforts to transcend ethnic or local affiliation. Any effective challenge to white settler domination, they felt, needed to come from a united African voice.

Hopes of establishing a Central African Congress in the 1940s soon faded when the Nyasaland Congress sent delegates to Southern Rhodesia and South Africa to establish external branches of their own organisation. The move to convene separate meetings rather than encourage Nyasaland migrants to join the Southern Rhodesian organisation was interpreted by Samkange as 'a resurgence of the old enemy of the Africans – tribalism'.[22] Samkange urged the leaders of the Nyasaland party not to create these outposts but instead work towards a 'Central Inter-Territory African

[18] Shula Marks, 'Southern Africa', Judith Brown and Wm Roger Louis (eds.), *The Oxford History of the British Empire, Volume IV: The Twentieth Century* (Oxford, 1999), p. 560.

[19] Ranger, *Are We Not Also Men?* p. 98.

[20] The majority of this correspondence is found in the Samkange Archive which remains closed but was used extensively by Ranger in '*Are We Not Also Men*'.

[21] *The Bantu Mirror*, 9 September 1944, Quoted in Ranger, ibid., p. 94.

[22] Ranger, *Are We Not Also Men?* p. 101.

Congress'.[23] Hastings Kamuzu Banda, future leader of the Nyasaland Congress who at this stage was living in the UK, was in full agreement with Samkange about the external branches of the Nyasaland Congress and exchanged correspondence with him on the subject:

> I agree with you in everything you say. Disunity will only ruin us whilst unity will build us, politically, economically and socially...We must think in terms of a Central African Nation rather than in terms of tribalism or even territories...Africans of Nyasaland in Southern Rhodesia should not organise a separate political or industrial body from that organised by their brethren in the Colony...they should wholeheartedly support the organisation already in existence in Southern Rhodesia.[24]

Nonetheless, the Nyasaland and Northern Rhodesian African Congress movements continued with their plans and opened branches in Salisbury in 1946 and 1948, respectively.

Hastings Kamuzu Banda had himself left Nyasaland at a young age in 1915 to seek work in the south.[25] Banda worked as a sweeper at a hospital in Hartley (Chegutu) where he first became inspired to pursue a medical career. After 18 months Banda continued south to Johannesburg where he was employed by the Witwatersrand Deep Mine at Boksburg between 1917 and 1925. From Johannesburg, Banda travelled to the United States where he completed high school at an African American Methodist College and later obtained a university degree, funded by several wealthy white philanthropists. After his first degree, Banda studied medicine in Edinburgh and later worked as a doctor in Scotland and England in the 1940s. He was an outspoken critic of plans for amalgamation (and later federation) having experienced racism in Southern Rhodesia and South Africa. The Colonial Office suspected Banda was responsible for influencing educated Africans with an interest in politics back in Nyasaland. While in England, Banda had regular communication on political matters with Dr Rita Hinden, Secretary of the Fabian Society's Colonial Bureau,

[23] Ibid.

[24] Quoted in Ranger, *Are We Not Also Men?* p. 102. Ranger quotes at length from letters to *The Bantu Mirror* between 1945 and 1946, *Are We Not Also Men?* pp. 100–102.

[25] Markku Hokkanen, *Medicine, Mobility and the Empire Nyasaland Networks, 1859–1960* (Manchester, 2017), pp. 167–169.

and in one letter he voiced strong disapproval of Colonial Office policy in the Central African territories under the Labour government:

> Twelve months ago if anybody had told me that a British Labour Government would approve of the segregation law in Southern Rhodesia, that it would resort to detentions and deportation in Uganda, as an instrument of administrative policy, that it would continue the conservative policy of favouring ignorant and reactionary chiefs in Nyasaland, as opposed to educated and progressive Africans, I would have denied it with both force and anger...But to my bitter surprise, a Labour Dominion Secretary has approved a law in Southern Rhodesia, which to the Africans at any rate is in no way different from any law passed by Hitler's Government on the continent of Europe.[26]

Banda continued to challenge the idea of federation until he left the UK for the Gold Coast, disillusioned by the Colonial Office decision to proceed with their plans against the wishes of the African majority.

Charles Matinga, founding member of the Nyasaland Congress, travelled widely in South Africa and Southern Rhodesia to enlist 'financial and spiritual support' from Nyasaland migrants working in Cape Town, Johannesburg and Bulawayo.[27] By the time of the third annual conference in Salima in 1946, Matinga announced that the Southern Rhodesian government had agreed to allow a new branch of the Nyasaland Congress to be established in Salisbury. The first meeting was held on the 14 September, 1946.[28] Mr A. B. Kapila, head clerk to the Nyasaland Government Representative in Salisbury, explained the purpose of the external branches: 'Congress has been established here not as a business to take money, but as a channel to the Nyasaland Government through which its

[26] MNA 60/HKB/1/1/2(a) Letter dated 20 September 1946 from H. K. Banda to Dr Rita Hinden, Secretary for the Fabian Society Colonial Bureau. Presumably the letter refers to the 1946 Native Urban Areas Registration and Accommodation Act in Southern Rhodesia.

[27] Rotberg, *The Rise of Nationalism*, p. 198. Matinga attempted to persuade Dr Xuma of the South African National Congress to sponsor a Pan-African Congress but was unsuccessful.

[28] MNA PCC1/4/1, 'Nyasaland African Congress, 1945–1952', Report from the Third Annual Conference, 21–25 September 1946.

people can direct their complaints or views'.[29] The Nyasaland Congress was able to acquire new members in Southern Rhodesia through the burial and mutual aid societies. The external branches became a valuable asset to the central office in terms of their financial contribution. Congress leaders were aware that higher membership fees and donations could be made by migrant workers in the south whose wages were considerably better than members employed in the Protectorate. By the 1950s the Mashonaland and Johannesburg branches had become a crucial source of financial support, particularly following the withdrawal of Dr Banda's personal contributions when he left for the Gold Coast. All three African Congress movements established branches in South Africa over the course of the next ten years, and the South African government closely monitored any contact between them, and the South African ANC, throughout the 1950s.[30]

The early Congress organisations of Southern Rhodesia and Nyasaland contrasted with the political agitations of the ICU (and later RICU) and the more radical nationalist politics of the 1960s. The external congress branches were small and their demands moderate, emphasising cooperation with the government, despite strong disapproval of colonial policies. A tone of 'controlled anger' was set by mission-educated elites who were largely behind the organisations.[31] Members discussed the need for greater educational opportunities in Nyasaland and Southern Rhodesia, and direct political representation for Africans on the Nyasaland Legislative Council. They were aware of the threat of 'closer association' but were not seen to pose any real political threat to the territorial governments. When Mr E. C. Barnes, Labour officer of the Nyasaland Government wrote to the deputy Chief Native Commissioner for Salisbury in the late 1940s, he mentioned the Nyasaland Congress but was dismissive about its political aims:

[29] MNA PCC1/4/1 min of the Special Meeting of the Nyasaland African Congress, Salisbury Branch, 1946.

[30] For a more detailed examination of Nyasas in South Africa, particularly Johannesburg, see Henry Dee, 'Nyasa Leaders, Christianity and African Internationalism in 1920s Johannesburg', *South African Historical Journal*, 70, 2 (2018), pp. 383–406.

[31] West, *The Rise of an African Middle Class*, pp. 152–153. On the rhetorical strategies of African politicians and nationalists in Southern Rhodesia before 1960, see Scarnecchia, *The Urban Roots of Democracy and Political Violence, Harare and Highfield, 1940–1964* (Rochester, 2008), p. 6.

> I assured Mr Powys Jones that I did not think that the Salisbury Branch of the Congress contemplated taking any active political part in Native Affairs in Southern Rhodesia, but thought their sole aim was concerned with the welfare of Nyasaland Natives in Southern Rhodesia.[32]

Some years later, a combined meeting of the Nyasaland and Northern Rhodesia African Congresses took place in Harare African Township in 1951.[33] Nophas Kwenje had been resident in Salisbury since the early 1940s where he was employed as an editor at the *Bantu Mirror*. Lewis Mataka, the Reverend Hanock Phiri (uncle of Dr H. K. Banda) and Kwenje together called for a meeting of NAC to discuss federation. It was attended by around thirty Africans who took the opportunity to voice their frustrations over the 1948 Migrant Workers Act.[34] Plans for closer association were discussed, but the Nyasaland Government Representative for Salisbury felt that Nyasas in Southern Rhodesia generally had more pressing concerns:

> ... it can safely be said that with the exception of a few intelligentsia, the ordinary Nyasaland African in Southern Rhodesia is displaying very little interest in the closer association proposals.[35]

Much stronger feelings were expressed against federation from chiefs, the young and educated and returned migrant men and women in both the rural and urban areas of Nyasaland and Northern Rhodesia. A statement from the Church of Central Africa, Presbyterian (CCAP) outlined the feelings of ordinary Nyasaland Africans in the mid-1950s. The racial discrimination migrants experienced in Southern Rhodesia was important in informing their views of federation, and those of their families:

> The people may not be politically articulate or active but they see Federation making Nyasaland like Southern Rhodesia or South Africa. Almost every family has at least one member who has worked there. They don't

[32] MNA S15/1/7/1 Nyasaland African Congress, 1945–47, Extract from Report on Visits to Lourenço Marques, Johannesburg and Salisbury by Mr E. C. Barnes.

[33] MNA Transmittal Files: 3.3.7F/1295, Nyasaland Government Representative for Salisbury, Reports, Vol. 1.

[34] MNA Transmittal Files: 3.3.7F/1295, Nyasaland Government Representative Reports, Vol. 1.

[35] Ibid.

> want that kind of white domination, race segregation and discrimination here.[36]

At a chiefs' conference in Lilongwe in 1952 a petition was signed by over one hundred Nyasaland chiefs representing their people. Their objections were presented to the Nyasaland government:

> Large numbers of our people have migrated to Southern Rhodesia and have worked there and have returned to Nyasaland. In Southern Rhodesia they see the discrimination by the European government and people against Africans, a discrimination which does not exist in Nyasaland. They have told others in Nyasaland of that discrimination. We fear that if we have 'closer association' with Southern Rhodesia that that discrimination will spread.[37]

Kanyama Chiume, who would later become one of the key figures within the Nyasaland African Congress from 1956, later described how 'the treatment given to Africans in Southern Rhodesia was no different from that in South Africa'. His comments further highlighted one of the consequences of regional migration: 'There was hardly a family in Nyasaland who did not have a member who had been to either Rhodesia or South Africa. They knew well enough, therefore, what conditions in those countries were like'.[38]

On the eve of federation in 1952, the Nyasaland Congress held a large meeting in Blantyre that was attended by over one thousand Africans, including several chiefs.[39] The delegates spoke unanimously against the creation of a federation with Southern and Northern Rhodesia. Representatives of NAC branches across Nyasaland, as well as from Southern Rhodesia and South Africa were present. African delegates from Nyasaland and Northern Rhodesia boycotted official talks held in London

[36] ZNA MS841/6/4 Personal correspondence of Sir Malcolm Barrow (Minister of Home Affairs 1954–1955) Statement from the CCAP, Blantyre Synod, 1954–1957.

[37] SOAS (Special Collection Archives) PPMS Fox-Pitt, Box 5 Nyasaland African Chiefs Conference, Lilongwe, 15th and 16th November 1952.

[38] Chiume, *Kwacha*, p. 178.

[39] Rhodes House Library (RHL) 'The Africa Bureau' MSS 240/1 Letter from N.D. Kwenje to Dr Banda.

between 1951 and 1952, while Southern Rhodesian African representatives accepted the invitation and sent delegates Joshua Nkomo and Jaspar Savanhu.[40]

Opposition towards proposals for federation was less clearly articulated in Southern Rhodesia than in either Nyasaland or Northern Rhodesia. Local political organisations were preoccupied with territorial concerns and continuing grievances related to the 1930 Land Apportionment Act and the 1946 Urban Areas Act. The passing of the 1951 Land Husbandry Act was also met with widespread opposition from both the rural and urban African communities.[41] Zimbabwean nationalist Nathan Shamuyarira recalled why federation held more appeal for Africans in Southern Rhodesia, especially during the first few years of the scheme:

> ... for most of the hitherto oppressed Southern Rhodesian Africans the prospect of federation with the British Protectorates of Northern Rhodesia and Nyasaland seemed full of promise: the new policy of partnership would bring to a speedy end the segregation, humiliation and indignation...[42]

Africans in the north feared the adoption of Southern Rhodesian policies in their territories, whereas Africans in Southern Rhodesia hoped that the more liberal policies in the northern territories would pressurise the Southern Rhodesian government into breaking down racial barriers. Reuben Jamela would later recall how some of the discriminatory legislation in Southern Rhodesia was relaxed during the federation.[43] The

[40] Leys and Pratt offer a comprehensive and contemporary account of events leading up to and responses towards Federation in *A New Deal in Central Africa*.

[41] George Nyandoro (founding member of the Salisbury City Youth League in 1956) writing for Dissent—a short-lived mimeographed broadsheet started in Southern Rhodesia after the banning of Congress in 1959—later suggested that the Land Husbandry Act was the best recruiter the Southern Rhodesian Congress could have wished for, as it was met with such strong dissatisfaction from so many sections across African society. *Dissent* provided a critical voice of government policies, in the absence of any African political party after the banning of Congress. *Dissent*, No. 19, 9 June 1960.

[42] Nathan M. Shamuyarira, *Crisis in Rhodesia* (London, 1965), p. 15.

[43] ZNA AOH/63 (Oral Histories), Interview with Reuben Jamela, 11 January 1980.

Liquor Act was amended, and the State Lottery opened up, both as concessions to the growing African middle class.[44]

The Federation of Rhodesia and Nyasaland was finally established in 1953 against the wishes of the African majority. Each territory retained control over its domestic affairs, such as land policy and education, and the federal government held jurisdiction over the external affairs of the three territories. The Federal Assembly in Salisbury included representatives from the settler communities of each territory, plus a small number of African seats in the Federal Parliament. The Central African Council (CAC) set up in 1944, had already brought closer collaboration between the northern and southern colonies' settler communities on issues of mutual interest such as labour, trade, transport, immigration and general economic development in the region. The economic boom following the Second World War acted as a catalyst for an agreement to be reached to allow the British to capitalise on industrial and commercial strengths in Central Africa. A federal government, the British hoped, would combine the profits of the copper and coal mining industries in Northern and Southern Rhodesia, with the plentiful labour supply provided by Nyasaland. In addition to the economic benefits, federation promised a political 'partnership' between the races. This promise was the basis upon which federation was sold to the international community.[45] In reality, however, interpretations of the official policy of 'partnership' varied greatly between the different parties involved. Sir Roy Welensky, Prime Minster of Federation from 1956–1963 and one of its most vehement advocates, famously likened the concept of partnership to that between a rider and his horse, 'The European must be the senior partner by virtue of his ability, initiative and capital'.[46]

Harry Nkumbula, leader of the Northern Rhodesian African Congress, arranged for a meeting of the three Congress movements to decide on a

[44] Nathan Shamuyarira, *Crisis*, p. 15; M. West, 'Liquor and Libido: Joint Drinking and the Politics of Sexual Control in Colonial Zimbabwe, 1920s–1950 s', *Journal of Social History*, 30, 3 (1997), pp. 645–667.

[45] The idea of 'partnership' and how crucial it was in 'selling' the federation scheme is explored in Robert I. Rotberg, 'The Partnership Hoax: How the British Government Deprived Central Africans of their Rights', *Journal of Southern African Studies*, 45, 1 (2019), pp. 89–110.

[46] Roy Welensky, *Welensky's 4000 Days: The Life and Death of the Federation of Rhodesia and Nyasaland* (London, 1964), p. 35.

joint course of action in 1953. Stanlake Samkange attended on behalf of the Southern Rhodesian Congress and unanimously they agreed to launch a campaign of civil disobedience and passive resistance. Demonstrations in Nyasaland and Northern Rhodesia included chiefs' resignations, non-cooperation with government officials and the boycott of labour recruiters.[47] Yet in Southern Rhodesia the campaign never took off. Federal intelligence kept close surveillance over those in Nyasaland and Northern Rhodesia who were 'fanatical in their insistence on full African rights...'[48] In the first few years of federation pan-African solidarity was evident, but the individual nationalist movements were weak and divided, and lacking the broad support base needed to pursue political struggle.

African Nationalism and Middle-Class Networks, 1956–1959

The emerging African middle class was important in stepping up the intensity of the anti-federation campaign in the mid-1950s, and in creating a more coherent and broad-based anticolonial movement across the region. Many of those involved with the Nyasaland African Congress had lived, worked or pursued higher education outside of the colony. The same was true of a number of Northern Rhodesians who, along with certain Nyasas and Southern Rhodesian Africans, formed a prominent new social class in Salisbury in the 1950s. Elias Mtepuka, like Nophas Kwenje (mentioned above), had been working in the city since the 1940s. Mtepuka was particularly active in the Salisbury branch of the Nyasaland Congress in the early 1950s. He worked as editor for the African newspaper *African Weekly*, mixing with other educated and respectable Southern Rhodesian Africans, including prominent journalist Lawrence Vambe, and political figure and editor of the *Bantu Mirror*, Jaspar Savanhu. Vambe described Mtepuka's highly political editorials as 'a source of great discomfort to the municipal and central government administrators', as it was clear that they were written under the

[47] Violent outbreaks occurred in several Nyasaland districts in response to Federation. See Power, *Political Culture*, pp. 55–75.

[48] RHL MSS 'Welensky Papers', Box 239/8, Federal Intelligence and Security Bureau (FISB), Report by Mr Spicer on Nyasaland, September 1953.

influence of the Congress movements.[49] Mtepuka travelled to London with a Congress delegation for the Federal conference in 1952 and was monitored by Federal Intelligence agents from 1953 onwards.[50] Mtepuka joined the Inter Racial Association (IRA) in 1955 during a period of disillusionment with Congress. Others in Salisbury experimented with membership of multiracial associations like the IRA or the Capricorn Africa Society.[51] In the mid-1950s, politically conscious Africans looked to multiracial organisations as a means of improving their social mobility. These organisations promised other routes to progress, besides the nationalist path. Aaron Jacha, previous secretary of the SRBC (who had encouraged both Congress movements to work more closely in the mid-1940s) joined the Capricorn Africa Society in the 1950s.[52] The society held their annual convention in Salima, along the shores of Lake Nyasa, although in contrast to the popularity of the multiracial group in Southern Rhodesia, few Nyasaland Africans engaged with this type of multiracial politics. In Nyasaland, the term 'Capricorn' was more commonly used to refer to 'a sell-out', a collaborator with colonialism or to describe the settlers of Southern Rhodesia.[53]

By the mid-1950s the nature of urban politics was changing fast. Charles Mzingeli, leader of the Reformed Industrial and Commercial Workers' Union (RICU) and a popular local politician in Salisbury from the mid-1940s, was seen by a younger more radical cohort to have failed to keep up with the demands of his young supporters.[54] The RICU and its members dominated the African Township Advisory Boards, but they were later discredited by the Salisbury City Youth League, a group

[49] ZNA Oral/233 Interview with Lawrence Vambe, 1–13 June 1983.

[50] RHL, Box 238/2, FISB Affairs, Letter to the Private Secretary of the Acting PM, 8th December 1955 Mtepuka's name appeared on a list of African leaders. Laurence Vambe and M. M. Hove also held prominent positions working for the African run press in Southern Rhodesia.

[51] Ibid. The Capricorn Africa Society was explored in Luise White, *The Assassination of Herbert Chitepo: Texts and Politics in Zimbabwe* (Bloomington, 2003).

[52] Jacha later became a member of the United Federal party and held a seat in the Federal Parliament. ZNA AOH/14 Aaron Jacha, 14th July 1977.

[53] Shamuyarira, *Crisis*, p. 20; White, *The Assassination of Herbert Chitepo*, p. 71. The *Gule Wamkulu* even had a character representing the two-faced Capricorn.

[54] Scarnecchia, *The Urban Roots of Democracy*, pp. 12–28.

of young African intellectuals who had grown impatient with Mzingeli's conservative approach to politics. The demise of the organisation signalled an end to the more strictly urban-based movements, which had represented the interests of individuals and groups, including poor urban women. An older type of patronage politics, which attempted to transcend class cleavages, was replaced by a nationalist movement, led by the new intelligentsia with a more male-dominated agenda.

Zimbabwean nationalist Maurice Nyagumbo (himself a migrant worker in South Africa in the 1940s), was initially sceptical of the Salisbury Youth League. He envisaged an association run by 'irresponsible town gangsters' and explained, 'I had a wrong picture of city-dwellers and used to think that most of the Africans who lived in towns were not to be trusted'.[55] Nyagumbo's opinion changed the day he met with Robert Chikerema who took him to the Youth League office in Salisbury. He was surprised to find a meeting place used by a group of intellectuals, including Dunduzu Chisiza from Nyasaland, who had been educated at the Livingstonia Mission, and George Nyandoro—both respectable men with good jobs. These men of a similar social class had reached the limits of upward social and occupational mobility in Salisbury and were channelling their energies into political activism.

The City Youth League was an alliance of frustrated teachers, shopkeepers and white-collar workers, dissatisfied with the political strategy of the RICU. Founding members included James Chikerema, George Nyandoro, Paul Mushonga and Dunduzu Chisiza. Chisiza worked as a clerk in the Indian High Commissioner's office until he was deported in 1956. He was noted for 'his nationalist endeavours [which] during his year of residence in this colony [Southern Rhodesia] culminated in his attempting to subvert African members of the British South Africa Police'.[56] Back in Nyasaland Chisiza played a pivotal role bringing together the nationalist movements across territorial boundaries. Before working in Southern Rhodesia Chisiza had spent a year working in Tanganyika, and time studying in Uganda. His involvement in politics dated back to his student days and his later political career was shaped by his experience of travel around the region.

[55] Maurice Nyagumbo, *With the People* (London, 1980), pp. 101–102.

[56] Many Africans working for the BSA Police were from Nyasaland, which may explain why Chisiza was suspected of subversion. RHL FISB Affairs Box 239/8 'Memorandum concerning Dunduzu K. Chisiza', 1 August 1956.

The first meeting of the Youth League attracted many people with speeches from James Chikerema, George Nyandoro and Dunduzu Chisiza on 'why men should be free'.[57] The Youth League mobilised urban workers and attempted to politicise the African townships on a large scale with the 1956 Bus Boycott. This violent demonstration resulted in the biggest display of urban African protest seen since the 1948 General Strike. *African Weekly* described it as 'The Worst Riot in the history of African Township'—its leaders, they suggested, were nowhere to be seen. The 'lawlessness and hooliganism' was said to be the result of open-air meetings which addressed 'large numbers of spivs and loafers who hardly understand'.[58] A group of angry young demonstrators targeted African men and women who ignored calls for a boycott. Several African women residing at the Carter House Hostel were among those most brutally attacked. The women's hostel in Harare African Township had recently opened, close to the single male hostels. Non-indigenous labour migrants, seen as a threat to the respectable classes, were blamed for the rioting and the violent attacks against women at Carter House. Crowds were alleged to have shouted in Chinyanja while rampaging through the streets.[59] The violence against women seen during the protest was indicative of increased gender tensions in the urban areas. The greater presence of women in urban employment came at a time of rising unemployment and further competition over housing and resources.

Widespread participation in the boycott and a new kind of militancy seen with the tactics employed by the Youth League marked the beginning of a more radical phase in Southern Rhodesian African politics. Leaders of the Youth League aimed to transform their organisation into a national movement in 1957 by amalgamating with the Bulawayo-based Southern Rhodesian African National Congress, relaunched under the leadership of Joshua Nkomo. The renewed Southern Rhodesian African National Congress (SRANC) successfully combined

[57] *African Weekly*, 16 May 1956.

[58] Ibid, 19 September 1956.

[59] Timothy Scarnecchia, 'Poor Women and Nationalist Politics: Alliances and Fissures in the Formation of a Nationalist Political Movement in Salisbury, Rhodesia, 1950–6', *Journal of African History*, 37, 2 (1996), p. 302.

general African urban and rural discontent.[60] It also brought the previously redundant Southern Rhodesia Congress into line with its more progressive African Congress sister movements in the region.[61] Ignatius Takaidza Chigwendere suggested that the new kind of militancy displayed in the nationalist movement from 1956 was a result of the African National Congress movements in the northern territories:

> There were quite a lot of examples in the neighbouring countries of our Federation, in Malawi and before that in Nyasaland. After all some of the people who were responsible for forming the Youth League were from there...they started the Nyasaland African Congress, then the Malawi Congress Party and then there were those from Zambia. They helped to create the kind of militants that were the basis [of the Zimbabwean nationalist movement].[62]

The central executive of the Nyasaland African Congress also enjoyed a renewal of its membership in the mid-1950s. Congress had been fairly inactive at the national level, but things began to change from 1955 when acts of defiance again became part of a coordinated programme of resistance.[63] Flax Musopole, the 'self styled military general', took control of the Misuku branch of NAC in Karonga District in the northern region, using the Misuku Coffee Producers Co-operative Society to organise a nationalist support base.[64] Musopole was another returned migrant worker from South Africa where he was closely involved with the South

[60] For more on the rise of the City Youth League and politics in Salisbury during the 1950s see: Brian Raftopoulos, 'Nationalism and Labour in Salisbury 1953–1965', *Journal of Southern African Studies*, 21, 1 (1995), pp. 79–94.

[61] 'The vanguardist tendencies of the Youth League and the Southern Rhodesian African National Congress followed the pattern of the Nyasaland, the South African and the Northern Rhodesian National Congresses'. Scarnecchia, 'Poor Women and Nationalist Politics', p. 302.

[62] ZNA Oral/228, Interview with Ignatius Takaidza Chigwendere, 24th May 1974.

[63] Whilst the central body of NAC was experiencing a quiet phase, some of the individual branches were busy building up important grass roots support in their localities. Joey Power, 'Building Relevance: The Blantyre Congress, 1953–56', *Journal of Southern African Studies*, 28, 1 (2002), pp. 45–65.

[64] *The Nyasaland Times*, Tuesday 27 October 1959. On Flax Musopole, see John McCracken, 'The Ambiguities of Nationalism: Flax Musopole and the Northern Factor in Malawian Politics, c.1956–1966', *Journal of Southern African Studies*, 28, 1 (2002), pp. 67–87; Owen Kalinga, 'The General from Fort Hill': Katoba Flax Musopole's Role

African ANC and the Defiance Campaign. Back in Nyasaland he sought to employ similar tactics within his local Congress branch in Karonga.[65] Musopole was later joined by Gilbert Kumtumanje, president of the Mashonaland branch of the Nyasaland Congress until his expulsion from Southern Rhodesia in December 1957. Kumtumanje had lived in Salisbury for ten years following service as a corporeal medical orderly during the Second World War. He and Musopole along with other emerging nationalists, Kanyama Chiume and R. R. Chumia, opened new branches throughout the Northern Province, building up a substantial following in Karonga and Nkhata Bay.[66] Similarly, Henry Masauko Chipembere became an active member of Congress in 1955 soon after his return to Nyasaland from Fort Hare University in South Africa. By 1957 he was an executive figure in the Nyasaland Congress as well as a member of the Legislative Council. Chipembere was one of several central African nationalist figures to have studied at Fort Hare.[67] He recalled the importance of his experiences in terms of his nationalist career and pan-African ambitions:

> Fort Hare remained the training ground of future leaders in South Africa. There was enough political activity and awareness to transform each student into a much more radicalised and politically enlightened person by the time he completed his studies. The vast majority of African leaders in South Africa and, for some time, in Central Africa, were alumni of Fort Hare. I became one when I returned to Malawi.[68]

as an Anti-colonial Activist and Politician in Malawi', *Journal of Southern African Studies*, 46, 2 (2020), pp. 301–317.

[65] The Defiance Campaign was organised by the African National Congress Youth League in South Africa in 1952. It was an attempt to bring about the repeal of the National Government's unjust laws by openly defying them. Huge rallies and marches were held daily until the campaign was eventually crushed by government and police brutality. The Campaign succeeded in bringing a certain amount of international attention to the situation in South Africa, William Beinart, *Twentieth Century South Africa* (Oxford, 2001), pp. 148–155.

[66] Chiume, Musople and Chumia were described by colonial office intelligence as 'the main driving force' behind congress in the Northern Province. The National Archives (UK) CO 1015/1748 'Nyasaland African Congress Intelligence Reports', Extract from Nyasaland Intelligence Report for the Quarter Ending, 31 December 1957.

[67] On Fort Hare University, see S. Morrow and K. Gxabalashe, 'The Records of the University of Fort Hare', *History in Africa*, 27 (2000), pp. 481–497.

[68] Robert Rotberg (ed.), *Hero of the Nation: Chipembere of Malawi—An Autobiography* (Blantyre, 2002), p. 137; Terence Ranger, *Are We Not Also Men?*, pp. 105–106. Southern

Chipembere was elected to the Legislative Council along with Kanyama Chiume who had recently returned to Nyasaland from East Africa. Chiume studied education at Makerere University College in Uganda and like Chipembere and Musopole he had also been active in politics during his stay abroad. This new generation of nationalists included the recent deportee from Southern Rhodesia, Dunduzu Chisiza and together they transformed the Nyasaland Congress into a popular and more widespread organisation. Collectively, 'the young Turks' as they came to be known, injected a new vigour into the central office of the Nyasaland African Congress and they sought to radicalise African nationalism throughout the Central African Federation.

Most government officials remained unconvinced that Congress posed much of a threat to the success of federation, although its improved organisation into 'action groups' was noted and some feared it could become dangerous under a more coherent leadership.[69] The federal government moved an intelligence officer to Nyasaland, stationed within the Special Branch, in order to keep a closer eye on events.[70] In July 1958, Dr Banda returned to Nyasaland to provide the movement with the strong leadership it had been lacking. He was greeted by a crowd of three thousand supporters demonstrating new levels of support for the nationalist movement. A statement made by the Blantyre Synod of the CCAP suggested that anti-federation sentiment was now widespread: 'It is untrue to say that this unrest is confined to the educated Africans; it is found in every village'.[71]

From 1958 the external branches of the Nyasaland and Northern Rhodesian Congresses became an important channel through which African nationalists throughout the federation could coordinate their campaign. Combined meetings became more frequent and were arranged between the executive committees of all three congress parties. Prominent individuals from one congress would often attend and speak at the

Rhodesian Africans at Fort Hare protested in 1945 about the fact that senior teaching positions in schools would be closed to Africans.

[69] The National Archives CAB/129/89, 'Report by the Secretary of State for Commonwealth Relations on his Visit to the Federation of Rhodesia and Nyasaland in October, 1957'.

[70] RHL Welensky Papers, 239/8.

[71] RHL Box 239/8, 'Statement of the Synod of Blantyre of the CCAP Concerning the Present State of Unrest in Nyasaland, 1957'.

meetings of another territorial group. In June 1958 a meeting of the Harare Branch of the Nyasaland Congress was attended by over 500 people who gathered to hear anti-federation speeches. George Nyandoro's presence was noted by federal security.[72] It was not uncommon for Southern and Northern Rhodesian Africans to attend NAC meetings alongside Nyasa migrants. Through singing, dancing and drumming and some animated and impassioned speeches from key figures, the Nyasaland Congress grabbed the attention of a wider section of African urban society. A meeting held at the Vashi Hall, in honour of Wellington Manoah Chirwa (member of NAC and Federal MP for Nyasaland), in August 1956, for example, drew crowds of around 800 people with political speeches, drums and singing. *The Chronicle* described 'A roll of drums and thunderous shouts of Africa! Africa!' as Chirwa shouted to the crowds of Southern Rhodesian and Nyasaland Africans: 'When we succeed, we will help you too to become free!' Chirwa appealed to local leaders to come forward and lead their people: 'Have we no Nkrumah here? Have we no Gandhi? Have we no Moses? Come forward and lead your people!'[73] He was greeted with huge applause.

Another Nyasaland Congress meeting at the Stanley Hall in Bulawayo in January 1957 had begun with a performance of the Congress choir. Provincial President, Mr Jere, spoke at the event:

> The Provincial President of the Nyasaland African Congress, Mr Jele [sic], told us that people in Nyasaland are doing famously while those in Southern Rhodesia are doing nothing except eating sugar and drinking beer and they think they are Lords and Masters not knowing the dangers confronting them…[74]

At a meeting of thirty Nyasaland Congress members the following month a long memorandum drawn up by James Sangala (founding member of NAC) and T. D. T. Banda (Secretary General of NAC) was read to the crowd. The memorandum addressed to the Colonial Secretary attacked the Federal government for repression and discrimination and warned

[72] ZNA F120/L343/1 Security Situation Reports, December 1959—It was noted that, 'the Nyasaland ANC in and around Salisbury succeeds in attracting large crowds who applaud the extreme statements of the speakers'.

[73] Bulawayo Files, S.O. 8 Vol. T Box 100 (Archival notes from Terence Ranger).

[74] Ibid.

against 'turning the Protectorate into a miserable colony of Southern Rhodesia'.[75] The language used at the annual conference of the Southern Rhodesian branches of NAC in 1958 had become more striking than the early meetings of the 1950s. Kachunjulu, an executive member of Congress addressed the audience of sixty delegates and exclaimed, 'The Congressmen are not only for the freedom of Nyasaland, but also for the freedom of the African continent'.[76]

Pan-African Solidarity and the 1959 Emergency

Branches of the Nyasaland Congress in Blantyre and Limbe organised celebrations to mark a year since Ghana gained independence in March 1957.[77] Members of the Northern and Southern Rhodesian and Nyasaland African Congress movements travelled to Accra for the All African Peoples' Conference in Ghana in 1958, which they had sponsored together with many other African nationalist organisations across the continent.[78] Publicity Secretary Kanyama Chiume and Dr Banda went on behalf of NAC. Keen member of Congress, C. B. B. Kachunjulu was unable to attend because of restrictions placed on him entering Southern Rhodesia (flights to Accra from Nyasaland went via Salisbury).[79] African leaders gathered in Ghana from across the continent under the banner of pan-African unity and it was decided that firm action should be taken to break up the Central African Federation. The conference delegates declared that full support would be given to 'all fighters for freedom in Africa'.[80] Chiume described how deeply honoured he was to attend the conference, where hundreds of representatives of progressive political, nationalist, trade union, cooperative, youth, women and other African organisations came together to discuss the 'tactics and strategy

[75] Ibid. Meeting in Stanley Hall, Bulawayo, 10 February 1957.

[76] Ibid. Report of the Annual Conference of NAC in Southern Rhodesia, 11 May 1958.

[77] *The Nyasaland Times*, 7 March 1958.

[78] Chiume, *Kwacha*, p. 99.

[79] *The Nyasaland Times*, Friday 7 March 1958.

[80] Colin Baker highlights the significance of this declaration; while the nationalists in southern Africa advocated the use of non-violent means in order to gain independence they went one step further at this conference, claiming they would not rule out the use of force in retaliation, or if peaceful means did not gain results. Colin Baker, *State of Emergency: Crisis in Central Africa, Nyasaland 1959–60* (London, 1997), pp. 8–9.

of the African non-violent revolution' that would lead to a Pan-African Commonwealth of Free Independent United States of Africa.[81]

Dr Banda was deliberately delayed on his return from Ghana by the Nyasaland government that was worried by the large crowds that might gather in Chileka (Blantyre Airport) at the weekend. The Federal authorities forced Banda's flight to stop in Salisbury, where he stayed for a couple of nights. Back in Nyasaland he recounted his experiences to the crowds awaiting him:

> …at first I was angry but by Sunday I felt happy that I did not come because my stay in Salisbury brought us and our people in Southern Rhodesia [together – sic]; and I don't mean the Nyasaland Africans working in Southern Rhodesia but the Mashonas, Matabeles and Makarangas gathered together…they said that I was not just your leader here in Nyasaland but their leader in Southern Rhodesia as well. I didn't even stay with the Nyasas in Salisbury. The Mashonas kept me with them… they said we the Africans of Southern Rhodesia do not recognise the Federation so this is our leader for everybody in Central Africa.[82]

Writing to the Commander Fox-Pitt (previously Provincial Commissioner in Northern Rhodesia before he was dismissed for his criticism of the government's racial policy) Dr Banda reiterated how pleased he had been with the reception from SRANC leaders and the Southern Rhodesian people:

> Incidentally the authorities did a stupid thing…my stay in Salisbury proved to be a blessing in disguise. The Africans in Salisbury received me with such enthusiasm that even the Nyasas were a bit jealous. I stayed with Southern Rhodesian Congress leaders. George Nyandoro, the Secretary of the Southern Rhodesian Congress, himself, told his people that I was not only the leader of the Africans of Nyasaland but also of those of Southern Rhodesia, and that from Sunday onwards, we would work together as a team.[83]

[81] Chiume, *Kwacha*, p. 99.

[82] ZNA MS 841/32 'ANC Information and Reports, 1959–62', Dr Banda's speech at Chileka Airport in Blantyre, 28 December 1958.

[83] RHL Box 241 File 1 Letter to Commander Fox-Pitt from Dr Banda, 30 December 1958.

Previously, Dr Banda had publicly derided Africans in Southern Rhodesia as 'Capricorns', but his attitude changed following this encounter.[84] Shortly after his visit Banda was prohibited from entering Southern Rhodesia and Northern Rhodesia under the Inter-Territorial Movement of Persons Act. He was described as a 'danger to peace' having spoken violently against Federation on his latest visit to Salisbury.[85] The Harare branch of the Nyasaland African Congress Women's League gathered in Harare Township in protest. They declared their intention, 'to unite in support of our Messiah, Banda'.[86] A march in honour of Dr Banda was also arranged in Highfield, where Banda claimed there had been crowds of up to ten thousand people listening to his address.[87]

The increased radicalism of the nationalists in the north with their powerful anti-federation rhetoric alarmed the federal administration. Federal intelligence gradually revealed how African political figures in Southern Rhodesia were aligning themselves more closely with their neighbours in the north. J. C. Malifa was described by the Federal Intelligence and Security Board as:

> ...a militant African nationalist whose activities as an executive of the African National Congress in Southern Rhodesia have been noted by the security branch for the last five years. He signed a lengthy 'Declaration of Independence of Nyasaland Africans' which came to light in December, 1955, and is regarded as the driving force behind the Mashonaland Branch of the Nyasaland African Congress which is the most active branch in Southern Rhodesia and gives considerable financial support to the central body in Nyasaland. Malifa is regarded as the leader of the Nyasas in this colony and the danger of his continued residence here lies in his ability to

[84] RHL MSS Afr.S 1681 Box 240/1 In a letter from Dr Banda to Mr David Astor in January a year before he was prohibited from Southern Rhodesia, Banda wrote, 'They [Southern Rhodesian Africans] lack the proper spirit and are used to being spoon fed by Europeans. I entirely agree with him on this. The Africans in Southern Rhodesia, even the best of them are stooges...', Letter, 17 January 1958.

[85] *The Nyasaland Times*, 6 January 1959.

[86] ZNA Federal Archives F120/L343/1, 'Security Situation Reports, 1959'.

[87] SOAS Fox-Pitt, Box 9, 'The Africa Bureau' Southern Rhodesia African National Congress meeting 'in protest against the action taken by the Southern Rhodesian and Northern Rhodesian governments in banning Dr Hastings Banda...and other African leaders and in denying them even transit facilities', 18th January 1959.

> incite Africans resident in this colony to follow the course of subversion dictated by African National Congress of Nyasaland.'[88]

George Nyandoro returned to Southern Rhodesia after another visit to Nyasaland in 1958. He spoke to a meeting of the Harare branch of SRANC and encouraged the formation of a Women's League and a Youth wing, just as they had done in Nyasaland.[89] In January 1959 Chipembere planned to travel to Southern Rhodesia again to meet with the other Congress leaders, but the Southern Rhodesian government was fore-warned by the Colonial Office: 'You will know that Chipembere is the first lieutenant of Dr Banda who has just been made a prohibited immigrant…'[90] Suspicious of Chipembere's visit, and fearful of the political capital that could be made of the situation for NAC if he was also prohibited from entering Southern Rhodesia, the Colonial Office advised the Southern Rhodesian government that a decision be taken very carefully:

> …we think that, in present political circumstances the balance of advantage to us and to the federation as a whole would lie in letting Chipembere visit Southern Rhodesia. You could then keep a very close watch on his activities there and, if he oversteps the mark, prosecute him for a breach of the law and subsequently declare him a prohibited immigrant. In this way it will be demonstrable that while there is freedom of movement between the territories, those who abuse the hospitality of a territory must accept all the consequences.[91]

Chipembere was banned from entering Southern Rhodesia only a week after Dr Banda's restriction order was issued.[92] The inter-territorial Congress meeting was postponed and relocated to Blantyre, yet federal restriction orders made it difficult to find a suitable location anywhere

[88] RHL FISB Affairs Box 239/8, 'Memorandum concerning Joshua Chirwa Wellington MALIFA', 1 August 1956.

[89] Carl F. Hallencreutz, *Religion and Politics Religion and Politics in Harare, 1890–1980* (Uppsala, 1999), p. 331.

[90] ZNA F120 Letter from P. W. Youens, Deputy Chief Secretary for Nyasaland to the Official Secretary to the Prime Minister of Southern Rhodesia, 9 January 1959.

[91] ZNA F120 Letter from P. W. Youens, Deputy Chief Secretary for Nyasaland to the Official Secretary to the Prime Minister of Southern Rhodesia, 9 January 1959.

[92] *The Nyasaland Times*, 16 January 1959, 'African M.L.C. Banned in Southern Rhodesia'.

in the Central African Federation. In a letter to Chiume, Chipembere explained their eventual success in finding a meeting place for the executive members of the three congress movements:

> George [Nyandoro] being determined to have the meeting, arranged that it takes place in Blantyre, but then a sudden ban descended on Sipalo – he was arrested and sent back to Northern Rhodesia! ...it was decided that Du [Dunduzu Chisiza] and George should go to Fort Manning and meet Sipalo there. This has at last been achieved. The Imperialists are quite baffled. Police have been enquiring where George and Du are![93]

By early 1959 the federal and territorial governments were anxious to prevent further contact between the congress movements and to avoid the damaging influence of the more radical Africans in the north on growing African political consciousness in Southern Rhodesia. According to Banda, 'Sir Edgar Whitehead and his government [are] panicking like a lot of rabbits...'[94] The Federal Immigration Act of 1954 gave wider powers to the government to restrict the movement of nationalists and confine activists to their own territories. In Nyasaland in 1958 a bill was passed to extend police powers following bitter debate in the Legislative Council.[95] Dr Banda challenged the government's restrictions against leaders of Congress when he addressed a crowd of five thousand on the Palombe plains in Mlanje District (see Map 2.3): 'If Todd and Welensky can come to Nyasaland...why are we not allowed to meet for talks on politics?'[96] Congress leaders continued to busily coordinate their efforts and build pressure on the Federal government, in the face of increasing tensions. The atmosphere in Nyasaland just prior to the declaration of an emergency in Southern Rhodesia, was described by Chipembere: 'Brother, you cannot imagine the state of Nationalism now.

[93] The National Archives, CAB/129/98, Report of the Nyasaland Commission of Inquiry, 6 April 1959 (Hereafter—The Devlin Commission). Appendix One, Letter from Chipembere to Chiume, 2 February 1959. Munukayumbwa Sipalo was a radical member of the Zambia Congress. Rotberg, *The Rise of African Nationalism*, p. 291.

[94] *The Nyasaland Times*, 16 January 1959.

[95] These powers included the ability to stop and order assemblies and processions to disperse, and prohibited the carrying of weapons, see *The Nyasaland Times*, 5 December 1958.

[96] *The Nyasaland Times*, 10 February 1959, 'Banda in Mlanje'. Sir Garfield Todd was Prime Minister of Southern Rhodesia from 1953 to 1958.

If we are not careful, the whole thing might go out of hand. Boys are really, really hot and determined'.[97]

On the 24 January 1959 an emergency meeting of the Nyasaland African Congress was convened in Blantyre. The next day the meeting moved to a private location near Limbe where, according to the unreliable testimony of the colonial authorities, a notorious 'massacre plot' was hatched. The meeting became known as 'the secret bush meeting' where nationalists devised their plan to kill Europeans in Nyasaland.[98] African Congress officials denied the accusations claiming they had in fact met to discuss plans in the event of Dr Banda's arrest, which had been rumoured since his prohibition from Southern Rhodesia. Funding was of primary concern at the meeting as it was suggested that the Nyasaland African Congress would soon be banned in Southern Rhodesia, meaning an end to donations and subscriptions from Nyasas abroad. George Nyandoro was present at the bush meeting, having managed to evade government surveillance. Nyandoro reportedly offered the full support of the Southern Rhodesian African National Congress, including, if necessary, the use of violence.[99]

Welensky had previously informed his close advisors that they were expecting 'serious trouble' in Nyasaland. Welensky doubted whether the Nyasaland police could be relied upon in an emergency and raised the matter at the Federal Prime Minister's meeting on the 19 January 1959: 'The Federal Government must be in a position to exercise its responsibilities in the event of trouble, and play its part in maintaining internal security'.[100] A plan was devised to send Federal and Southern Rhodesian troops to Nyasaland, but only after they had 'secured the situation' in Southern Rhodesia.[101] Sir Edgar Whitehead (Prime Minister of Southern Rhodesia) predicted that moving federal troops to Nyasaland could provoke unrest elsewhere.[102] Robert Armitage, the Governor

[97] The Devlin Commission, Appendix One Letter from Chipembere to Chiume, 2 February 1959.

[98] The Devlin Commission.

[99] RHL Welensky Papers, Box 240/1.

[100] Ibid. Box 239/9 Federal PM's meeting, 19 January 1959.

[101] Ibid.

[102] Their prediction was correct. Dr Banda exploded in reaction to the movement of troops into Nyasaland to put down unrest in the Northern region. In a letter to the Governor of Nyasaland, Banda wrote, 'I protest in the strongest possible terms against

of Nyasaland, also warned of the possibility of joint action on behalf of the African congresses: '... nor can we discount the possibility of sympathetic disorders being staged in Northern and Southern Rhodesia, indeed if George Nyandoro is to be believed...'[103]

The Federal government decided to pre-empt any violent protest by congress members. Welensky felt that swift action in Southern Rhodesia would clear the way for strong action to be taken against the more militant and dangerous activists in Nyasaland. However, in contrast to parts of Nyasaland, the atmosphere in Salisbury and throughout the territory remained relatively calm. Therefore, Whitehead, under pressure from Welensky to act decisively, was left to find justification for using emergency measures against African congress supporters. A state of emergency was declared in Southern Rhodesia on the 26 February 1959. The declaration came as a shock to Congress members. During the first wave of arrests 495 people were rounded up by police and security forces; 307 were members of the Southern Rhodesian Congress; 105 officially belonged to the Nyasaland movement; and 83 were of the Northern Rhodesian Congress.[104] African journalist Lawrence Vambe described the emergency as arriving 'like a bolt from the blue'.[105] Leaders and members were rounded up and taken into detention with relative ease. Vambe continued, 'I was shocked and I felt extremely angry. It had not occurred to me or any of my friends, black and white that Sir Edgar Whitehead, who claimed to support the policy of partnership, would be so misguided as to resort to these draconian measures'.[106]

Welensky pushed for Whitehead to close the external branches of NAC in Southern Rhodesia in order to cut off its main source of funding. Ultimately the emergency in Southern Rhodesia was called to enable security forces to tackle the more radical Congress elements in Nyasaland without repercussions throughout the rest of the Federation.

the sending of outside troops, particularly, troops from Southern Rhodesia, to Karonga, Fort Hill and anywhere else in this country...Nowhere in the country has law and order been so broken down as to necessitate the calling in of troops from Southern Rhodesia, either federal or territorial...' RHL Welensky Papers 239/9, 23 February 1959.

[103] RHL MSS Welensky 240/1 Letter to Roy Welensky from Government House Zomba, 18 February 1959.

[104] These figures were confirmed in the Devlin Commission Report.

[105] ZNA Oral/233 Interview with Lawrence Vambe, 1–13 June 1983.

[106] Ibid.

The Southern Rhodesian emergency allowed the Federal government to weaken all three nationalist bases in Southern Rhodesia and the northern territories. The Unlawful Organisations Act was passed through hurriedly in Southern Rhodesia, banning all African Congress movements in the settler colony.[107] Overnight it became an offence for anyone to hold a membership card for any of the African Congress parties in central Africa.

An emergency was declared in Nyasaland on the 3 March 1959, in order to tackle disturbances in isolated parts of the territory.[108] The government aimed to stamp out Congress by arresting its 'hard core' members. Protests ensued at the arrests of local leaders and the Nyasaland government had to call in support from Federal security forces and the British South Africa Police (BSAP) in order to restore law and order. Over the course of a few days there were a number of deaths and many casualties, most of which occurred as a result of action taken by troops, and not in the course of any large scale disturbances.[109] Soldiers of the Kings African Rifles (KAR) and the Rhodesian African Rifles (RAR) were deployed in Limbe, Ncheu and Lilongwe, three of the Nyasaland Congress stronghold districts.[110] A number of detainees from Nyasaland were taken and held in Southern Rhodesia, but kept separately from the 'hard core' (the Chisiza brothers, Dunduzu and Yatuta, Chipembere and Dr Banda), and away from the Southern Rhodesian detainees.[111] Sometime later when a letter was smuggled from Southern Rhodesian Congress activist Edson Sithole to Dunduzu Chisiza, it caused such a stir from the authorities that visits to the 'hard core' in Gwelo Prison were temporarily prohibited.[112]

[107] *The Nyasaland Times*, 27 February 1959. The emergency powers allowed the government to detain people, prohibit gatherings of more than three, control movement of people and supplies of weapons, impose a curfew and control the publication of information about the movement or actions of the security forces.

[108] For a more detailed account of both the Southern Rhodesian and Nyasaland emergencies in 1959, see Baker, *State of Emergency*; The Devlin Commission Report, and the early editions of *Dissent*.

[109] The Devlin Commission, p. 5.

[110] Baker, *State of Emergency*, p. 29.

[111] Headline in *The Nyasaland Times* read: 'How They Live at Khami Prison—Detainees Are Kept in Two Separate Blocks, Nyasas in One, Southern Rhodesians in the Other, They Are Not Allowed to Mix', 24 March 1959.

[112] Mackay, *We Have Tomorrow*, p. 32.

Nyasaland detainees arrested in Southern Rhodesia were deported when they were no longer considered a threat by the authorities. Thirty Nyasas were released in April, although another 146 remained in detention in Southern Rhodesia and 66 were deported to Nyasaland in May.[113] Those arrested in Salisbury were respectable middle-class Africans working as teachers, ministers and shop keepers. Among those deported several months later, was Aleke K. Banda, a young man of only nineteen years. Aleke was born in Northern Rhodesia to Nyasaland parents who were both from Nkhata Bay. He was raised in Southern Rhodesia where his father worked at Moss Mine near Que Que and had never even been to Nyasaland before his release in 1959.[114] Aleke had become interested in politics soon after the federation was declared in 1953 and by the age of fifteen was secretary of his local Southern Rhodesian branch of NAC. During his short detention in Khami prison he became closely acquainted with several leading NAC activists and was able to expand on his political education. Soon after his release, along with Orton Ching'oli Chirwa, he helped to establish the Malawi Congress Party (MCP).

Keeping Nyasaland detainees in Southern Rhodesia isolated them from their families, who were either sent back to Nyasaland or left in the care of relatives in Salisbury. Rose Chibambo, founder of the NAC Women's League, was among those arrested and charged with conspiring over the 'massacre plot'. Rose was sent to prison in Zomba moments after leaving the hospital where she had just given birth to her daughter. She was later joined by Vera Chirwa (NAC activist and wife of lawyer Orton Chirwa) who was briefly incarcerated in Salisbury, along with Gertrude Rubadiri (activist and wife of David Rubadiri) and four other women activists from Nyasaland, Northern and Southern Rhodesia before being relocated to Zomba Central Prison.[115] Several months after the emergencies were declared another ninety Nyasaland Africans were arrested in Salisbury under the new Unlawful Organisations Act.[116] These men and women had been found collecting funds on behalf of NAC to go towards the

[113] *The Nyasaland Times*, 17th April and 5 May 1959.

[114] *Tsopano*, No. 11, September 1960.

[115] Vera Mlangazua Chirwa, 'The Nyasaland State of Emergency of 1959/60: My Own Eye Witness Perception', in Kings M. Phiri, John McCracken, and Wapulumuka O. Mulwafu (eds.), *Malawi in Crisis: The 1959/60 Nyasaland State of Emergency and Its Legacy* (Zomba, 2012), pp. 330–331.

[116] *Dissent*, No. 6, 25 June 1959.

defence and relief of Nyasaland detainees. The editors of *Dissent* noted the obscurity of the men arrested:

> Here are none of the African notables who made up so considerable a proportion of the original 495 detainees – no leading politicians or trade unionists; no teachers, no ministers of religion; no journalists; no shopkeepers. The ninety now arrested are small men known only to their immediate circle, typical rank and file members rather than leaders…[117]

These congress members had built networks organised around common workplaces, factories, township houses and bible and prayer groups, demonstrating the extent to which Congress had infiltrated the lives of ordinary urban dwellers in Salisbury.

The strength and organisation of NAC was noted in an issue of *Dissent* when its 'superior survival value' was contrasted with the Southern Rhodesian Congress.[118] Southern Rhodesian nationalists took longer to re-group following the 1959 emergency. Chigwendere described the impact of the emergency:

> I think the ban came as a surprise to many people. It shattered quite a lot of people's hopes and it also took a long time to recover from the ban. It was the first experience of an African organisation being banned…But I think it also gave them time to think. The ban in Nyasaland resulted in the formation of the Malawi Congress Party, which later developed to lead Malawi to independence. Kaunda's Zambia National Congress was banned. He was also like Banda brought to Rhodesia for their prison terms. After that it seemed like they were making some kind of headway and I suppose it gave the feeling to people in Southern Rhodesia that they were also no exception. The length of time I can only say was a response to the shock and unpreparedness of the people for such a move…[119]

The National Democratic Party (NDP), successor to the SRANC, was formed in January 1960, whereas the Malawi Congress Party (MCP), successor to NAC, was already up and running by September 1959. By March 1960 the MCP was described as, 'a proper political party for

[117] Ibid.

[118] Ibid.

[119] ZNA Oral/228 Interview with Chigwendere, 24 May 1974.

hundreds of Nyasaland Africans both in the protectorate and outside'.[120] Lengthier detentions were imposed on African leaders in Southern Rhodesia and restrictive legislation made virtually all effective challenges to the settler regime illegal after 1959. The powers of the police in Southern Rhodesia to search, seize and arrest at random were extended and the Preventive Detention Act meant that anyone suspected of involvement in subversive activities could be imprisoned. Prior to the emergency, the Nyasaland African Congress had become a far more popular and radical organisation than SRANC. In Nyasaland there were 47 branches of congress; 34 of those were in the Northern Province where the most violence occurred during the emergency.[121] According to membership, NAC strongholds were in Blantyre, Limbe, Zomba and Mashonaland. These offices combined with other external branches in Southern and Northern Rhodesia and South Africa to provide a solid foundation on which the MCP could build.

The new nationalist parties emerged in Southern Rhodesia and Nyasaland within a different context to that of their predecessor organisations. The atmosphere throughout central Africa and the continent was rapidly changing by 1960. The influence of external events was noted in the Devlin Report:

> [Nationalism in Nyasaland] has been immensely encouraged by recent developments in Ghana, the Sudan, Nigeria and Uganda. We do not pause to enquire what difference there may be between conditions in these countries and in Nyasaland; the fact is that the success of African nationalism there has stimulated Africans elsewhere to believe that self-government is within their grasp and to behave accordingly.[122]

Relations between the nationalist organisations and the trajectories of all three federated territories changed over the ensuing years. Nyasaland, Northern and Southern Rhodesian Africans together celebrated the successes of Malawi and Zambia and their achievement of self-government

[120] *Tsopano*, No. 6, March 1960—Letter from W. A. Mhlaba Sambo in Bulawayo, Southern Rhodesia.

[121] ZNA F120/L341, 'Nyasaland Security Appreciation, 4 March 1959'.

[122] The Devlin Commission Report, p. 16.

and the dissolution of federation in 1963.[123] When the Southern Rhodesian NDP was formed *Drum* magazine had reported: 'It signals the arrival of the most determined form of nationalism the quietest of the three federal states has ever known – a party determined to stand alongside the Malawi Congress of Nyasaland and the United National Independence Party of Northern Rhodesia as the voice of the Federation's 8,000,000 blacks'.[124] Relations between the NDP and MCP were never as strong as those between the African Congress movements in the late 1950 s. Nyasaland newspaper, *Bwalo La Nyasaland* reported how 'differences between the NDP and the MCP' had to be 'ironed out', clearing the way for the MCP to open a new office in Salisbury in 1961.[125]

Salisbury experienced a great deal of unrest from 1960 onwards. Riots and demonstrations involved thousands of African men and women.[126] The NDP was banned in December 1961 and was quickly replaced with the Zimbabwe African People's Union (ZAPU) which was proscribed in September the following year. The Zimbabwean nationalist movement suffered a major split in 1963, with the Zimbabwe African National Union (ZANU) and the People's Caretaker Council (PCC) forming in August. ZANU broke away from those who remained loyal to ZAPU. Finally, federation was dissolved in December 1963. The MCP was banned in Southern Rhodesia in 1964 and Dr Banda (as Prime Minister of Malawi) made no attempt to hide his dismay over the divisions in the Zimbabwean nationalist movement.

Salisbury After the Emergency, 1959–1965

This chapter has so far explored the connections between the nationalist movements at the executive levels of Congress, highlighting the connections forged by middle-class migrants quite apart from the more typical image of the Nyasa labour migrant of this time. However, the political upheaval of federation brought changes not just to the lives

[123] 'NDP in Support of Banda and MCP Victory', *Bulawayo Chronicle*, 17 August 1961.

[124] Tom Hopkinson and Tim Couzens (eds.), *Zimbabwe: The Search for Common Ground since 1890* (Cape Town, 1992), p. 65.

[125] 'Malawi Congress Party', *Bwalo La Nyasaland*, 24 October 1961.

[126] For a first-hand account of 'the troubles' in Salisbury in the early 1960 s, see Mackay, *We Have Tomorrow*.

of influential members of political movements, but to more ordinary men and women who were trying to make a living in Salisbury. Labour migrants were involved in local politics in the 1950s when organisations, including church groups, mutual aid and burials societies became more highly politicised as so many aspects of life in Salisbury were subsumed by the nationalist agenda. Nationalist politics infiltrated into people's daily lives through the burial societies, which sometimes affiliated to political groups.

International evangelist Stephen Lungu was born in Salisbury to a Nyasaland father and Northern Rhodesian mother. He grew up in the city in the 1950s and 1960s, and he remembered how the burial societies could be a useful disguise for political meetings after the Congress movements were banned.[127] The Northern Province or Dowa Burial Society was formed in Salisbury after the 1959 emergency. It collected money for the wives and families of some of the political detainees and was accused of breaking the law as members were found to have Congress membership cards during the second wave of arrests in the city.[128]

As the political situation in Nyasaland became more intense, northern migrants in Salisbury were regarded with suspicion by their Southern Rhodesian employers. Ibrahim (whose life history was discussed in Chapters 4 and 5) recalled how there was a lot of discrimination (*tsankho*) in Southern Rhodesia during the federation years. In 1958 a new economic policy in Southern Rhodesia distinguished between labourers by territory, or nationality.[129] He described the reputation that became Nyasas/Malawians became associated with in Salisbury after the emergency:

> Malawians were not really wanted there. In order for you to get a job you did need some kind of identification. Malawians were never allowed to look for jobs within town. They were told to look for jobs ten miles outside of town and stay there. It was only if you were approached by a white person and he was happy with the way you were working, then that

[127] Interview with Stephen Lungu, Chatham, Kent, November 2006. Also, Stephen Lungu with Anne Coomes, *Out of the Black Shadows: The Amazing Transformation of Stephen Lungu* (London, 2001).

[128] *Dissent*, No. 7, 16 July 1959.

[129] Bill Paton, *Labour Export Policy in the Development of Southern Africa* (Harare, 1995), p. 124.

> person would take you to the District Commissioner. He would organise for you to be given identification so that you could become like a citizen of the country. The reason for the ten-mile thing was that in 1963 in Malawi they were heading towards independence. They were worried that if we were allowed to enter the towns, we would give people the same ideas and people would begin to push for the same things they were in Malawi.[130]

Nyasa migrants living in the city after the emergency felt that they were branded 'troublesome Nyasaland nationalists' and some struggled to find work. The political uncertainty of the early 1960s led to a slowdown in industrial growth. An advisor in the federal government's Department on Race Affairs claimed that 'every worker laid off becomes a new potential rioter'.[131] Nyasaland migrants became increasingly disadvantaged within the formal employment market in Salisbury.

For Stephen Lungu, the federation was also a period of unity among Africans before the divisions between the various nationalist groups in Zimbabwe in the 1960s, '...we felt united during the Federation before there was a split and the fighting came on'.[132] He and other young people were inspired by angry nationalist speeches. Many people recalled Dr Banda's visits to Salisbury to speak about 'the stupid federation'. Lungu described the appeal of Banda's speeches at that time:

> In 1958 Dr Banda came to Zimbabwe, to address the rally there. Later on he was arrested and put into Gwelo prison. It was there that the fireworks started because the white people thought by arresting him it was going to be a quiet thing, that it would destroy all of the noise from the black people. That was a big mistake, because that's when everything was an explosion...

Many people admired Banda's outspokenness; he was 'aggressive' and 'the first political leader who challenged white people in public'.[133] Everyone took notice as Banda articulated how angry people were with the racial discrimination that they faced:

[130] Interview with Ibrahim, Dedza, 2008.

[131] ZNA F128/L15 'Race Affairs, African Opinion, 1961–63', Commentary by J. D. Kenan, Advisor to the Federal Government on Race Affairs—African Unemployment, 30 May 1962.

[132] Interview with Stephen Lungu, Chatham, Kent, November 2006.

[133] Ibid.

> He said we have come to do two things here: One is to break this stupid federation. To call it stupid in public... ooooh, it was fireworks! With white soldiers around him, telling them I don't fear you and I have come to break this stupid federation and to attend to our own independence, to stand on our own. He spoke about being humiliated. It was the first time a black man had heard another black man saying all that was inside us. You should have been there to see it, ooh the excitement! The anger! You know that meeting didn't finish well because we started stoning all of the police cars and we just took hold of stones, because now there was no fear.'[134]

Some young men, like Stephen Lungu, were coerced into youth gangs in Salisbury and some became homeless when they could not find work. Lungu and other young men struggled to survive on the streets but found that they were able to carve out new roles for themselves within the political struggle: '...in the beginning we got involved because we were all under the Rhodesian Federation and Nyasaland. So, we thought more or less the same way, to fight the same enemy'.[135] In the early 1960s, Lungu became a member of a youth gang, which he described as acting informally on behalf of all the African organisations. They were known as 'the Black Shadows' and were not officially attached to any organised youth wing but were a group of young men with a common experience of growing up in a racially segregated and prejudiced city. For Lungu, resentment had built up since his childhood. By 1960 his father had left the family and gone back to Nyasaland; his mother was poor and unable to provide for her children on her own in the city. Eventually, he was abandoned. For Lungu, involvement in the youth gang was about finding a sense of belonging:

> [T]he Black Shadows was a gang which formed like a family. We were all like orphans. We had nothing to lose. We started breaking into homes, breaking into cars, stealing... So when I came to the political struggle there was fighting for freedom, but partly for me it was revenge, personal...[136]

[134] Ibid.

[135] Ibid.

[136] Ibid.

The Black Shadows were used by nationalist groups not only to assert pressure on the administration, but also to act against 'sell outs' and collaborators with the settler state.

A lot of Nyasas and later Malawians living in Salisbury avoided direct involvement with politics before and after the emergency, especially during the troubles of the early 1960 s and into the years of the liberation war. Nyasas were deported from Southern Rhodesia and others feared losing their jobs and homes if they attended rallies or joined political groups, including the MCP.[137] It was still possible to obtain work as domestic servants and many men found work as 'garden boys' in the white suburbs of the city. Some white settlers in the city even preferred to hire Malawians to work in their homes over Southern Rhodesian Africans because it was less likely they would be politically active; this was especially true during Zimbabwe's liberation struggle in the late 1960s and 1970s.[138] Better paid and more respectable employment had become harder to find as the urban economy suffered during these years. A Nyasaland government representative in Salisbury observed in 1959: 'Since the Nyasaland emergency became known there has been a disinclination amongst private and small commercial employers to accept Nyasa Africans'.[139] Later in 1961 the FISB warned about rumours of a planned walk out of farm labour in Northern and Southern Rhodesia. It would be the Malawi Congress Party rather than the National Democratic Party, they suggested, because the farm labour mostly came from Nyasaland.[140] Any strike action was assumed to be organised by nationalist groups.

Labour migrants from Nyasaland became entangled in the political disputes between African nationalists and the white settler government of Southern Rhodesia during the last years of the federation. A commentary written for a 1960 edition of *Tsopano* discussed the consequences for Nyasaland labour if the colony seceded from federation:

[137] Interview with Mr Binga, CCAP, Harare, August 2009.

[138] John Pape, '*Chimurenga* in the Kia: Domestic Workers in the Liberation Struggle in Zimbabwe', *Sites of Struggle* (Harare, 1999), p. 263.

[139] MNA 14239 (Secretariat Dept.) 2/27/6F/2357 Nyasaland Government Representative for Salisbury, Reports, Vol. 2, 1959.

[140] RHL Welensky Papers, FISB Affairs, Box 238/3.

> The Prime Minister of Southern Rhodesia stated that the day Nyasaland secedes from Federation, Southern Rhodesia would close its borders to Nyasaland labour. Sir Edgar of course was just being spiteful...[141]

Tsopano (meaning 'now' in Chinyanja) was a monthly publication produced and managed in Salisbury by two Europeans, Peter Mackay and Jimmy Skinner.[142] The magazine, founded in October 1959, published material in English that was critical of the federal and Nyasaland governments, and sympathetic towards African nationalist movements in the region. Mackay intended the publication to provide 'a voice for Nyasaland', similar to *Dissent* published in Southern Rhodesia, and *Contact* in South Africa.[143] In 1962, Whitehead threatened to ban Nyasas from Southern Rhodesia.[144] African nationalists were aware of Southern Rhodesia's dependence on Nyasaland labour, particularly when it came to the farms and mines. Commercial farmers were concerned by the very real possibility of labour shortages if nationalists in Nyasaland were to force the withdrawal of labour from Southern Rhodesia once they gained self-government. Nyasaland nationalists responded defiantly to Whitehead's warnings stating that, 'Nyasaland is unperturbed by Whitehead's threat...the unvarnished truth is that Nyasaland labour is as indispensable as Northern Rhodesia's copper is to Southern Rhodesia'.[145] An article in the Bulawayo *Chronicle* in 1962, stressed the importance of retaining good relations between Zomba and Salisbury, regardless of the political outcome.[146]

African Congress members from both northern territories had been strongly critical of labour export policy during discussions on their respective legislative councils. Labour migration, they argued, was to blame for the lack of development in Nyasaland and in certain rural areas of Northern Rhodesia. Although federation had promised increased investment, the number of labour migrants leaving Nyasaland on a yearly basis

[141] *Tsopano*, No. 5, February 1960, Commentary by Mlonda.

[142] Andrew C. Ross, *Colonialism to Cabinet Crisis: A Political History of Malawi* (Zomba, 2009), p. 198.

[143] Peter Mackay, *We Have Tomorrow*, pp. 38–43.

[144] 'Whitehead threatens to Ban Nyasas in S.R'. *The Daily News*, 18 July 1962.

[145] *Tsopano*, No. 6, March 1960.

[146] 'Tete a Tete in Zomba', *The Chronicle*, 28 March 1962.

had continued to rise throughout the 1950s.[147] Furthermore, the decision to locate a new hydro-electric dam at Kariba in Southern Rhodesia, as opposed to the Shire River site in Nyasaland, was seen at the time by Congress leaders as another example of the failure of the federal government to honour promises of development for Nyasaland. Ten thousand Nyasaland migrants were employed at Kariba during its construction, further exacerbating their frustrations.[148] The new Malawi Congress Party promised economic development for the future:

> [W]hen Nyasaland secedes from Federation, any lessening of the number of Nyasa people entering Southern Rhodesia will be solely due to the great surge of economic development which will then begin in Nyasaland.[149]

In 1960 and again the following year, the Nyasaland government raised the quota for labour recruitment in the territory, despite the protests of the MCP; the number of *Mthandizi* and *Wenela* contracts reached a record high.[150] African agriculture in Nyasaland in the early 1960 s was in decline, due to a lack of investment and large scale out-migration. The MCP, in line with its predecessor organisation the NAC, was opposed to all forms of labour recruitment and their official policy was to increase awareness of the exploitative nature of the colonial migrant labour system in southern Africa.[151]

Malawian migrants in Salisbury, along with other urban dwellers, were marginalised from the Zimbabwean nationalist struggle after 1965. Non-indigenous migrants were excluded from nationalist parties, which in any case were forced to operate underground from this point onwards, and

[147] Paton, *Labour Export Policy*, p. 45. These figures are for recruited labour and did not include *machona* or those who had independently migrated without passes and official documentation.

[148] On the building of the Kariba Damn see Julia Tischler, *Light and Power for a Multiracial Nation: The Kariba Damn Scheme in the Central African Federation* (New York, 2013).

[149] *Tsopano*, No. 6 March 1960.

[150] Paton, *Labour Export Policy*, p. 47.

[151] ZNA F236/CX29/2/2 African Labour Policy, Vol. 3, 'Nyasaland and RNLSC (Mthandizi), 7 September 1961. The Nyasaland Government had decided not to renew RNLSC permits at the end of the year. The announcement was made by Harry Bwanausi, Minister of Labour and Social Development in the new government.

the interests of women and trade unions in many ways became subordinate to the nationalist agenda.[152] The struggle for national liberation in Zimbabwe moved out of the city, into the rural areas and across the country's borders, following the pronouncement of UDI.[153] Elube from Ntcheu lived with her husband in Gatooma, Southern Rhodesia. They had secured married accommodation in the 1950s through her husband's employers and raised their family of eight children in the mining town.[154] Elube recalled how peaceful life had been in the 1950s when they first arrived. Everything changed when the freedom fighters came:

> Soldiers started coming door to door and killing people in their houses. The groups I attended were associated with the church, and we didn't take any role in politics. When the time of war came we formed a group known as *Molale*. It was a group for those who didn't originate in Zimbabwe, those who used identity cards to move around. If you went outside the gate of the mines without an identity card and someone attacked you or killed you it was your own fault. The soldiers would come to our houses at night and bang on the doors. If they came and they knew that you were Malawian you were ok, but if they didn't know anything about you, you could be killed. If they found members of Nkomo's party or Mugabe's party, they would kill people who weren't with them. So it was important to be identified as a Malawian.[155]

Zimbabwean nationalism became increasingly exclusive and narrowly defined. Politics in Malawi was also transformed with the coming of independence and the strengthening of African nationalism, through the project of state-building. These dynamics are explored in the final chapter.

Conclusion

In the formative years of African nationalism in Central Africa, several attempts were made to establish a more coherent movement that transcended arbitrary colonial boundaries. The long history of migration from

[152] Raftopoulos, 'Nationalism and Labour in Salisbury, 1953–1965', *Sites of Struggle*, p. 144.

[153] The position of non-indigenous migrants during the period of the liberation struggle, from 1965 to 1980 and after independence is discussed in Chapter 7.

[154] Interview with Elube, Ntcheu District, February 2008. Second name unknown.

[155] Ibid.

Nyasaland fostered the growth of pan-African solidarity among early political leaders. African elites endeavoured to work across borders in building their opposition to federation, and later in demanding freedom from white minority rule. Early attempts to create an organisation in the 1940s to represent Africans throughout the region, and not just at the territorial level, were largely unsuccessful, and the ideal of a 'Central African Congress' was never truly realised. However, efforts towards this end became important again in the late 1950s.

During the early years of the Federation, many Nyasas were involved in politics outside of the Protectorate. Like many Nyasas, B. K. Manda first became active in African nationalist politics in South Africa.[156] He was later deported and sent home to Nyasaland where he continued to be politically active. Manda maintained that 'nationalism knows no country of origin'.[157] His experiences suggest that nationalisms could hold a universal appeal. African leaders recognised the strength in uniting all three Congress parties in their common struggle against Welensky and his 'stupid federation'. These sentiments were underlined at the high-level conference held by leaders of the Southern Rhodesia, Northern Rhodesia and the Nyasaland African Congresses in Lusaka in 1958. A presidential report on the progress made by SRANC since its revival in 1957 explained how: 'The success of this conference marked the beginning of an interchange of information between the three Congresses'. It was decided that this level of cooperation must continue in order to 'coordinate one general policy of the Congress movement'.[158] A new unanimity was established between the Congress movements, centred on pan-African sentiments in the wake of Ghanaian independence in 1957 and the All African People's Conference in 1958, which inspired and gave optimism to the nationalists in central Africa. Nationalists who had lived and worked outside of their home territories, either as labour migrants, preachers or students were concerned for the freedom of Africans from white settler and colonial domination. Nonetheless, the strength of solidarity between the different nationalist groups was to be short lived, as

[156] *Tsopano*, No. 4, January 1960.

[157] Ibid.

[158] 'Southern Rhodesia African National Congress: Presidential Report on Progress and Expansion During 1957–8. First Annual Delegates Conference, 12–14 September 1958', published in Christopher Nyangoni and Gideon Nyandoro (eds.), *Zimbabwe Independence Movements. Select Documents* (London, 1979), p. 17.

repressive action taken by the federal state succeeded in driving the territorial movements apart. Internal disputes and disagreements over strategy and the future of their respective postcolonial states also played a role in the failure of the movements to work together effectively after the 1959 emergency.

Following the 1959 emergency, the Devlin Commission found that anti-Federation sentiment was deeply rooted in Nyasaland and not just confined to a group of intellectual agitators:

> The issue touches, or appears to touch, the African, whether he is educated or uneducated, on a point where he is particularly sensitive...The partly educated, who have been to Southern Rhodesia and to the Union of South Africa as labourers, dislike the ways and attitudes that they have seen there...Federation means the domination of Southern Rhodesia; the domination of Southern Rhodesia means the domination of the settler; the domination of the settler means the perpetuation of racial inferiority and of the threat to the Africans' land.[159]

Federation provided a strong rallying point for Central African nationalists. The leaders of the Nyasaland African Congress used federation to politicise Africans on a wider scale. N. D. Kwenje, President of the Salisbury branch of NAC, realised the value of anti-federation propaganda when he reported to Dr Banda in 1952: 'The Federation question has done a great deed for us Africans. It has united us far more closely than any other question would have accomplished'.[160] The political culture created by NAC from the mid-1950s, in the build up to the state of emergency in 1959, was again reshaped by Banda and the new mechanisms of the MCP in the 1960s. More on this in the final chapter.

The radicalism and militancy of one nationalist movement inevitably impacted on others in the region. The early establishment of the Nyasaland and Northern Rhodesian African Congresses certainly influenced the development of African political organisation in Southern Rhodesia and was noted at the time in *Dissent*: 'The issue of Federation only came to assume significance in Southern Rhodesian African politics with the increasing degree of co-operation between the three territorial Congresses

[159] The Devlin Commission, p. 22.

[160] RHL MSS Africa Bureau Box 240.

in 1958'.[161] Connections between the Congress movements were a growing concern for the colonial and settler governments during federation. The draconian measures taken against NAC and SRANC during the emergency were also shaped by wider regional and international events, such as escalating tensions in South Africa and the Mau Mau revolt in Kenya in the 1950s. Ultimately, nationalist politics was moulded as much by the repressive responses from individual states, as it was created by Africans themselves.

Finally, the nationalist movement in Nyasaland made an important contribution to African nationalisms elsewhere in the Central Southern African region. Middle ranking and senior members of the early African Congress in Nyasaland kept close networks abroad and pursued an inclusive strategy with their fellow Congress members in the south. By 1960 Nyasaland was effectively charting a new course towards secession from federation advanced by the Malawi Congress Party (MCP). African majority rule and self-governing status were achieved in 1963. Independence followed for Malawi (and Zambia) in 1964. In Southern Rhodesia the struggle for African independence was only just beginning as white settler politics 'swung in an increasingly racist direction'.[162] The feelings of many Africans in Southern Rhodesia at this time were aptly summarised in *Drum* magazine:

> No matter how law abiding the mass of Southern Rhodesian Africans may be, they cannot forget that Kenneth Kaunda and Hastings Banda have emerged from prison to be recognised as national leaders by the British government and they wonder whether Southern Rhodesia, too, must not embark upon a road of militant nationalism before the black man begins to share the good things in life.[163]

A period of open mass nationalist activity in Southern Rhodesia ended in 1965, by which point racial tensions had dramatically worsened. Ian Smith and the right-wing Rhodesian Front (RF) gradually tightened their control of Rhodesian society following the end of Federation in 1963. In 1965 with the illegal Unilateral Declaration of Independence (UDI), the path to national liberation for Zimbabwe changed course entirely.

[161] Terence Ranger and John Reed in *Dissent*, No. 19, 9 June 1960.

[162] Ibid, p. 74.

[163] Hopkinson and Couzens (eds.), *Zimbabwe: The Search*, p. 69.

CHAPTER 7

Citizenship and Belonging in Malawi and Zimbabwe

Chivinda Banda went to Malawi for the first time in 1998. He only planned to go for a short visit but stayed to be closer to his parents after he was offered a job at a school in Chinteche in the north of Malawi—the area his father was from. Chivinda was born in Rhodesia in the 1970s during the liberation struggle.[1] He grew up in a small mining town in Lomagundi District in Mashonaland West, where his father had worked from the mid-1950s until his retirement in the early 1990s. Chivinda and all of his siblings left Zimbabwe in the late 1990s. One moved to Zambia while the others relocated to Malawi. Chivinda kept in close contact with friends in Harare and dreamt about one day returning to Zimbabwe.

Thousands of second and third generation Malawians, like Chivinda Banda, were born in Rhodesia, and later Zimbabwe. Former migrant workers and their families were initially welcomed to remain in Zimbabwe at independence in 1980, along with other minority groups, including white settlers. Yet, the country's citizenship laws became increasingly exclusive leaving many Malawian migrants and their descendants politically disenfranchised and labelled 'aliens' by the state. Some Malawians decided to leave Zimbabwe when the political and economic climate deteriorated in the late 1990s and early 2000s. Those who returned to Malawi

[1] Southern Rhodesia became known as Rhodesia in 1964 after the break up of federation.

Z. R. Groves, *Malawian Migration to Zimbabwe, 1900–1965*, Cambridge Imperial and Post-Colonial Studies Series,
https://doi.org/10.1007/978-3-030-54104-0_7

usually had a house to go back to and a community to welcome them home. In contrast to Zimbabwe, the mid-1990s marked a moment of optimism in Malawi, with the end of Banda's one-party rule and the beginning of multi-party democracy.[2] However, many Malawians lacked the connections and resources to go back while others were determined to remain in Zimbabwe. For second and third generation Malawians born in the country, Zimbabwe was the only place they had ever known as home.

This final chapter offers an overview of events after the break-up of the federation in 1963, during the years of the liberation struggle in Zimbabwe, and following independence in 1980. It traces migration to and from Malawi after independence in 1964 and explores issues of citizenship and belonging for people of Malawian (or Nyasaland) origin and descent in Zimbabwe the postcolonial era.[3] The chapter highlights the fraught xenophobic tensions in southern Africa and the effect this has had on people's lives and prospects. Finally, the book ends with a discussion of the Malawian diaspora in southern Africa.

After Federation

With the demise of federation, two key areas of debate for Rhodesia and Nyasaland (soon to become Malawi) were constitutional change and the nature of the new states to emerge. New governments grappled with questions over citizenship rights alongside concerns about economic viability. The economies of the three former federal territories were strongly interconnected, which made it hard for newly independent Malawi and Zambia to impose full sanctions against the 'pariah state' of Rhodesia after the Unilateral Declaration of Independence (UDI) in 1965. Several attempts between the British and the white-dominated settler government to negotiate a constitution that would lead to Rhodesian independence failed in the 1960s.[4] The relatively small number of

[2] On Malawi's political transition see Harri Englund (ed.), *A Democracy of Chameleons: Politics and Culture in the New Malawi* (Stockholm, 2002).

[3] The question of citizenship and belonging for Malawians in Zimbabwe is examined in more detail here: Zoë Groves, 'Zimbabwe is my home': Citizenship and Belonging for 'Malawians' in Post-Independence Urban Zimbabwe, *South African Historical Journal* (2020). https://doi.org/10.1080/02582473.2020.1773521.

[4] See Josiah Bronwell, *The Collapse of Rhodesia: Population Demographics and the Politics of Race* (London, 2010), p. 4. On this period of Rhodesian history, see Luise White,

white settlers in Rhodesia when compared with the African population, as well as divisions within the white population, meant that race was never a sufficient basis on which to build a strong Rhodesian state.[5] For this reason, the ruling party, the Rhodesian Front, was compelled to make some concessions in order to retain power, for example, with the inclusion of minority groups—namely 'Coloureds and Asians'—on the 1969 voters' roll, and with the co-opting of the African middle classes in various ways. These gestures were part of a policy of 'inclusive exclusion' whereby non-white groups were included in political structures without allowing them any real political power.[6] Meanwhile, African nationalists, either in prison, exile, or operating underground, were engaged in their own process of imagining the nation, drawing heavily on discourses of race and origin, using race as a means of exclusion.[7] Africans were portrayed by Zimbabwean nationalists as the true 'sons and daughters of the soil' (*mwana wevhu*), with whites or Europeans and other groups delegitimised as 'settlers' on indigenous land. These exclusive ideas about who belonged and who did not belong to Zimbabwe were to have dramatic consequences in the post-independence era, which this chapter will turn to below.

Labour and the legacies of labour migration were crucial issues for the post-federation states. The federal government had promoted the migration of workers and their families even more strongly during the federation years. By 1965, an estimated 300,000 Malawians worked in Rhodesia.[8] Leader of the Rhodesian Front and Prime Minister of

Unpopular Sovereignty: Rhodesian Independence and African Decolonisation (Chicago, 2015).

[5] At its height the white population in Rhodesia reached 277,000. To put this in perspective, the number of Malawians in Rhodesia after federation were estimated to be between 240,000 and 300,000. Bronwell, *The Collapse of Rhodesia*, p. 3. Statistics on the number of Malawians are taken from Robert E. Christiansen and Jonathan G. Kydd, 'The Return of Malawian Labour from South Africa and Zimbabwe', *The Journal of Modern African Studies*, 21, 2 (1983), p. 319; Joseph Mtisi, Munyaradzi Nyakuda and Teresa Barnes, 'Social and Economic Developments in the UDI Period', in Brian Raftopoulos and Alois Mlambo (eds.), *Becoming Zimbabwe: A History from the Pre-Colonial Period to the Present* (Harare, 2009), p. 135.

[6] Mtisi, Nyakuda and Barnes, 'Social and Economic Developments in the UDI Period', p. 123.

[7] Ibid, p. 124.

[8] Thousands of Zambian workers were in fact repatriated in 1965 and those who remained had restrictions placed on where they could find employment. Ibid., p. 137.

Rhodesia (1964–1979), Ian Smith, threatened to repatriate Malawian and Zambian workers and their families if the Rhodesian economy was to suffer through British government action. The Smith regime introduced new restrictions on the employment of 'alien' Africans within different sectors in the 1960s and again in 1976. Between 1962 and 1969, the number of Malawians in Salisbury declined quite significantly from 41,530 to 28,830.[9] However, the demands for labour in mining and agriculture meant attempts to push foreign labour out of the country were once again unsuccessful. In 1972, Malawians made up just over twenty per cent of agricultural workers, and they remained the largest group of foreign workers employed in the country.[10]

In newly independent Malawi, President Banda abandoned earlier pan-African visions of inclusive nationality when he defined citizenship by race and origin in the 1966 Malawi Citizenship Bill. One of the consequences of the new bill was the exclusion of Asians and Europeans despite long histories of residence going back two generations in some cases. Citizenship could be granted on application to the government, but it was not guaranteed. As John McCracken put it: 'Only Africans or people born of an African mother could be Malawian citizens as of right'.[11] But it was not only other racial groups whose entitlement to belong to Malawi was brought into question. Banda weaponised the discourse of foreignness to discredit his political opponents. Henry Masauko Chipembere was one of the prominent African nationalist leaders to emerge during the federation years and also one of Banda's closest allies until the 1964 Cabinet Crisis, which led to the dramatic resignation of six cabinet ministers soon after independence.[12] Chipembere was ridiculed by Banda who called him 'a foreigner from Mozambique'. To counter the narrative that he and others with Mozambican ancestral ties were any less Malawian,

[9] According to these statistics, the number of Malawians in Salisbury fell from 39 to 10 per cent of the total African population in the city. Tsuneo Yoshikuni, *African Urban Experiences in Colonial Zimbabwe: A Social History of Harare before 1925* (Harare, 2005), p. 160.

[10] Alois Mlambo, 'A History of Zimbabwean Migration to 1990', in Jonathan Crush and Daniel S. Tevera (eds.), *Zimbabwe's Exodus: Crisis, Migration, Survival* (Cape Town, 2010), p. 66.

[11] John McCracken, *A History of Malawi, 1859–1966* (Woodbridge, 2012), p. 457.

[12] On the shift in political culture from 1960 and the events surrounding the 1964 Cabinet Crisis, see Joey Power, *Political Culture and Nationalism in Malawi: Building Kwacha* (Rochester, 2010), pp. 177–201.

Chipembere produced a pamphlet about the history of his ancestors to prove that he was a real Malawian. The insinuation behind Banda's attack was that Chipembere was of freed slave heritage and therefore had no kin, rendering him ineligible for citizenship status.[13] Banda was himself accused of being an inauthentic Malawian by those wary of his leadership when he first returned to Nyasaland in 1958; because he had spent so many years outside of Malawi and lost touch with his homeland, Banda was seen as one of the *machona*.[14] Rumours circulated that Banda was really from the United States or Ghana.[15]

Hundreds of Malawians went into political exile in the years after independence. The Cabinet Crisis (also known as 'the Revolt of the Ministers') occurred due to Banda's autocratic style of governing as well as disagreements over key policies, such as Banda's insistence on maintaining diplomatic relations with the white minority regimes in the region.[16] Many of these ministers and their supporters were intimidated and forced into exile with their families. Political opponents who remained were imprisoned, assaulted and in some cases murdered.[17] The Banda government used spies and informers to report on disloyalty and dissent. Political exiles were depicted in negative terms as *zigawenga* (rebels). Those who left were dismissed as traitors who were disloyal to Malawi.[18] Unlike the federation years when Nyasas in Southern Rhodesia had played a major role in building the nationalist movement back home, Malawians outside of the country became cautious of involvement with the Malawi Congress Party (MCP) after independence. David Ngowe recalled how people in Zimbabwe shied away from Malawian politics

[13] McCracken, *History of Malawi*, p. 458; The pamphlet is reproduced in Colin Baker, *Chipembere: The Missing Years* (Zomba, 2008), pp. 242–263.

[14] See for example, McCracken, *History of Malawi*, p. 383; M. W. Kanyama Chiume, *Kwacha: An Autobiography* (Nairobi, 1975), p. 89.

[15] Brooks Marmon, 'Fallout from the Fallacious Accusation of Hastings Kamuzu Banda's West African Origins, 1960', *Society of Malawi Journal* (forthcoming).

[16] For a recent re-examination of Hastings Banda's political thought and practice, see Clive Gabay, 'The Radical and Reactionary Politics of Malawi's Hastings Banda: Roots, Fruit and Legacy', *Journal of Southern African Studies*, 43, 6 (2017), pp. 1119–1135.

[17] Power, *Political Culture and Nationalism*, pp. 180–181.

[18] John Lwanda, 'Diaspora, Domicile and Debate: A Preliminary Artistic and Cultural Search for a Malawi Identity from Pre-Colonial Times to 2014', *Society of Malawi Journal*, 67, 1 (2014), p. 37.

because of rumours that 'people would come hunting for you… Sometimes we would hear stories of people who were caught and sent back to Malawi'.[19] David's account chimed with the experiences of Malawians in political exile in Zambia, Tanzania, the United States and the UK.[20]

Malawians working abroad were encouraged by Banda and the MCP to return home after independence, and in the 1960s and 1970s many did for a variety of reasons. The country's development strategy saw the expansion of large-scale estate agriculture and the production of cash crops—mainly tobacco and sugar—which created a much greater demand for wage labour. Even though wages were still very low in comparison with other countries in the region, between 1966 and 1977, 333,000 'economically active individuals' returned to Malawi.[21] Nonetheless, despite Banda's political speeches discouraging international labour migration, the number of Malawians outside of the country in 1972 was still an estimated ten per cent of the population (487,000).[22] Wages in Malawi remained very low when compared to other countries in the region. In the early 1970s, 124,000 Malawians were under contract with TEBA (The Employment Bureau of Africa, previously Wenela) working on the mines in South Africa. Banda later prohibited Malawian citizens taking up contract labour in South Africa following the 1974 Francistown air crash in which 74 Malawian miners were killed in Botswana on their way back home. Although labour recruitment was reinstated in 1977 it never reached the same levels as before.[23] By the 1980s, the South African mining industry had gradually reoriented towards the recruitment of local labour. Malawian labour was no longer the important resource it had once been for the Chamber of Mines. Increasing numbers of Malawian workers were repatriated from the South African mines from

[19] Interview with David Ngowe, Ntcheu, February 2008.

[20] Power, *Political Culture and Nationalism in Malawi*, pp. 188–198.

[21] Employment in estate agriculture were not necessarily the incentive that led individuals to return. Robert E. Christiansen and Jonathan G. Kydd, 'The Return of Malawian Labour from South Africa and Zimbabwe', *The Journal of Modern African Studies*, 21, 2 (1983), p. 312.

[22] Ibid., p. 313. Between 1972 and 1977, approximately 212,000 people retuned to Malawi.

[23] On labour migration to South Africa after 1974, see Harvey C. Banda, 'The Dynamics of Labour Migration from Northern Malawi to South Africa since 1974', PhD Thesis, University of the Witwatersrand, 2017.

1988.[24] The official reason was that large numbers of Malawian miners had tested positive for HIV/AIDS. The Malawian government refused to allow migrants to be screened for HIV/AIDS before leaving the country, as requested by the Chamber of Mines, and this effectively brought an end to formal labour recruitment in Malawi. Malawi gradually reduced its economic dependence on South Africa but the retrenchment of workers in the 1980s and 1990s still had an impact on livelihoods and the rural economy.[25] In the 2000s, some Malawians looked back with nostalgia for the era of labour recruitment and the opportunities that had once existed.[26]

Finally, the escalating military conflict of the liberation wars in the 1970s, which created huge numbers of displaced people and refugees throughout the region, also saw Malawians returning from Mozambique and Zimbabwe. A significant number of Malawians also returned from Zambia in the decade from the late 1960s to the late 1970s when the policy of Zambianisation was enacted in the mining industry. Malawians had been employed in the Zambian mines since the 1940s and many people considered Malawian by the Zambian government had in fact been born in Zambia to Malawian fathers.[27] Chipembere was seemingly unaware of the consequences of this policy when he wrote 'an expression of admiration for the people of Zambia' in his 1969 pamphlet (authored while in exile and mentioned above):

> They [Zambians] have accepted not only Dr Kenneth Kaunda, the Zambian-born leader of the Zambian nation, whose parents came from Malawi and were born of Malawian parents, but have accepted thousands of Malawians to work in Zambia and even to hold key positions in the public service, in the party, on the mines, in commerce and industry, and

[24] For a detailed examination of this episode, see Wiseman Chijere Chirwa, 'Aliens and Aids in Southern Africa: The Malawi-South Africa Debate', *African Affairs*, 97, 386 (1998), pp. 53–79.

[25] See also Wiseman Chijere Chirwa, '"No TEBA ...Forget TEBA": The Plight of Malawian Ex-Migrant Workers to South Africa, 1988–1994', *International Migration Review*, 31, 3 (1997), pp. 628–654.

[26] Daniel Wroe, 'Remembering Kamuzu: The Ambiguity of the Past in Malawi's Central Region', *Journal of Southern African Studies*, 46, 2 (2020), pp. 247–261.

[27] Duncan Money, 'Aliens on the Copperbelt: Zambianisation, Nationalism and Non-Zambian Africans in the Mining Industry', *Journal of Southern African Studies*, 45, 5 (2019), pp. 859–875.

> in the Church ... Malawians are said to form 15 per cent of the total labour force in Zambia. Zambia has demonstrated its belief in the oneness of Africa by this invaluable act of kindness and magnanimity.[28]

Zambian nationalism was no exception in the region when it came to narrow and exclusive definitions of citizenship and belonging. This was seen even more dramatically when Kenneth Kaunda, president of the country from 1964 to 1991—regarded by many as the 'Father of the modern Zambian nation'—was prevented from running for office in the 1996 elections following a recent change to the constitution which had resulted in him being declared no longer a Zambian citizen.[29] Kaunda later successfully challenged this ruling in the Supreme Court of Zambia and his citizenship was reinstated, however, this was not the last time that citizenship in Zambia would be abused for political purposes.[30]

Zimbabwe After Independence

Zimbabwean politics in 1980 publicly promoted a spirit of national reconciliation. All those residing in the country on a permanent basis were welcomed as citizens of the state, 'regardless of race, colour or creed'.[31] Dual citizenship was endorsed in the first Zimbabwean constitution (the Lancaster House constitution) negotiated under the close watch of the British at the close of the liberation struggle. Unlike the special restrictions protecting white Zimbabweans from widespread land redistribution for the first decade of majority rule, dual citizenship was not specifically guarded.[32] Subsequently, by 1982 the government sought to amend the

[28] Baker, *Chipembere*, p. 263.

[29] Beth E. Whitaker, 'Citizens and Foreigners: Democratisation and the Politics of Exclusion in Africa', *African Studies Review*, 48, 1 (2005), pp. 112–117.

[30] Money, 'Aliens on the Copperbelt', p. 861.

[31] Robert Mugabe's address to the nation. 4 March 1980. http://www.politicsweb.co.za/politicsweb/view/politicsweb/en/page71619?oid=164016&sn=Detail (1 July 2014).

[32] Bronwen Manby, *Struggles for Citizenship in Africa* (London, 2009), pp. 40–41.

constitution and remove the right to hold dual citizenship.[33] The government argued that a policy of 'mono-citizenship' was intended to inculcate a sense of belonging and a common unity in the newly independent nation and to break down the historic separation between 'colonist and colonised', and the hierarchy of citizenship that characterised the settler-colonial period.[34] Holders of dual citizenship were seen by the state as 'half-hearted citizens'[35] who opposed and resisted the state's nationalist policies.[36] The 1984 citizenship bill was therefore presented by the government as an opportunity for all citizens to express their loyalty and commitment to the nation. It was openly targeted towards white commercial farmers, many of whom held citizenship rights in Britain, but it also had implications for former labour migrants and their families who had settled in the country. Further amendments were made to the constitution in the early 2000s with major consequences for people of Malawian origin and descent. Essentially, citizenship came to be defined by descent rather than place of birth.[37]

By the early 2000s, the atmosphere in Zimbabwe had changed dramatically. Political tensions had intensified from 1999 as a series of mostly white-owned farms were invaded by war veterans and peasants, later receiving the support of government forces as part of the new 'fast track' land reform programme. At the same time, urban areas had seen rising discontent over inflated food prices, high unemployment and increased living costs. Drawing on these grievances, the Movement for Democratic Change (MDC) was formed in 1999 to create a platform for political

[33] Constitutional Amendment No. 13 of 1983, Section 2: 'no citizen of Zimbabwe who is of full age and sound mind is entitled to be a citizen of a foreign country'. Manby, *Struggles for Citizenship*, pp. 39–41; J. L. Fisher, *Pioneers, Settlers, Aliens, Exiles: The Decolonisation of White Identity in Zimbabwe* (Canberra, 2010), pp. 108–115; Angela P. Cheater, 'Transcending the State? Gender and Borderline Constructions of Citizenship in Zimbabwe', in Thomas M. Wilson and Hastings Donnan (eds.), *Border Identities: Nation and State at International Frontiers* (Cambridge, 1998), pp. 191–214.

[34] Fisher, *Pioneers, Settler, Aliens, Exiles*, pp. 103–115.

[35] Musiwaro Ndakaripa, 'The State and Contested Citizenship in Zimbabwe, 1980–2011', in Sabelo Ndlovu-Gatsheni and Fenix Ndlovu (eds.), *Nationalism and National Projects in Southern Africa: New Critical Reflections* (Pretoria, 2013), p. 294.

[36] Fisher, *Pioneers, Settlers, Aliens, Exiles*, p. 109.

[37] For a summary of Zimbabwe's citizenship laws from the settler-colonial era to the 2019, see Bronwen Manby, Report on Citizenship Law: Zimbabwe, January 2019, available online: http://hdl.handle.net/1814/60436, date accessed 28 August 2020.

opposition. With the new electoral challenge from the MDC in the early 2000s, a more violent and coercive politics ensued. The government sought to further amend the country's citizenship laws with the new Citizenship of Zimbabwe Act, No. 12 of 2001.[38] This strengthened the demand for renunciation of foreign citizenship under the relevant foreign law, allowing six months for individuals to comply with the new regulations, or else forfeit their Zimbabwean nationality. The act was given some publicity by the government and human rights groups in towns and cities, however, many people in outer lying areas, especially farm workers (whose citizenship status had remained ambiguous) were not aware of the requirements until after the deadline of January 2002. The state-owned media claimed that 'those with dual citizenship are behind efforts to discredit the Government economically and politically by enlisting foreign governments to use diplomatic and other means to topple the ZANU-PF government'.[39] Government critics argued that the state was acting against white Zimbabwean farmers, so-called 'foreign' farmworkers, and those who had voted for the MDC in the 2000 parliamentary elections, with the aim to disenfranchise opposition supporters prior to the 2002 presidential election.[40] More than the previous changes in citizenship, this act was potentially the most devastating for second and third generation Zimbabweans. The Registrar-General's office, responsible for civil registration, identity documents, citizenship and the voters' roll, insisted that any *possible* claim to citizenship must be renounced in order to retain Zimbabwean citizenship.

Former migrants from Malawi and their descendants were not necessarily the main targets of the exclusionary citizenship laws, however, many people were angered by the changes as they were left vulnerable without a political voice. Prince Law Kavuli described how Malawians had initially been welcomed in Zimbabwe and invited to join the celebrations following ZANU-PF victory at the polls after independence, 'but people of Malawian descent are no longer able to vote, having "alien" stamped on their citizenship cards'.[41] Prince and his brother Blessings said they

[38] Manby, *Struggles for Citizenship*, pp. 43–44.

[39] *Sunday Mail* quoted in *Zimbabwe Human Rights Bulletin*, Issue 5, Zimbabwe Lawyers for Human Rights, September 2001.

[40] Zimbabwe Lawyers for Human Rights, 'The Path to Disenfranchisement', *Pambazuka News*, 21 March 2002.

[41] Interview with Prince Law Kavuli, Nkhata Bay, 2008.

were discriminated against because of their Malawian heritage. Prince was born in Zimbabwe in 1983. Before the law changed, he was entitled to Zimbabwean citizenship, or he could claim Malawian citizenship up until his 21st birthday. Prince's father had migrated to Rhodesia from Nkhata Bay in 1967 to work at Trojan mine in Bindura. Thirty years on, in 1998, Prince's father returned to Malawi. Prince and his brother Blessings joined their parents several years later having decided to leave Zimbabwe because of the politics. Before Prince and Blessings relocated, they were granted Malawian passports. Both of their parents were Malawian, and they were fortunate to have the documentation to prove it. The Malawi Embassy in Harare required applicants to sit an exam where they were questioned about the chiefs and headmen in the area that they claimed to be from. 'It was difficult for some people', Prince explained, 'if they were second or third generation Malawians [born in Zimbabwe] and if their parents had long died. These people had to wait a long time [before they could leave Zimbabwe] and they found it very difficult to obtain a passport'. When Prince and Blessings moved to Malawi in 2002, it was the first time they had ever visited the country.

Just as it became difficult for second and third generation Malawians to access Zimbabwean citizenship documents, it was also complicated for them to claim Malawian citizenship. Anyone born in Zimbabwe who had not applied for Malawian citizenship before their 21st birthday was no longer eligible. Few people had copies of their parents' birth certificates or evidence of their parents' arrival in the country before independence, especially when their parents had migrated independently of recruitment agents and without official documentation. Zimbabwe's new citizenship laws violated international law and rendered many people stateless. Pressure from the Southern African Development Community (SADC) eventually led the Zimbabwe government to amend the 2001 Citizenship Act. In 2003, a new clause was introduced to effectively safeguard nationality for anyone born in Zimbabwe to parents from a SADC country who had migrated to Zimbabwe for work before independence. This was a direct acknowledgement of the legacies of colonial-era labour migration. Nonetheless, confusion and uncertainty ensued as the Registrar-General's office continued to reject applications and unlawfully declined to renew passports. Some applicants were asked to pay a restoration of citizenship fee, which they could not afford.[42]

Stephen Tsinambuto's story highlights the difficulties faced by Malawians who had long ago migrated to Zimbabwe. Stephen had lived in Zimbabwe for almost forty years by the time he moved back to Malawi. He reflected on the reasons why Malawians went to Zimbabwe and their intentions: 'Some Malawians who migrated to Zimbabwe wanted to stay there permanently. Those people didn't want to think of themselves as Malawians anymore. They wanted to stay in Southern Rhodesia living as they did without any distinction or separation'.[43] Stephen never planned to spend so long away from Malawi, but the money was good, and he was able to provide for his family. Similarly, for David Ngowe, migration was a strategy to escape poverty in Malawi. David worked as a teacher in Nyasaland before he left during federation to work in Southern Rhodesia where he knew he could earn more money. He worked at the Cold Storage Company and stayed for 39 years before he returned to his village in Ntcheu in Malawi's Central Region. David shared his reflections on why people from Malawi migrated and how things had changed:

> Malawians are decent people (*KuMalawi kuno kuli anthu a ulemu*). At first people in Zimbabwe used to be decent but then they changed. The good thing about Zimbabwe is you can earn a good wage and things are cheap. You can easily get what you want there. The problem here in Malawi is that it is a very poor country …
>
> The way you felt about Zimbabwe depended on your intentions and what you wanted to achieve by staying there. For those who felt Zimbabwe was their home it was because they had planned when they left home [Nyasaland] not to return, because of the poverty back home. If you knew you would return home one day then you knew that Zimbabwe was not your home. There were some people who had made up their mind that once they went there, they would marry there, and never go home, even if they had a wife and children back home. That's why the government would try to trace the husband in Zimbabwe and bring him back to his family in Malawi.[44]

[42] Rumbidzai Dube, 'Identity, Citizenship and the Registrar General: The Politicking of Identity in Zimbabwe', A Report by the Research Advocacy Unit, Harare (2012), pp. 3–6.

[43] Interview with Stephen Tsinambuto, Ntcheu, February 2008.

[44] Interview with David Ngowe, Ntcheu, February 2008.

Andu Pangani was one of those who left Nyasaland with no intention to return. He migrated during the federation in 1962 and considered both places as 'home'. Andu described his frustrations with the poor economy in Zimbabwe that had made it harder to maintain contact with his relatives back in Malawi:

> I used to visit home almost every year and they always used to celebrate my visit because I would take them back blankets, bicycles, clothes and shoes. My standard of living definitely improved [in the 1980s]. But later things started to change, I think from the mid-1990s. I then started to visit home after every two or even three years. But the last time I went there now was in 2001. It is worrying me because I am missing my family and I know that they are wondering why I have not been home for so long. But it is because of the economy here and the fact that things change so quickly. It is impossible to save up enough for the bus fare. I am even struggling just to look after myself these days. I used to give letters to people I knew who were going back but now most of them don't go and it is difficult to keep in contact. My family, back at home is too poor to have a cell phone and in my rural home there are no pay phones.[45]

On numerous occasions, former President Robert Mugabe spoke out publicly against descendants of foreign nationals. He accused township residents of supporting the opposition party, the MDC, and labelled them 'totem-less elements of alien origin'.[46] Mugabe attempted to highlight the cultural differences between Malawians and Zimbabweans by using the trope of 'totem-less elements' and playing on the historic rivalry between Shona and Malawians, which dated back to the ethnic stereotypes and competition in the colonial-era labour market.[47] The predominance of Malawians, Mozambicans and Zambians in urban areas, also meant they were associated with opposition politics. Cities were an MDC stronghold during the 2000s and government critics saw this

[45] Interview with Andu Pangani, Harare, June 2008.

[46] *Daily News*, 14 October 2002, quoted in James Muzondidya, '"Zimbabwe for Zimbabweans": Invisible Subject Minorities and the Quest for Justice and Reconciliation in Post-Colonial Zimbabwe', in Brian Raftopoulos and Tyrone Savage (eds.), *Zimbabwe: Injustice and Political Reconciliation* (Harare, 2004), p. 227.

[47] See Anusa Daimon, 'Totemless Aliens': The Historical Antecedents of the Anti-Malawian Discourse in Zimbabwe, 1920s–1979s', *Journal of Southern African Studies*, 44, 6 (2018), pp. 1095–1114.

as one of the reasons behind the state's urban demolition campaign in 2005, Operation *Murambatsvina* (a Shona term, meaning 'clean up the dirt'). The relatively poor high-density suburbs of Mbare, Epworth and Dzivarasekwa—areas where Malawians, Zambians and Mozambicans were disproportionately represented—were especially badly affected by the so-called 'clean-up' campaign, which played on popular perceptions in Zimbabwe that if you were born in the city (*born-rukesheni* – literally, in the location) and did not have a rural home (*kumusha*), you were 'rootless and uncultured'.[48] During this campaign, the government claimed to be enforcing urban planning regulations by removing backyard shacks and informal extensions to houses. These back rooms were often rented out by the homeowners to guarantee an income every month. When people complained that their homes had been destroyed, the government played on the colonial idea that Africans belonged in rural areas and if they did not have a rural home in Zimbabwe, they should go back to where they came from.[49] Enersei Machienda was one of the 700,000 residents who lost their home or main source of income in 2005 when the backyard cottage built onto her three-roomed house in Dzivarasekwa was destroyed by the government:

> It is hard to survive these days here in Zimbabwe, especially for us old people. And, also for us who are not pure Zimbabweans. I am not employed. I just do my gardening and sell the vegetables here at my house. Back in the day we had built some cottages outside here in our yard that we used to rent out. This would guarantee us money every month. We never used to struggle for money until they were destroyed by Operation *Murambatsvina*.[50]

[48] Panashe Chigumadzi describes this in her book *These Bones Will Rise Again* (London, 2018), pp. 42–45.

[49] For more in depth analysis of events, see Maurice Vambe (ed.), *The Hidden Dimensions of Operation Murambatsvina* (Harare, 2008); Deborah Potts, '"Restoring Order"? Operation Murambatsvina and the Urban Crisis in Zimbabwe', *Journal of Southern African Studies*, 32, 2 (2006), pp. 273–291; Michael Bratton and Eldred Masunungure, 'Popular Reactions to State Repression: Operation Murambatsvina in Zimbabwe', *African Affairs*, 106, 422 (2006), pp. 21–45; Joost Fontein, 'Anticipating the Tsunami: Rumours, Planning and the Arbitrary State', *Africa: Journal of the International African Institute*, 79, 3 (2009), pp. 373–374.

[50] Interview with Eneresi Machienda, Harare, June 2008.

Ownership of a rural home and participation in the liberation struggle came to signify indigeneity and the right to belong in Zimbabwe. For Malawian residents born in Harare or other towns in Zimbabwe, their urban roots and their Malawian ancestry led them to be branded 'totemless' outsiders.

Xenophobic tensions were at their most extreme during the fraught elections of 2008 (at the time of this research), when according to Zimbabwean historian Alois Mlambo, 'Shona nationalists were even denouncing Ndebeles who were critical of ZANU-PF policies as recent newcomers to the country who had no stake in it, telling Ndebeles they should go back to Zululand where they originally came from'.[51] The 2008 elections coincided with the height of hyperinflation, further economic decline and unprecedented levels of political violence in Zimbabwe. In June 2008 South Africa also experienced one of the worst outbreaks of xenophobic violence in townships across the country, resulting in the deaths of 62 people. Hundreds more were injured and tens of thousands were displaced. Many fled across borders and according to one Malawian reporter, 15,000 Malawians were evacuated.[52] Johani Jobson emphasised the importance of keeping ties in Malawi, in case he was one day forced to leave Zimbabwe, like those who had been bussed out of South Africa in 2008:

[51] Alois Mlambo, 'Becoming Zimbabwe or Becoming Zimbabwean: Identity, Nationalism and State-Building', *African Spectrum*, 48, 1 (2013), p. 62.

[52] Akwete Sande, 'The Golden Glitter of South Africa Is Gone', *Pambazuka News*, 12 June 2008. Available at: https://www.pambazuka.org/land-environment/golden-glitter-south-africa-gone, date accessed 12 August 2020. On xenophobia and the politics of citizenship in South Africa, see Francis Nyamnjoh, *Insiders and Outsiders: Citizenship and Xenophobia in Contemporary Southern Africa* (London, 2006); Shireen Hassim, Tawana Kupe, and Eric Worby (eds.), *Go Home or Die Here: Violence, Xenophobia and the Reinvention of Difference in South Africa* (Johannesburg, 2008); Michael Neocosmos, *From 'Foreign Natives' to 'Native Foreigners': Explaining Xenophobia in Post-Apartheid South Africa* (Dakar, 2010); Aiden Mosselson, '"There Is No Difference Between Citizens and Non-citizens Anymore": Violent Xenophobia, Citizenship and the Politics of Belonging in Post-Apartheid South Africa', *Journal of Southern African Studies*, 36, 3 (2010), pp. 641–655; Loren Landau (ed.), *Exorcising the Demons Within: Xenophobia, Violence and Statecraft in Contemporary South Africa* (Johannesburg, 2011). On the historical origins of citizenship and its evolution in South Africa, see Jonathan Klaaren, 'A View from the Past: The Future of South African Citizenship', *African Studies*, 69, 3 (2010), 385–401.

> Those people especially from Malawi who have come here to Zimbabwe and spent many years without going back … it is a bad thing for them to do that because if they ever were to go back to Malawi no one would remember them. And yet, even if they spend so many years here in Zimbabwe – that does not entitle them to be Zimbabweans. In the end they will have nowhere to call their home … if the South African situation were to happen here in Zimbabwe they would still have nowhere to go because they would not be accepted both in Malawi and in Zimbabwe.[53]

People in Zimbabwe with vulnerable citizenship status observed the violence in South Africa and worried that they could be rejected from their homes and communities in Harare, just as others like them were pushed out of the townships and neighbourhoods in Johannesburg, Pretoria and Cape Town. The extreme political tensions in Zimbabwe in 2008 began to ease with the signing of the Global Political Agreement between ZANU-PF and the MDC in 2009. Before new elections could be held, the coalition government had to agree upon a new constitution. Eventually, in March 2013 a new constitution was approved by referendum, however, the provisions for citizenship still fell short of protecting those born in Zimbabwe to foreign parents.[54]

The Malawian Diaspora in Southern Africa

The backdrop of intensifying xenophobic violence in South Africa makes evident the need to understand the region's history of migration and integration. Migration came to define the Malawian historical experience in the twentieth century as almost every person was affected by migration in some way. Labour migration and the mobility that preceded colonial rule have continued to shape postcolonial southern Africa well into the twenty-first century. Malawians constitute one of the largest diasporas among migrant groups that settled in Zimbabwe during the colonial era. Much of Malawi's diasporic history elsewhere in the southern African region and further afield remains to be explored. Governments in postcolonial southern Africa, like elsewhere around the world, have too often treated migration as a crisis and a phenomenon which threatens the

[53] Interview with Johani Jobson, Mount Pleasant, Harare, Zimbabwe, June 2008.

[54] For more detail on the provision of citizenship in the new constitution and the issues surrounding this see Manby, Report on Citizenship Law: Zimbabwe, January 2019.

nation-state. This study has shown that migration in fact played an important part in building the nationalist movements of Malawi, just as different forms of mobility and regional solidarity were crucial during the liberation struggles of southern Africa, more broadly. Migration helped to expand political communities based on broader pan-African and anticolonial solidarities. Although migration is often presented as an aberration, it has long been the norm in southern Africa (and beyond), and this remains the case in the region today.

Malawian migration in southern Africa of course tells us a great deal about the history of Malawi, as well as the ways in which Malawi's history mattered (and continues to matter) beyond its borders. Studying the receiving-end of a migrant community can, of course, shed light on the place of origin, however, such connections are not always made by historians. The history of the Malawian diaspora has not always been embraced as part of the history of the nation, which can in part be explained by Malawi's postcolonial politics under Banda. But this does not reflect the outward looking nature of many Malawians, including *machona*, or the long-standing culture of mobility in Malawi. Malawian nationalist Kanyama Chiume described 'the migrant nature' of Malawians.[55] Malawian author John Lwanda argued that notions of travel have always been important within Malawian culture.[56] Through colonial-era migration, men and women came to identify themselves as Nyasas. Malawi's diasporic and migrant history demonstrates that it is vital to hold together an internal and external perspective when considering what it means to be Malawian.

As this book has shown, the study of the African diaspora—including African migrations within Africa—can provide an important corrective to inward looking nationalisms, as well as a push back against the assumption that Africans have only played the role of victim in global history. This book contributes towards these objectives with the hope that historians will continue to explore the fuller extent of Malawian and other African diaspora histories and dynamics within the continent and beyond, both spatially and temporally.

[55] Chiume, Kwacha, p. 240.

[56] For an interesting discussion of inclusion and exclusion in precolonial Malawi, see Lwanda, 'Diaspora, Domicile and Debate', pp. 21–24.

Note on Terminology

Throughout the book I have used the place names and spellings that were current in the times under discussion. 'Nyasa' and 'Malawian' are both used to describe the inhabitants and people with origins in the modern state of Malawi.

Boma—British administrative station
Capitão—Portuguese word meaning 'captain', also used to describe the African 'boss-boy'
Ganyao—Portuguese word meaning 'bonus' and refers to the labour system used in southern Nyasaland. The system required that you work in exchange for accommodation and food

Z. R. Groves, *Malawian Migration to Zimbabwe, 1900–1965*, Cambridge Imperial and Post-Colonial Studies Series,
https://doi.org/10.1007/978-3-030-54104-0

Glossary

Chishona

Chechi yama Chawa—the church of the 'Chawa', the Muslim church or Mosque
Kia—accommodation for domestic employees, usually a small dwelling at the back of the European employer's house
Kumusha—home, place of origin
Matevera Njanji—those who follow the railway line on foot, colloquially means foreigners
Mangoromera—a medicine to make one strong and powerful. A concoction used by boxers in the African townships
Murambatsvina—the name given to the Zimbabwean Government's 'Operation Clean-Up' in 2005, but more literally translated as 'getting rid of the filth' or 'drive out the rubbish'
Roora—bride price, custom of giving money to the bride's family before marriage

Chichewa/Chinyanja

Ankhoswe—Marriage guardians
Askari—African soldiers in the British South Africa Police
Azungu—white people, or Europeans (plural)

Z. R. Groves, *Malawian Migration to Zimbabwe, 1900–1965*, Cambridge Imperial and Post-Colonial Studies Series,
https://doi.org/10.1007/978-3-030-54104-0

Chawa—a term used in Malawi to describe children of Chewa and Yao parents; sometimes derogatory. In Zimbabwe the term is sometimes used to describe Yao Muslims.
Chibuku—traditional beer made from sorghum
Chinamwali—coming of age ceremony for girls
Chikokeyani—Another word for traditional beer
Cibalo—(along with *isibalo*, *shibaru* and *chibaro*) term widely used throughout the region to refer to contract labour, forced labour and slavery
Gule Wamkulu—the great dance; the dance of the *Nyau* society
Gumbagumba—term used for a big old radio, like a gramophone
Juju—magic or witchcraft
Kachasu—traditionally brewed spirit, made in the rural areas. Very strong and thought to have powerful hallucinatory effects if consumed too heavily.
(Ku)malova—house for the unemployed. *Lova* = loaf, literally, the house for 'loafers'
Kumudzi—home, place of origin
Lobola—bride price (as above)
Mabhurandaya—one from Blantyre
Mabwidi—a stranger, foreigner, one without a rural home
Machona—'the lost ones.' Used in reference to migrant workers who left Nyasaland and never returned.
Madobadoba—unofficial recruitment agents
MaNyasarande—one from Nyasaland
Mboni za Yehovah—Jehovah's Witnesses
Mthandizi—colloquial term for the Rhodesia Native Labour Supply Company, meaning 'helper'
Mzungu—white person, or European
Nchito—work
Ndalama—money
Nyasa—one from Nyasaland
Tenga tenga—porters or carriers
Thangata—term used for system of labour in Nyasaland, literally meaning 'help'
Ulendo—literally translates as 'journey' and used to refer to groups of migrant workers travelling south from Nyasaland
Ulere—meaning 'free'; the lorry transport service provided by the Southern Rhodesian Government for migrant workers

Wenela—popular name for the Witwatersrand Native Labour Association
Zigawenga—rebels
Zilombo—Wild animals; term used to describe *nyau* dancers

Bibliography

National Archives, Malawi (MNA)

District Administration files
Labour Office
Pamphlets
Private Papers
Provincial Commissioner Files
Secretariat Files

National Archives, Kew (TNA)

Cabinet Files (CAB)
Colonial Office papers

Rhodes House Library, Oxford

Africa Bureau papers
Hoole papers
Welensky papers

School of Oriental and African Studies, London (SOAS)

Fox-Pitt papers

Z. R. Groves, *Malawian Migration to Zimbabwe, 1900–1965*, Cambridge Imperial and Post-Colonial Studies Series,
https://doi.org/10.1007/978-3-030-54104-0

National Archives, Zimbabwe (ZNA)

Chief Native Commissioner files
Committees and Commissions of Enquiry
Federal Archives (Including Central African Council)
Historical Manuscripts
Internal Affairs
Local Government
Oral History Archives:
John Mzembe Macpherson, 18 February 1977
Jaspar Zengeza Savanhu, 28 February 1977
Aaron Jacha, 14 July 1977
Patrick Gwara Pazarungu, 24 May 1979
Reuben Jamela, 11 January 1980
Ignatius Takaidza Chigwendere, 24 May 1974
Lawrence Vambe, 1–13 June 1983
Mr Claypole, date unknown
John Hartley (Jack) Howman, 7–14 July 1983
Police Headquarters (CID and Salisbury Central)

Centre for African Studies (CAS), Edinburgh University

Central Africa: News and Views (A quarterly Record of the Life and Work of the Blantyre and Livingstonia Missions of the Church of Scotland) 1, 4 (April 1936), pp. 13–19.

Perham, Marjory, Margaret Read and Mary Stuart, 'Migrant Labour in Africa Today', in Philip Mairet and Alec Vidler (ed.), *The Frontier: A Christian Commentary on the Common Life*, 1, 7 (July 1950), pp. 253–262.

Wits Historical Papers, University of the Witwatersrand

Collection AD1715 South African Institute of Race Relations (SAIRR), 1892–1974.

Official Publications

Nyasaland Natives in the Union of South Africa and in Southern Rhodesia by J. C. Abraham Published for the Government of Nyasaland by the Crown Agents for the Colonies (London, 1937).

Nyasaland Native Labour in Southern Rhodesia by G. N. Burden (Zomba: Government Printer, 1938).

Federation of Rhodesia and Nyasaland, Census Report, 1956 (Salisbury: Government Printer, 1956).
Hansard, 23 November 1908.
Nyasaland Protectorate Census Report, 1931 (Zomba: Government Printer, 1931).
Nyasaland Protectorate Census Report, 1945 (Zomba: Government Printer, 1945).
Report of the Committee appointed by His Excellency the governor to enquire into Emigrant Labour, 1935 (Zomba: Government Printer, 1936).
Report of the Urban African Affairs Commission, 1958 (Salisbury: Government Printer, 1958).

Interviews

Stephen Lungu, Chatham, Kent, November 2006 (conducted by Zoë Groves)
Malawi:
(Interviews conducted by Zoë Groves)

Mr Katoki, Lilongwe, October 2007
D.D. Phiri, Blantyre, October 2007
Molly Dzabala, November 2007

(Interviews by Lucy Phiri and Zoë Groves)

Ibrahim, Dedza District, Malawi, February 2008
James Mwale, Dedza District, February 2008

Steven Ntsinambuto, Ntcheu District, Malawi, February 2008
Mrs Tsinambuto, Ntcheu District, February 2008
Mr Gilidala Galatiya Kathyole, Ntcheu District, February 2008
Agnes Galatiya, Ntcheu District February 2008
Felistas Ngowe, Sharpvale, Ntcheu District, February 2008
David Ngowe, Sharpvale, Ntcheu District, February 2008
Litness Huwa, Sharpvale, Ntcheu District, February 2008
Gladyss Huwa, Sharpvale, Ntcheu District, February 2008
Judith Huwa, Sharpvale, Ntcheu District, February 2008
Mulauzi Chikoya, Ntcheu District, February 2008
Matthews Kasankha, Ntcheu District, February 2008
Elube, Ntcheu District, February 2008 (surname not disclosed)
Nazione Kamdima, Ntcheu District, February 2008
Eden Mbewe, Ntcheu District, February 2008
Anderson Molande, Ntcheu District, February 2008
Geoffrey Mpinganjira, Ntcheu District, February 2008
Mr. Kasale, Ntcheu District, February 2008 (first name not disclosed)

Alfred Zingwa, Ntcheu District, February 2008
Veronica Mofolo, Ntcheu District, February 2008

Dzoole Bello, Thyolo District, February 2008
Daniel Likhobwe, Thyolo District, February, 2008
Daniel Ndalama, Thyolo District, February 2008
Martha Kataya, Thyolo District, February 2008

Mr Kataya, Tyholo District, February 2008 (first name not disclosed)
Chivinda Banda, Nkhata Bay District, August 2008
Sophie Jeyala, Nkhata Bay District, August 2008
Mary Nyalongwe, Nkhata Bay District, August 2008
Mr Kavuli, Nkhata Bay District, August 2008
Prince Law Kavuli, Nkhata Bay District, August 2008
Blessed Kavuli, Nkhata Bay District, August 2008

Zimbabwe:
(Interviews conducted by Margaret Goreraza and Fortune Sithole)

Johani Jobson, Harare, May 2008
Freton Phiri, Harare. June 2008
Andu Pangani, Harare, June 2008
Grey Areas, Harare, June 2008
Josphat Banda, Dzivarasekwa, Harare, June 2008
Jafari Daimi, Harare, June 2008
Jenny Blande, Harare, June 2008
Doris Marikwa, Harare, June 2008
Eneresi Machienda, Harare, June 2008
Emily Milanzi, Harare, June 2008

(Interviews conducted by Zoë Groves)

Members of the CCAP Harare Synod in Harare, August 2009 (first names not disclosed)
Mr Chimoyo
Mr Binga
Rev Juma
Mr Tembo
Mr Misanja
Mr Cinde
Rev Boloma

Newspapers and Magazines

African Weekly
Bulawayo Chronicle
Bwalo La Nyasaland
The Chronicle
The Daily News (Salisbury)
The Daily News (Harare)
The Daily Times (Blantyre)
Dissent
The Financial Gazette (Harare)
The Gwelo Times
The Herald (Harare)
The Malawi News ('Voice of the Malawi Congress Party')
Mapolisa (The Official Magazine of the African Regiment of the British South Africa Police)
The Nation (Blantyre)
The Nyasaland Times
The Rhodesia Herald
Tsopano
The Zimbabwean Independent

Books, Chapters in Books and Articles

Aiyar, Sana, *Indians in Kenya: The Politics of Diaspora* (Cambridge, MA: Harvard University Press, 2015).

Alexander, Jocelyn, *The Unsettled Land: State-Making and The Politics of Land in Zimbabwe* (Oxford: James Currey, 2006).

Alexander, Jocelyn and JoAnn McGregor, 'Modernity and Ethnicity in a Frontier Society: Understanding Difference in Northwestern Zimbabwe', *Journal of Southern African Studies*, 23, 2 (1997), pp. 187–203.

Alexander, Jocelyn, JoAnn McGregor and Blessing-Miles Tendi, 'The Transnational Histories of Southern African Liberation Movements: An Introduction', *Journal of Southern African Studies*, 43, 1 (2017), pp. 1–12.

Allina, Eric, *Slavery by Any Other Name: African Life under Company Rule in Colonial Mozambique* (Charlottesville: University of Virginia Press, 2012).

Alpers, Edward, *Ivory and Slaves in East Central Africa* (Berkeley, 1975).

Amrith, Sunil S., *Crossing the Bay of Bengal: The Furies of Nature and the Fortunes of Migrants* (Cambridge, MA: Harvard University Press, 2015).

Anderson, Benedict, *Imagined Communities: Reflections on the Origin and Spread of Nationalism* (London: Verso, 1983).

Anderson-Morshead, A. E., *History of the Universities' Mission to Central Africa Volume I, 1859–1909* (London: Bracton Books, 1955).

Andersson, Jens A., 'Informal Moves, Informal Markets: International Migrants and Traders from Mzimba District, Malawi', *African Affairs*, 105, 420 (2006), pp. 375–397.

Anonymous, 'Recruiting and Native Welfare in Nyasaland', *International Labour Review*, 33 (1936), pp. 849–861.

Arsan, Andrew, *Interlopers of Empire: The Lebanese Diaspora in Colonial French West Africa* (London: Hurst, 2014).

Badenhorst, Cecile and Charles Mather, 'Tribal Recreation and Recreating Tribalism: Culture, Leisure and Social Control on South Africa's Gold Mines, 1940–1950', *Journal of Southern African Studies*, 23, 3 (1997), pp. 473–489.

Baker, Colin, *State of Emergency: Crisis in Central Africa, Nyasaland 1959–60* (London: I.B. Tauris, 1997).

Baker, Colin, *The Revolt of the Ministers: The Malawi Cabinet Crisis, 1964–65* (London: I.B. Tauris, 2001).

Baker, Colin, *Chipembere: The Missing Years* (Zomba: Kachere Series, 2008).

Baker, William J. and James A. Mangan eds., *Sport in Africa: Essays in Social History* (London: Africana Publishing, 1987).

Bakewell, Oliver and Naluwembe Binaisa, 'Tracing Diasporic Identifications in Africa's Urban Landscapes: Evidence from Lusaka and Kampala', *Ethnic and Racial Studies*, 39, 2 (2016) pp. 280–300.

Banda, Harvey C. Chiboda. *Migration from Malawi to South Africa: A Historical and Cultural Novel* (Bamendna, Cameroon: Langaa RPCIG, 2018).

Barnes, Terri and Everjoyce Win, *To live a Better Life: An Oral History of Women in the City of Harare, 1930–70* (Harare: Baobab Books, 1992).

Barnes, Teresa, '"So That a Labourer Could Live with His Family": Overlooked Factors in Social and Economic Strife in Urban Colonial Zimbabwe, 1945–1952', *Journal of Southern African Studies*, 21, 1 (1995), pp. 95–113.

Barnes, Teresa A., "*We Women Worked So Hard" Gender, Urbanization and Social Reproduction in Colonial Harare, Zimbabwe, 1930–1956* (London: Heinemann, 1999).

Bayly, Chris, Sven Beckert, Matthew Connelly, Isabel Hofmeyer, Wendy Kozol, Patricia Seed, 'American Historical Review Conversation: On Transnational History', *American Historical Review* (2006), pp. 1441–1464.

Beach, David, 'The Shona Economy: Branches of Production', in Robin Palmer and Neil Parsons eds., *The Roots of Rural Poverty in Central and Southern Africa* (Berkeley: University of California Press, 1977), pp. 37–65.

Beinart, William, 'Worker Consciousness, Ethnic Particularism and Nationalism: The Experiences of a South African Migrant, 1930–1960', in Shula Marks and Stanley Trapido, eds., *The Politics of Race, Class and Nationalism in Twentieth Century South Africa* (London: Longman, 1987), pp. 286–309.

Beinart, William, *Twentieth Century South Africa* (Oxford: Oxford University Press, 2001).

Bhebe, Ngwabi, *B. Burombo. African Politics in Zimbabwe, 1947–1958* (Harare: College Press, 1989).

Bhebe, Ngwabi and Terence Ranger, eds., *The Historical Dimensions of Democracy and Human Rights in Zimbabwe. Volume One: Pre-Colonial and Colonial Legacies* (Harare: University of Zimbabwe Publications, 2001).

Birmingham, David and Terence Ranger, 'Settlers and Liberators in the South, 1953–1980', in David Birmingham and P. M. Martin, eds., *History of Central Africa, Vol. Two* (London: Longman, 1983), pp. 336–382.

Boeder, Robert, '"We won't die for fourpence": Malawian Labour and the Kariba Dam', *Journal of Modern African Studies*, 15, 2 (1977), pp. 310–315.

Boeder, Robert, 'Malawi Burial Societies and Social Change in Zimbabwe', *Journal of Contemporary African Studies*, 1, 2 (1982), pp. 239–348.

Bonner, Philip, 'Labour, Migrancy and Urbanisation in South Africa and India, 1900–1960', *Journal of Asian and African Studies* 44, 1 (2009), pp. 69–95.

Bonner, Philip, Jonathan Hyslop and Lucien Van Der Walt, 'Rethinking Worlds of Labour: Southern African Labour History in International Context', *African Studies*, 66, 2–3 (2007), pp. 137–167.

Bozzoli, Belinda with Mmantho Nkotsoe, *Women of Phokeng. Consciousness, Life Strategy and Migrancy in South Africa, 1900–1983* (London: James Currey, 1991).

Brantley, Cynthia, 'Through Ngoni Eyes: Margaret Read's Matrilineal Interpretations from Nyasaland', *Critique of Anthropology*, 17, 2 (1997), pp. 147–169.

Bratton, Michael and Eldred Masunungure, 'Popular Reactions to State Repression: Operation Murambatsvina in Zimbabwe', *African Affairs*, 106, 422 (2006), pp. 21–45.

Bravman, Bill. *Making Ethnic Ways. Communities and Their Transformations in Taita, Kenya, 1800–1950* (Oxford: James Currey, 1998).

Bronwell, Josiah, *The Collapse of Rhodesia: Population Demographics and the Politics of Race* (London, Bloomsbury, 2010).

Brown, Judith and Wm Roger Louis, eds., *The Oxford History of the British Empire, Vol. IV: The Twentieth Century* (Oxford: Oxford University Press, 1999).

Brubaker, Rogers and Frederick Cooper, 'Beyond "Identity"' *Theory and Society*, 29 (2000), pp. 1–47.

Bryceson, Deborah F., 'Ganyu in Malawi: Transformation of Local Labour Relation under Famine and HIV/AIDS Duress', in J. Abbink, ed., *Fractures and Reconnections: Civic Action and the Redefinition of African Political and Economic Spaces* (Leiden, African Studies Centre/Zurich: Lit Verlag, 2012), pp. 37–59.

Buell, Raymond Leslie, *The Native Problem in Africa* (New York: The Macmillan Company, 1928).

Cheater, Angela P., 'Transcending the State? Gender and Borderline Constructions of Citizenship in Zimbabwe', in Thomas M. Wilson and Hastings Donnan, eds., *Border Identities: Nation and State at International Frontiers* (Cambridge: Cambridge University Press, 1998), pp. 191–214.

Chigumadzi, Panashe, *These Bones Will Rise Again* (London: Indigo Press, 2018).

Chikowero, Mhoze, *African Music, Power and Being in Colonial Zimbabwe* (Indiana and Bloomington: Indiana University Press, 2015).

Chirwa, Vera Mlangazua, 'The Nyasaland State of Emergency of 1959/60: My Own Eye Witness Perception', in Kings M. Phiri, John McCracken and Wapulumuka O. Mulwafu, eds., *Malawi in Crisis: The 1959/60 Nyasaland State of Emergency and its Legacy* (Zomba: Kachere Press, 2012), pp. 322–337.

Chirwa, Wiseman Chijere, 'Alomwe and Mozambican Immigrant Labour in Colonial Malawi, 1890s–1945', *The International Journal of African Historical Studies*, 27, 3 (1994), pp. 525–550.

Chirwa, Wiseman Chijere, 'The Malawi Government and South African Labour Recruiters, 1974–92', *Journal of Modern African Studies*, 33, 4 (1996), pp. 623–642.

Chirwa, Wiseman Chijere, '"No TEBA ...Forget TEBA": The Plight of Malawian Ex-Migrant Workers to South Africa, 1988–1994', *International Migration Review*, 31, 3 (1997), pp. 628–654.

Chirwa, Wiseman Chijere, 'Aliens and Aids in Southern Africa: The Malawi-South Africa Debate', *African Affairs*, 97, 386 (1998), pp. 53–79.

Christiansen, Robert E. and Jonathan G. Kydd, 'The Return of Malawian Labour from South Africa and Zimbabwe', *Journal of Modern African Studies*, 21, 2 (1983), pp. 311–326.

Chiume, M. and W. Kanyama, *Kwacha: An Autobiography* (Nairobi: East African Publishing, 1975).

Clarke, Duncan G., *Domestic Workers in Rhodesia: The Economics of Masters and Servants* (Salisbury: Mambo Press, 1974).

Clutton-Brock, Guy, *Dawn in Nyasaland* (London: Hodder and Stoughton, 1959).

Cohen, Andrew, *The Politics and Economics of Decolonization in Africa: The Failed Experiment of the Central African Federation* (London, I.B. Tauris, 2017).

Coleman, Gilroy, 'International Labour Migration from Malawi, 1875–1966', *Journal of Social Science*, 2 (1972), pp. 31–46.

Collins, Michael, 'Decolonisation and the "Federal Moment"', *Diplomacy and Statecraft*, 24 (2013), pp. 21–40.

Cook, D. J., 'The Influence of the Livingstonia Mission Upon the Formation of Welfare Associations in Zambia, 1912–31', in T. O. Ranger and John Weller, eds., *Themes in the Christian History of Central Africa* (Berkeley: University of California Press, 1975), pp. 98–134.

Cooper, Frederick, *The Struggle for the City: Migrant Labour, Capital and the State in Urban Africa* (Beverly Hills, CA: Sage, 1983).

Cooper, Frederick, 'Conflict and Connection: Rethinking Colonial African History', *American Historical Review*, 99, 5 (1994), pp. 1516–1545.

Cooper, Frederick, *Decolonisation and African Society: The Labour Question in French and British Africa* (Cambridge: Cambridge University Press, 1996).

Cooper, Frederick, 'What Is the Concept of Globalisation Good for? An African Historians Perspective', *African Affairs*, 100, 399 (2001), pp. 189–213.

Cooper, Frederick, *Africa Since 1940: The Past of the Present* (Cambridge: Cambridge University Press, 2002).

Coplan, David, *In the Time of Cannibals: The Word Music of South Africa's Basotho Migrants* (Chicago: Chicago University Press, 1995).

Crush, Jonathan, 'Migrations Past: An Historical Overview of Cross-Border Movement in Southern Africa', in David A. McDonald, ed., *On Borders: Perspectives on Cross-Border Migration in Southern Africa* (New York: St. Martins Press, 2000), pp. 12–24.

Crush, Jonathan and Charles Ambler, *Liquor and Labour in Southern Africa* (Athens, OH: Ohio University Press, 1992).

Crush, Jonathan and Daniel Tevera, *Zimbabwe's Exodus: Crisis, Migration and Survival* (Cape Town: Southern African Migration Project, 2010).

Crush, Jonathan, Alan Jeeves and David Yudelman, *South Africa's Labour Empire: A History of Black Migrancy to the Gold Mines* (Oxford, 1991).

Daimon, Anusa, 'Totemless Aliens': The Historical Antecedents of the Anti-Malawian Discourse in Zimbabwe, 1920s–1979', *Journal of Southern African Studies*, 44, 6 (2018), pp. 1095–1114.

Dee, Henry, 'Nyasa Leaders, Christianity and African Internationalism in 1920s Johannesburg', *South African Historical Journal*, 70, 2 (2018), pp. 383–406.

Dee, Henry, '"I Am a Bad Native": Masculinity and Marriage in the Biographies of Clements Kadalie', *African Studies*, 78, 2 (2019), pp. 183–204.

Delius, Peter, 'Sebatakgomo; Migrant Organisation, the ANC and the Sekhukhuneland Revolt', *Journal of Southern African Studies*, 15, 4 (1989), pp. 581–615.

Delius, Peter, *A Lion Amongst the Cattle: Reconstruction and resistance in the Northern Transvaal* (Portsmouth, NH: Heinemann, 1996).

Delius, Peter, Laura Phillips and Fiona Rankin-Smith, *A Long Way Home: Migrant Workers Worlds 1800–2014* (Johannesburg: Wits University Press, 2014).

Dotson, Floyd and Lillian O. Dotson, *The Indian Minority in Zambia, Rhodesia and Malawi* (New Haven and London: Yale University Press, 1968).

Duff, H. L., *Nyasaland under the Foreign Office* (London: George Bell and Sons, 1906).

Englund, Harri, *From War to Peace on the Mozambique-Malawi Borderland* (Edinburgh: Edinburgh University Press, 2002).

Englund, Harri, 'The Village in the City, the City in the Village: Migrants in Lilongwe', *Journal of Southern African Studies*, 28, 1 (2002), pp. 137–154.

Englund, Harri, ed., *A Democracy of Chameleons: Politics and Culture in the New Malawi* (Stockholm: The Nordic Africa Institute, 2002).

Epstein, A. L. *Politics in an Urban African Community* (Manchester: Manchester University Press, 1958).

Fasselt, Rebecca, 'Decolonising the Afropolitan: Intra-African Migrations in Post-2000 Literature', in Moradewun Adejunmobi and Carli Coetzee, eds., *Routledge Handbook of African Literature* (Routledge, 2019), chapter 6.

Fejzula, Merve, 'The Cosmopolitan Historiography of Twentieth Century Federalism', *The Historical Journal* (2020). https://doi.org/10.1017/S0018246X20000254.

Ferguson, James, 'Mobile Workers, Modernist Narratives: A Critique of the Historiography of Transition on the Zambian Copperbelt [Part One]', *Journal of Southern African Studies*, 16, 3 (1990), pp. 383–412.

Ferguson, James, 'Mobile Workers, Modernist Narratives: A Critique of the Historiography of Transition on the Zambian Copperbelt [Part Two]', *Journal of Southern African Studies*, 16, 4 (1990), pp. 603–621.

Fetter, Bruce, *The Creation of Elisabethville, 1910–1940* (Stanford: Hoover Institution Press, 1976).

Field, Sean, 'Doing Oral History in Africa' [Book Review: Paul Thompson with Joanna Bornat, *The Voice of the Past, Oral History*, fourth edition (Oxford: Oxford University Press, 2017)] *Journal of Southern African Studies*, 46, 2 (2020), pp. 384–386.

Fields, Karen E., *Revival and Rebellion in Colonial Central Africa* (Princeton, NJ: Princeton University Press, 1985).

Fisher, J. L., *Pioneers, Settlers, Aliens, Exiles: The Decolonisation of White Identity in Zimbabwe* (Canberra: ANU E Press, 2010).

Fontein, Joost, 'Anticipating the Tsunami: Rumours, Planning and the Arbitrary State', *Africa: Journal of the International African Institute*, 79, 3 (2009), pp. 373–374.

Freund, Bill, 'Labour and Labour History in Africa: A Review of the Literature', *African Studies Review*, 27, 4 (1984), pp. 1–58.

Freund, Bill, *The African Worker* (Cambridge: Cambridge University Press, 1988).

Gabay, Clive, 'The Radical and Reactionary Politics of Malawi's Hastings Banda: Roots, Fruit and Legacy', *Journal of Southern African Studies*, 43, 6 (2017), pp. 1119–1135.

Gluckman, Max, 'Tribalism in Modern British Central Africa', *Cahiers d'Etudes Africaines*, 1, 1 (1960), pp. 55–70.

Goodhew, David, 'Working-Class Respectability: The Example of the Western Areas of Johannesburg, 1930–1955', *Journal of African History*, 41, 1 (2000), pp. 241–266.

Gray, E., *The Early History of the Churches of Christ Missionary Work in Nyasaland, Central Africa, 1907–1930* (Cambridge: Church of Christ Historical Society, 1981).

Gray, Richard, *The Two Nations: Aspects of the Development of Race Relations in the Rhodesias and Nyasaland* (Oxford: Oxford University Press, 1960).

Groves, Zoë, 'Urban Migrants and Religious Networks: Malawians in Colonial Salisbury, 1920 to 1970', *Journal of Southern African Studies*, 38, 3 (2012), pp. 491–511.

Groves, Zoë, '"Zimbabwe Is my Home": Citizenship and Belonging for "Malawians" in Post-Independence Urban Zimbabwe', *South African Historical Journal* (2020). https://doi.org/10.1080/02582473.2020.1773521.

Gunner, Liz, Dina Ligaga and Dumisani Moyo, eds., *Radio in Africa: Publics, Cultures, Communities* (Woodbridge: James Currey, 2012).

Guthrie, Zachary Kagan, *Bound for Work: Labour, Mobility and Colonial Rule in Central Mozambique, 1940–1965* (Charlottesville, University of Virginia Press, 2018).

Hailey, Lord, *Native Administration in the British African Territories. Part II Central Africa: Zanzibar, Nyasaland and Northern Rhodesia* (London: HMSO, 1950).

Hallencreutz, Carl F., *Religion and Politics in Harare, 1890–1980* (Uppsala: Swedish Institute of Missionary Research, 1999).

Hamilton, Carolyn, ed., *The Mfecane Aftermath: Reconstructive Debates in Southern African History* (Pietermaritzburg, 1995).

Hammar, Amanda, JoAnn McGregor and Loren Landau, 'Introduction. Displacing Zimbabwe: Crisis and Construction in Southern Africa', *Journal of Southern African Studies*, 36, 2 (2010), pp. 263–283.

Hannerz, Ulf, 'Sophiatown: The View From Afar', *Journal of Southern African Studies*, 20, 2 (1994), pp. 181–193.

Harper, Marjory and Stephen Constantine, *Migration and Empire* (Oxford University Press, 2000).

Harries, Patrick, 'Exclusion, Classification and Internal Colonialism: The Emergence of Ethnicity Among the Tsonga-Speakers of South Africa', in Leroy Vail, ed., *The Creation of Tribalism in Southern Africa* (Berkeley: University of California Press, 1989), pp. 82–117.

Harries, Patrick, *Work, Culture and Identity: Migrant Labourers in Mozambique and South Africa c.1860–1910* (London: James Currey, 1994).

Hassim, Shireen, Tawana Kupe and Eric Worby, eds., *Go Home or Die Here: Violence, Xenophobia and the Reinvention of Difference in South Africa* (Johannesburg: Wits University Press, 2008).

Hinfelaar, Marja, *Respectable and Responsible Women: Methodist and Roman Catholic Women's Organisations in Harare, Zimbabwe (1919–1985)* (Zoetermeer: Uitgeverij Boekencentrum, 2001).

Hodgson, A. G. O., 'Notes on the Achewa and Angoni of the Dowa District of the Nyasaland Protectorate', *The Journal of the Royal Anthropological Institute of Great Britain and Ireland*, 63 (1933), pp. 123–164.

Hoerder, Dirk, *Cultures in Contact: World Migrations in the Second Millennium* (Durham, NC: Duke University Press, 2002).

Hokkanen, Markku, *Medicine and Scottish Missionaries in the Northern Malawi Region, 1875–1930: Quests for Health in a Colonial Society* (New York: Edwin Mellen Press, 2007).

Hokkanen, Markku, *Medicine, Mobility and the Empire: Nyasaland Networks, 1859–1960* (Manchester: Manchester University Press, 2017).

Hooker, James R., 'Welfare Associations and Other Instruments of Accommodation in the Rhodesias between the World Wars', *Comparative Studies in Society and History*, 9, 1 (1966), pp. 51–63.

Hopkinson, T. and T. Couzens, eds., *Zimbabwe: The Search for Common Ground since 1890: From the Pages of DRUM Magazine* (Lanseria, South Africa: Bailey's African Photo Archives, 1992).

Hyam, Ronald, 'The Geopolitical Origins of the Central African Federation: Britain, Rhodesia and South Africa, 1948–53', *The Historical Journal*, 31, 1 (1987), pp. 145–172.

Isaacman, Allen and Anton Rosenthal, 'Slaves, Soldiers and Police: Power and Dependency Among the Chikunda of Mozambique, ca.1825–1920', in Suzanne Miers and Richard Roberts, eds., *The End of Slavery in Africa* (Madison: University of Wisconsin Press, 1988), pp. 220–253.

James, Deborah, *Songs of the Women Migrants: Performance and Identity in South Africa* (Edinburgh: Edinburgh University Press, 1999).

Jeater, Diana, *Marriage, Perversion and Power: The Construction of Moral Discourse in Southern Rhodesia* (Oxford: James Currey, 1993).

Jeater, Diana, 'No Place for a Woman: Gwelo Town, Southern Rhodesia, 1894–1920', *Journal of Southern African Studies*, 26, 1 (2000), pp. 29–42.

Johnson, D. H., 'Criminal Secrecy: The Case of the Zande Secret Societies', *Past and Present*, 130, 1 (1991), pp. 170–200.

Johnson, Jessica, 'After the Mines: The Changing Social and Economic Landscape of Malawi-South Africa Migration', *Review of African Political Economy*, 44, 152 (2017), pp. 237–251.

Kadalie, Clements, *My Life and the ICU: The Autobiography of a Black Trade Unionist in South Africa* (London: Frank Cass and Company, 1970).

Kalinga, Owen, 'The General from Fort Hill': Katoba Flax Musopole's Role as an Anti-colonial Activist and Politician in Malawi', *Journal of Southern African Studies*, 46, 2 (2020), pp. 301–317.

Kaspin, Deborah, 'Chewa Visions and Revisions of Power: Transformations of the Nyau Dance in Central Malawi', in Jean Comaroff and John L. Comaroff, eds., *Modernity and its Malcontents: Ritual and Power in Postcolonial Africa* (Chicago: University of Chicago Press, 1993), pp. 34–57.

Kay, George and Michael Smout, eds., *Salisbury: A Geographical Survey of the Capital of Rhodesia* (Sevenoaks: Hodder and Stoughton, 1977).

Klaaren, Jonathan, 'A View from the Past: The Future of South African Citizenship', *African Studies*, 69, 3 (2010), pp. 385–401.

Kolk, M, ed., *Can You Tell Me Why I Went to War? A Story of a Young King's Rifle. Reverend Father John E.A. Mandambwe* (Zomba: Kachere Press, 2000).

Krishnamurthy, B. S., 'Economic Policy, Land and Labour in Nyasaland, 1890–1914', in Bridglal Pachai, ed., *The Early History of Malawi* (London: Longman, 1974), pp. 384–404.

Kuczynski, R. R., *A Demographic Survey of the British Colonial Empire. Volume II* (Oxford: Oxford University Press, 1949).

Landau, Loren, ed., *Exorcising the Demons Within: Xenophobia, Violence and Statecraft in Contemporary South Africa* (Johannesburg: Wits University Press, 2011).

Legassik, Martin, 'Gold, Agriculture, and Secondary Industry in South Africa, 1885–1970: From Periphery to Sub-Metropole as a Forced Labour System', in Robin Palmer and Neil Parsons, eds., *Roots of Rural Poverty in Central and Southern Africa* (Berkeley: University of California Press, 1977), pp. 175–200.

Leys, Colin and Cranford Pratt, eds., *A New Deal in Central Africa* (London: Heinemann, 1960).

Linden, Ian with Jane Linden. *Catholics, Peasants and Chewa Resistance in Nyasaland, 1889–1939* (London: Heinemann, 1974).

Lungu, Stephen, *Out of the Black Shadows: The Amazing Transformation of Stephen Lungu* (London: Monarch Books, 2001).

Lunn, Jon, 'The Meaning of the 1948 General Strike in Colonial Zimbabwe', in Brian Raftopolous and Tsuneo Yoshikuni, eds., *Sites of Struggle: Essays on Zimbabwe's Urban History* (Harare: Weaver Press, 1999), pp. 163–182.

Lwanda, John, 'Diaspora, Domicile and Debate: A Preliminary Artistic and Cultural Search for a Malawi Identity from Pre-Colonial Times to 2014', *Society of Malawi Journal*, 67, 1 (2014), pp. 16–45.

Mackay, Peter, *We Have Tomorrow: Stirrings in Africa, 1959–67* (Norwich: Michael Russel, 2008).

Macmillan, Hugh, 'The Historiography of Transition on the Zambian Copperbelt—Another View', *Journal of Southern African Studies*, 19, 4 (1993), pp. 681–712.

Macola, Giacom, *The Gun in Central Africa: A History of Technology and Politics* (Athens: Ohio University Press, 2016).

Mager, Anne Kelk, *Beer, Sociability and Masculinity in South Africa* (Bloomington: Indiana University Press, 2010).

Makambe, E. P., 'The Nyasaland African Labour *Ulendos* to Southern Rhodesia and the Problem of the African 'Highwaymen', 1903–1923: A Study in the Limitations of Early Independent Labour Migration', *African Affairs*, 79, 317 (2008), pp. 548–566.

Makoni, Sinfree, Janina Brutt-Griffler and Pedzisai Mashiri, 'The Use of 'Indigenous' and Urban Vernaculars in Zimbabwe', *Language in Society*, 36, 1 (2007), pp. 25–49.

Maloka, Tshidiso, 'Mines and Labour Migrants in Southern Africa: Review and Commentary', *Journal of Historical Sociology*, 10, 2 (1997), pp. 213–224.

Manby, Bronwen, *Struggles for Citizenship in Africa* (London: Zed Books, 2009).

Manchuelle, Francois, *Willing Migrants: Soninke Labour Diasporas, 1848–1960* (Athens, OH: Ohio University Press, 1997).

Mandala, Elias, 'Capitalism, Kinship and Gender in the Lower Tchiri (Shire) Valley of Malawi, 1860–1960: An Alternative Theoretical Framework', *African Economic History*, 13 (1984), pp. 137–169.

Mandala, Elias, *Work and Control in a Peasant Economy: A History of the Lower Tchiri Valley in Malawi, 1859–1960* (Madison: University of Wisconsin Press, 1990).

Mandivenga, E., 'The Migration of Muslims to Zimbabwe', *Journal of Muslim Minority Affairs*, 10, 2 (1989), pp. 507–519.

Marjoma, Risto, 'The Martial Spirit: Yao Soldiers in British Service in Nyasaland (Malawi), 1895–1939', *Journal of African History*, 44, 3 (2003), pp. 413–432.

Marks, Shula, 'Southern Africa', in Judith Brown and Wm Roger Louis, eds., *The Oxford History of the British Empire, Vol. IV: The Twentieth Century* (Oxford: Oxford University Press, 2001), pp. 545–573.

Marks, Shula and Stanley Trapido, eds., *The Politics of Race, Class and Nationalism in Twentieth Century South Africa* (London: Longman, 1987).

Marmon, Brooks, 'Fallout from the Fallacious Accusation of Hastings Kamuzu Banda's West African Origins, 1960', *Society of Malawi Journal* (forthcoming).

Maxwell, David, *Christians and Chiefs in Zimbabwe: A Social History of the Hwesa People, c.1870s–1990s* (Edinburgh: Edinburgh University Press, 1999).

Maxwell, David, *African Gifts of the Spirit: Pentecostalism and the Rise of a Zimbabwean Transnational Religious Movement* (Oxford: James Currey, 2006).

Mayer, Phillip and Iona Mayer, *Townsmen or Tribesmen: Conservatism in the Process of Urbanization in a South African City* (Oxford: Oxford University Press, 1974).

McCracken, John, 'African Politics in Twentieth Century Malawi', in Terence Ranger, ed., *Aspects of Central African History* (Portsmouth, NH: Northwestern University Press, 1968), pp. 190–209.

McCracken, John, 'Peasants, Planters and the Colonial State: The Impact of the Native Tobacco Board in the Central Province of Malawi', *Journal of Southern African Studies*, 9, 2 (1983), pp. 172–192.

McCracken, John, 'British Central Africa', in A. D. Roberts, ed., *The Cambridge History of Africa, Vol. 7 From 1905 to 1940* (Cambridge: Cambridge University Press, 1986), pp. 602–648.

McCracken, John, 'Economics and Ethnicity: The Italian Community in Malawi', *Journal of African History*, 32, 2 (1991), pp. 313–332.

McCracken, John, 'Democracy and Nationalism in Historical Perspective: The Case of Malawi', *African Affairs*, 97, 387 (1998), pp. 231–249.

McCracken, John, 'Blantyre Transformed: Class, Conflict and Nationalism in Urban Malawi', *Journal of African History*, 39, 2 (1998), pp. 247–269.

McCracken, John, *Politics and Christianity in Malawi, 1875–1940: The Impact of the Livingstonia Mission in the Northern Province* (Blantyre: CLAIM, 2000). Second Edition.

McCracken, John, 'The Ambiguities of Nationalism: Flax Musopole and the Northern Factor in Malawian Politics, c.1956–1966', *Journal of Southern African Studies*, 28, 1 (2002), pp. 67–87.

McCracken, John, 'The Exciting Times of a Central African Don Quixote', *Journal of Southern African Studies*, 35, 2 (2009), pp. 526–528.

McCracken, John, *A History of Malawi, 1859–1966* (Woodbridge: Boydell and Brewer, 2012).

McCulloch, Joch, *Black Peril, White Virtue: Sexual Crime in Southern Rhodesia, 1902–1935* (Bloomington: Indiana University Press, 2000).

McGregor, JoAnn, 'Associational Links with Home among Zimbabweans in the UK: Reflections on Long-Distance Nationalisms', *Global Networks*, 9, 2 (2009), pp. 185–208.

McGregor, J., *Crossing the Zambezi: The Politics of Landscape on a Central African Frontier* (Woodbridge: James Currey, 2009).

Mckeown, Adam, 'Global Migration, 1846–1940', *Journal of World History*, 15, 2 (2004), pp. 155–189.

Milford, Ismay, 'Federation, Partnership and the Chronologies of Space in 1950s East and Central Africa', *The Historical Journal* (2020). https://doi.org/10.1017/S0018246X19000712.

Mitchell, J. Clyde, 'The Political Organisation of the Yao of Southern Nyasaland', *African Studies*, 8, 3 (1949), pp. 141–159.

Mitchell, J. Clyde, *The Kalela Dance: Aspects of Social Relationships Among Urban Africans in Northern Rhodesia* (Manchester: Manchester University Press, 1956).

Mitchell, J. Clyde, *The Yao Village: A Study in the Social Structure of a Malawian People* (Manchester: Manchester University Press, 1956).

Mitchell, J. Clyde, *Social Networks in Urban Situations: Analysis of Personal Relationship in Central African Towns* (Manchester: Manchester University Press, 1969).

Mlambo, Alois S., 'From the Second World War to UDI, 1940-1965', in Brian Raftopoulos and Alois Mlambo, eds., *Becoming Zimbabwe: A History from the Pre-colonial Period to 2008* (Harare: Weaver Press, 2009), pp. 75–114.

Mlambo, Alois S., 'A History of Zimbabwean Migration to 1990', in Jonathan Crush and Daniel S. Tevera, eds., *Zimbabwe's Exodus: Crisis, Migration, Survival* (Cape Town: Unity Press, 2010), pp. 52–78.

Mlambo, Alois S., 'Becoming Zimbabwe or Becoming Zimbabwean: Identity, Nationalism and State-building', *African Spectrum*, 48, 1 (2013), pp. 49–70.

Money, Duncan, 'Aliens on the Copperbelt: Zambianisation, Nationalism and Non-Zambian Africans in the Mining Industry', *Journal of Southern African Studies*, 45, 5 (2019), pp. 859–875.

Moore, Henrietta and Megan Vaughan, *Cutting Down Trees: Gender, Nutrition, and Agricultural Change in the Northern Province of Zambia, 1890–1990* (London: James Currey, 1994).

Morrow, Sean and Khayalethu Gxabalashe, 'The Records of the University of Fort Hare', *History in Africa*, 27 (2000), pp. 481–497.

Mosselson, Aiden, '"There Is No Difference Between Citizens and Non-citizens Anymore': Violent Xenophobia, Citizenship and the Politics of Belonging in Post-Apartheid South Africa', *Journal of Southern African Studies*, 36, 3 (2010), pp. 641–655.

Msindo, Enocent, 'Ethnicity, Not Class? The 1929 Bulawayo Faction Fights Reconsidered', *Journal of Southern African Studies*, 32, 3 (2006), pp. 429–447.

Mtisi, Joseph, Munyuradzi Nyakuda and Teresa Barnes, 'Social and Economic Developments in the UDI Period', in Brian Raftopoulos and Alois Mlambo, eds., *Becoming Zimbabwe: A History from the Pre-Colonial Period to the Present* (Harare: Weaver Press, 2009), pp. 115–140.

Mudeka, Ireen, 'Gendered Exclusion and Contestation: Malawian Women's Migration and Work in Colonial Harare, Zimbabwe, 1930s to 1963', *African Economic History*, 44, (2016) pp. 18–43.

Murphy, Philip, ed., *British Documents on the End of Empire: Central Africa. Part 1: Closer Association, 1945–1958* (London: TSO, 2005).

Murray, Colin, *Families Divided. The Impact of Migrant Labour in Lesotho* (Cambridge: Cambridge University Press, 1981).

Murray, S. S. (Chief Clerk of the Nyasaland Government) *A Handbook of Nyasaland* (London: Crown Agents for the Colonies, 1922).

Musopole, Y. R., *The Church in Malawi* (Blantyre: Daystar Publications, 1964).

Muzondidya, James, 'Zimbabwe for Zimbabweans: Invisible Subject Minorities and the Quest for Justice and Reconciliation in Post-Colonial Zimbabwe', in Brian Raftopoulos and Tyrone Savage, eds., *Zimbabwe: Injustice and Political Reconciliation* (Cape Town: Institute for Justice and Reconciliation, 2004), pp. 213–235.

Ndakaripa, Musiwaro, 'The State and Contested Citizenship in Zimbabwe, 1980 2011', in Sabelo Ndlovu-Gatsheni and Fenix Ndlovu, eds., *Nationalism and National Projects in Southern Africa: New Critical Reflections* (Pretoria: Africa Institute of South Africa, 2013), pp. 294–320.

Neocosmos, Michael, *From 'Foreign Natives' to 'Native Foreigners': Explaining Xenophobia in Post-Apartheid South Africa* (Dakar: CODESRIA, 2010).

Nyagumbo, Maurice, *With the People: An Autobiography from the Zimbabwe Struggle* (London: Allison and Busby, 1980).

Nyamnjoh, Francis, *Insiders and Outsiders: Citizenship and Xenophobia in Contemporary Southern Africa* (London: Zed Books, 2006).

Nyangoni, Christopher and Gideon Nyandoro, eds., *Zimbabwe Independence Movements: Select Documents* (London: Collings, 1979).

Pachai Bridglal, ed., *The Early History of Malawi* (London: Longman, 1972).

Palmer, Robin and Neil Parsons, eds., *The Roots of Rural Poverty in Central and Southern Africa* (Berkeley: University of California Press, 1977).

Palmer, Robin, 'Johnston and Jameson: A Comparative Study in the Imposition of Colonial Rule', in Bridglal Pachai, ed., *The Early History of Malawi* (London: Longman, 1972), pp. 293–322.

Panofsky, Hans E., 'Migratory Labour in Africa—A Bibliographical Note', *Journal of Modern African Studies*, 1, 4 (1963), pp. 521–529.

Page, Melvin, 'The War of Thangata: Nyasaland and the East African Campaign, 1914–1918', *Journal of African History*, 19, 1 (1978), pp. 87–100.

Page, Melvin E., *The Chiwaya War: Malawians and the First World War* (Oxford, 2000).

Pape, John, '*Chimurenga* in the kia: Domestic Workers in the Liberation Struggle in Zimbabwe', in Brian Raftopoulos and Tsuneo Yoshikuni, eds., *Sites of*

Struggle: Essays in Zimbabwe's Urban History (Harare: Weaver Press, 1999), pp. 257–271.

Parry, Richard, 'Culture, Organisation and Class: The African Experience in Salisbury 1892–1935', in Brian Raftopoulos and Tsuneo Yoshikuni, eds., *Sites of Struggle: Essays in Zimbabwe's Urban History* (Harare: Weaver Press, 1999), pp. 53–94.

Paton, Bill, *Labour Export Policy in the Development of Southern Africa* (Harare: University of Zimbabwe Publications, 1995).

Phimister, Ian, *An Economic and Social History of Zimbabwe, 1890–1948: Capital Accumulation and Class Struggle* (London: Longman, 1988).

Phimister, Ian and Brian Raftopoulos, eds., *Keep on Knocking: A History of the Labour Movement in Zimbabwe, 1900–1997* (Harare: Baobab Books, 1997).

Phimister, Ian and Charles Van Onselen, 'The Political Economy of Tribal Animosity: A Case Study of the 1929 Bulwayo Location "Faction Fight"', *Journal of Southern African Studies*, 6, 1 (1979), pp. 1–43.

Phiri, D. D., *I See You. Life of Clements Kadalie, the Man South Africa, Malawi, Zimbabwe and Namibia Should Not Forget* (Blantyre: Kachere Press 2000).

Phiri, Kings M., John McCracken and Wapulumuka Mulwafu eds. *Malawi in Crisis: The 1959/60 State of Emergency and its Legacy* (Zomba: Kachere Books, 2013).

Potts, Deborah, *Circular Migration in Zimbabwe and Contemporary Sub-Saharan Africa* (Woodbridge: James Currey, 2010).

Potts, Deborah, '"Restoring Order"? Operation Murambatsvina and the Urban Crisis in Zimbabwe', *Journal of Southern African Studies*, 32, 2 (2006), pp. 273–291.

Power, Joey, 'Building Relevance: The Blantyre Congress, 1953–1956', *Journal of Southern African Studies*, 28, 1 (2002), pp. 45–65.

Power, Joey, *Political Culture and Nationalism in Malawi: Building Kwacha* (Rochester, NY: University of Rochester Press, 2010).

Probst, Peter, 'Expansion and Enclosure: Ritual Landscapes and the Politics of Space in Central Malawi', *Journal of Southern African Studies*, 28, 1 (2002), pp. 179–198.

Raftopoulos, Brian, 'Nationalism and Labour in Salisbury 1953–1965', *Journal of Southern African Studies* 21, 1 (1995), pp. 79–94.

Raftopoulos, Brian, 'Problematising Nationalism in Zimbabwe: A Historiographical Review', *Zambezia* 26, 2 (1999), pp. 115–134.

Raftopoulos Brian and Alois Mlambo, eds., *Becoming Zimbabwe: A History from the Pre-Colonial Period to 2008* (Harare: Weaver Press, 2009).

Raftopoulos, Brian and Tsuneo Yoshikuni, eds., *Sites of Struggle: Essays in Zimbabwe's Urban History* (Harare: Weaver Press, 1999).

Raftopoulos, Brian and Tyrone Savage, *Zimbabwe: Injustice and Political Reconciliation* (Cape Town: Institute for Justice and Reconciliation, 2004).

Rangeley, W. H. J., 'Notes on Chewa Tribal Law', *The Nyasaland Journal*, 1, 3 (1948), pp. 5–68.

Ranger, Terence, 'Missionaries, Migrants and the Manyika: The Invention of Ethnicity in Zimbabwe', in Leroy Vail, ed., *The Creation of Tribalism in Southern Africa* (Berkeley: University of California Press), pp. 118–150.

Ranger, Terence, 'African Politics in Twentieth Century Southern Rhodesia', in T. O. Ranger, ed., *Aspects of Central African History* (Portsmouth, NH: Northwestern University Press, 1968), pp. 210–245.

Ranger, Terence, *The African Voice in Southern Rhodesia, 1898–1930* (London: Heinemann, 1970).

Ranger, Terence, *Dance and Society in Eastern Africa 1890–1970: The Beni Ngoma* (Berkeley: University of California Press, 1975).

Ranger, Terence, 'Growing from the Roots: Reflections on Peasant Research in Central and Southern Africa', *Journal of Southern African Studies* 5, 1 (1978), pp. 99–133.

Ranger, Terence, 'The Invention of Tradition in Colonial Africa', in Eric Hobsbawm and Terence Ranger, eds., *The Invention of Tradition* (Cambridge: Cambridge University Press, 1983), pp. 211–262.

Ranger, Terence, *Peasant Consciousness and Guerrilla War in Zimbabwe* (Oxford: James Currey, 1985).

Ranger, Terence, 'Pugilism and Pathology: African Boxing and the Black Urban Experience in Urban Southern Rhodesia', in W. A. Baker and J. A. Mangan, eds., *Sport in Africa: Essays in Social History* (New York: Africana Publishing Co., 1987), pp. 196–213.

Ranger, Terence, 'The Invention of Tradition Revisited: The Case of Colonial Africa', in Terence Ranger and Olufemi Vaughan, eds., *Legitimacy and the State in Twentieth Century Africa* (Oxford: Oxford University Press, 1993), pp. 129–172.

Ranger, Terence, *Are We Not Also Men? The Samkange Family and African Politics in Zimbabwe, 1920–1964* (London: James Currey, 1995).

Ranger, Terence, 'The Meaning of Urban Violence in Africa: Bulawayo, Southern Rhodesia, 1890–1960', *Cultural and Social History*, 3, 2 (2006), pp. 193–228.

Ranger, Terence, *Bulawayo Burning: The Social History of a Southern African City* (Woodbridge: James Currey, 2010).

Read, Margaret, 'Tradition and Prestige among the Ngoni', *Africa: Journal of the International Africa Institute*, 9, 4 (1936), pp. 453–484.

Read, Margaret, 'Migrant Labour in Africa and its Effects on Tribal Life', *International Labour Review*, 45, 6 (1942), pp. 605–631.

Rockel, Stephen, *Carriers of Culture: Labour on the Road in Nineteenth Century East Africa* (Portsmouth: Heinemann, 2006).

Ross, Andrew, *Blantyre Mission and the Making of Modern Malawi* (Blantyre: Kachere Press, 1996).
Ross, Andrew with Jack Thompson, ed., *Colonialism to Cabinet Crisis: A Political History of Malawi* (Zomba: Kachere Press, 2009).
Rotberg, Robert, *The Rise of Nationalism in Central Africa: The Making of Malawi and Zambia, 1873–1964* (Oxford: Oxford University Press, 1965).
Rotberg, Robert I, ed., *Hero of the Nation. Chipembere of Malawi: An Autobiography* (Blantyre: Kachere Press, 2002).
Rotberg, Robert, 'The Partnership Hoax: How the British Government Deprived Central Africans of their Rights', *Journal of Southern African Studies*, 45, 1 (2019), pp. 89–110.
Rutherford, Blair, 'Another Side to Rural Zimbabwe: Social Constructs and the Administration of Farm Workers in Urungwe District, 1940s', *Journal of Southern African Studies*, 23, 1 (1997), pp. 107–126.
Rutherford, Blair, *Working on the Margins: Black Workers, White Farmers in Postcolonial Zimbabwe* (London: Zed Books, 2001).
Rutherford, Blair, 'Shifting Grounds in Zimbabwe: Citizenship and Farm Workers in the New Politics of Land', Sara Dorman, Daniel Hammet, Paul Nugent, eds., *Making Nations, Creating Strangers: States and Citizenship in Africa* (Leiden: Brill, 2007), pp. 105–122.
Saidi, William, *The Old Bricks Lives* (Harare: Mambo Press, 1988).
Sanderson, F. E., 'The Development of Labour Migration from Nyasaland, 1891–1914', *Journal of African History*, 2, 2 (1961), pp. 259–271.
Sapire, Hilary and Christopher Saunders, eds., *Southern African Liberation Struggles: New Local, Regional and Global Perspectives* (Claremont, UCT Press, 2013).
Scarnecchia, Timothy, 'Poor Women and Nationalist Politics: Alliances and Fissures in the Formation of a Nationalist Political Movement in Salisbury, Rhodesia, 1950–6', *Journal of African History*, 37, 2 (1996), pp. 283–310.
Scarnecchia, Timothy, *The Urban Roots of Democracy and Political Violence, Harare and Highfield, 1940–1964* (Rochester, NY: University of Rochester Press, 2008).
Schler, Lyn, Louise Bethlehem and Galia Sabar, 'Rethinking Labour in Africa, Past and Present', *African Identities*, 7, 3 (2009), pp. 287–298.
Schmidt, Elizabeth, *Peasants, Traders and Wives: Shona Women in the History of Zimbabwe, 1870–1939* (Heinemann: Portsmouth NH, 1992).
Schoffeleers, J. M., 'The Meaning and Use of the Name *Malawi* in Oral Traditions and Pre-colonial Documents', in Bridglal Pachai, ed., *The Early History of Malawi* (London: Longman, 1972), pp. 91–103.
Schoffeleers, M., 'The Interaction Between the M'Bona Cult and Christianity, 1859–1963', in Terence Ranger and John Weller, eds., *Themes in the Christian*

History of Central Africa (Berkeley: University of California Press, 1975), pp. 14–30.

Schoffeleers, M. and I. Linden, 'The Resistance of the Nyau Societies to the Roman Catholic Missions in Colonial Malawi', in Terence Ranger and I. Kimambo, eds., *The Historical Study of African Religion* (Berkeley: University of California Press, 1972), pp. 252–276.

Schumaker, Lyn, *Africanising Anthropology: Fieldwork, Networks and the Making of Cultural Knowledge in Central Africa* (London: Duke University Press, 2001).

Scott, Peter, 'Migrant Labour in Southern Rhodesia', *Geographical Review*, 44, 1 (1954), pp. 29–48.

Shamuyarira, Nathan M., *Crisis in Rhodesia* (New York: Transatlantic Arts, 1965).

Shepperson, George, 'The African Diaspora—Or the African Abroad', *African Forum: A Quarterly Journal of Contemporary Affairs*, 2, 1 (1966), pp. 76–93.

Shepperson, George and Thomas Price, *Independent African: John Chilembwe and the Origins, Setting and Significance of the Nyasaland Native Rising of 1915* (Edinburgh: Edinburgh University Press, 1958) First Edition (Blantyre: Kachere Press, 2000). Second Edition.

Short, Philip, *Banda* (London: Routledge, 1974).

Simelane, Hamilton Sipho, 'The State, Chiefs, and the Control of Female Migration in Colonial Swaziland, c.1930s–1950s', *Journal of African History*, 45, 1 (2004), pp. 103–124.

Soko, Boston, *Nchimi Chikanga: The Battle Against Witchcraft in Malawi* (Zomba: Kachere, 2002).

Spear, Thomas, 'Neo-Traditionalism and the Limits of Invention', *Journal of African History*, 44, 1 (2003), pp. 3–27.

Stapleton, Tim, 'The Composition of the Rhodesia Native Regiment during the First World War: A Look at the Evidence', *History in Africa*, 30 (2003), pp. 283–295.

Stichter, Sharon, *Migrant Laborers* (Cambridge: Cambridge University Press, 1985).

Thompson, P., *The Voice of the Past: Oral History* (Oxford: Oxford University Press, 2000), Third Edition.

Thompson, E. P., 'The Moral Economy of the English Crowd in the Eighteenth Century', *Past and Present*, 50, 1 (1971), pp. 76–136.

Thompson, T. Jack, *Christianity in Northern Malawi: Donald Fraser's Missionary Methods and Ngoni Culture* (Leiden: E.J. Brill, 1995).

Thornton, S., 'The Struggle for Profit and Participation by an Emerging Petty-Bourgeoisie in Bulawayo, 1893–1993', in Tsuneo Yoshikuni eds., *Sites of Struggle: Essays in Zimbabwe's Urban History* (Harare: Weaver Press, 1999), pp. 19–52.

Tischler, Julia, *Light and Power for a Multiracial Nation: The Kariba Dam Scheme in the Central African Federation* (New York: Palgrave Macmillan, 2013).

Tow, L., *The Manufacturing Economy of Southern Rhodesia: Problems and Prospects* (Washington, DC: National Academy of Sciences, 1960).

Turner, Rev. Dr W. Y., 'A Visit to Nyasaland Natives', *Central Africa: News and Views*, 1, 1 (July 1935), pp. 17–19.

Vail, Leroy, 'Railway Development and Colonial Underdevelopment: The Nyasaland Case', in Robin Palmer and Neil Parsons, eds., *The Roots of Rural Poverty in Central and Southern Africa* (Berkeley: University of California Press, 1977), pp. 365–395.

Vail, Leroy, ed., *The Creation of Tribalism in Southern Africa* (Berkeley: University of California Press, 1989).

Vail, Leroy, 'Introduction: Ethnicity in Southern African History', in Leroy Vail, ed., *The Creation of Tribalism in Southern Africa* (Berkeley: University of California Press, 1989), pp. 1–20.

Vail, Leroy and Landeg White, 'Tribalism in the Political History of Malawi', in Leroy Vail, ed., *The Creation of Tribalism in Southern Africa* (Berkeley: University of California Press, 1989), pp. 151–192.

Vail, Leroy and Landeg White, *Power and the Praise Poem: Southern African Voices in History* (Charlottesville: University of Virginia Press, 1991).

Vambe, Lawence, *From Rhodesia to Zimbabwe* (London: Heinemann, 1976).

Vambe, Maurice, '"*Aya Mahobo*": Migrant Labour and the Cultural Semiotics of Harare (Mbare) African Township, 1930–1970', *African Identities*, 5, 3 (2007), pp. 355–370.

Vambe, Maurice, ed., *The Hidden Dimensions of Operation Murambatsvina* (Harare: Weaver Press, 2008).

Van Breugel, J. W. M., *Chewa Traditional Religion* (Zomba: Kachere Press, 2001).

Van Onselen, Charles, 'Black Workers in Central African Industry: A Critical Essay on the Historiography and Sociology of Rhodesia', *Journal of Southern African Studies*, 1, 2 (1975), pp. 228–246.

Van Onselen, Charles, *Chibaro: African Mine Labour in Southern Rhodesia, 1900–1933* (London: Pluto Press, 1976).

Van Onselen, Charles, 'The Construction of a Rural life from Oral Testimony: Critical Notes on the Methodology Employed in the Study of Black South African Sharecropper', *Journal of Peasant Studies*, 20, 3 (1993), pp. 494–514.

Van Onselen, Charles, *The Seed is Mine: The Life of Kas Maine, a South African Share-Cropper, 1894–1985* (Oxford: James Currey, 1996).

Van Onselen, Charles, *New Babylon New Nineveh: Everyday Life on the Witwatersrand 1886–1914* (Johannesburg: Jonathan Ball Publishers, 2001).

Van Velsen, J., 'Labour Migration as a Positive Factor in the Continuity of Tonga Tribal Society', *Economic Development and Cultural Change*, 8, 3 (1960), pp. 265–278.

Van Velsen, J., *The Politics of Kinship: A study in Social Manipulation among the Lakeside Tonga of Nyasaland* (Manchester: Manchester University Press, 1964).

Vaughan, Megan, *The Story of an African Famine. Gender and Famine in Twentieth Century Malawi* (Cambridge: Cambridge University Press, 1987).

Vaughan, Megan, *Creating the Creole Island: Slavery in Eighteenth Century Mauritius* (London: Duke University Press, 2005).

Vertovec, Steven, 'Transnationalism and Identity', *Journal of Ethnic and Migration Studies*, 27, 4 (2001), pp. 573–582.

Vickery, Kenneth, 'The Rhodesia Railways African Strike of 1945, Part I: A Narrative Account', *Journal of Southern African Studies*, 23, 4 (1998), pp. 545–560.

Vickery, Kenneth, 'The Rhodesia Railways Strike of 1945, Part II: Cause, Consequence, Significance', *Journal of Southern African Studies*, 21, 1 (1999), pp. 49–71.

Webster, Eddie, 'Rethinking Migrant Labour' [Review article] *South African Historical Journal*, 28 (1993), pp. 292–299.

Welensky, Roy, *Welensky's 4000 Days: The Life and Death of the Federation of Rhodesia and Nyasaland* (London: Collins, 1964).

Werbner, Richard, *Tears of the Dead: The Social Biography of an African Family* (Edinburgh: Edinburgh University Press, 1991).

West, Michael O., 'Liquor and Libido: Joint Drinking and the Politics of Sexual Control in Colonial Zimbabwe, 1920s–1950s', *Journal of Social History*, 30, 3 (1997), pp. 645–667.

West, Michael, *The Rise of an African Middle Class: Colonial Zimbabwe, 1898–1965* (Bloomington: Indiana University Press, 2002).

Weyl, U., *Labour Migration and Underdevelopment in Malawi: Late Nineteenth Century to Mid-1970s* (Masvingo: Belmont Press, 1991).

Whitaker, Beth E., 'Citizens and Foreigners: Democratisation and the Politics of Exclusion in Africa', *African Studies Review*, 48, 1 (2005), pp. 109–126.

White, Landeg, '"Tribes" and the Aftermath of the Chilembwe Rising', *African Affairs*, 83, 333 (1984), pp. 511–541.

White, Landeg, *Magomera: Portrait of an African Village* (Cambridge: Cambridge University Press, 1987).

White, Luise, *The Comforts of Home: Prostitution in Colonial Nairobi* (London: University of Chicago Press, 1990).

White, Luise, *The Assassination of Herbert Chitepo: Texts and Politics in Zimbabwe* (Bloomington, IN: Indiana University Press, 2003).

White, Luise, Stephen F. Miescher and William David Cohen, eds., *African Words, African Voices: Critical Practices in Oral History* (Bloomington: Indiana University Press, 2001).

White, Luise and Miles Larmer, eds., *Mobile Soldiers and the Un-National Liberation of Southern Africa, Journal of Southern African Studies*, 40, 6 (2014).

White, Luise, *Unpopular Sovereignty: Rhodesian Independence and African Decolonization* (Chicago, University of Chicago Press, 2015).

Whitman, Jim, ed., *Migrants, Citizens and the State in Southern Africa* (London: Macmillan Press, 2000).

Wilson, Francis, *Labour on South African Gold Mines, 1911–1969* (Cambridge: Cambridge University Press, 1972).

Worby, Eric, 'Maps, Names and Ethnic Games: The Epistemology and Iconography of Colonial Power in Northwestern Zimbabwe', *Journal of Southern African Studies*, 20, 3 (1994), pp. 371–392.

Wroe, Daniel, 'Remembering Kamuzu: The Ambiguity of the Past in Malawi's Central Region', *Journal of Southern African Studies*, 46, 2 (2020), pp. 247–261.

Yoshikuni, Tsuneo, *African Urban Experiences in Colonial Zimbabwe: A Social History of Harare Before 1925* (Harare: Weaver Press, 2007).

Yoshikuni, Tsuneo, *Elizabeth Musodzi and the Birth of African Feminism in Early Colonial Zimbabwe* (Harare: Weaver Press, 2008).

Young, T. Cullen, *Notes on the History of the Tumbuka-Kamanga People's in the Northern Province of Nyasaland* (London: Religious Tract Society, 1932), First Edition.

Zinyama, Lovemore and Daniel Tevera, eds., *Harare: The Growth and Problems of the City* (Harare: University of Zimbabwe Publications, 1993).

Unpublished Dissertations/Theses/Seminar Papers

Banda, Harvey C., 'The Dynamics of Labour Migration from Northern Malawi to South Africa Since 1974', PhD Thesis, University of the Witwatersrand, 2017.

Boeder, Robert, 'Malawians Abroad: The History of Labour Emigration from Malawi to Its Neighbours, 1890 to the Present', PhD Thesis, Michigan State University, Ann Arbour, 1974.

Chirwa, W., '"Theba Is Power": Rural Labour, Migrancy and Fishing in Malawi, 1890s–1985', PhD Thesis, Queen's University, 1992.

Cross, Sholto, 'The Watch Tower Movement in South Central Africa, 1908–1945', DPhil Thesis, Oxford University, 1973.

Gawanani, Precious, 'Coping with the Absence of Men: The Experiences of Migrants' Wives in Madisi, Dowa District, 1936–1987', BEd Thesis, University of Livingstonia, 2007.

MacDonald, Andrew, 'Colonial Trespassers in the Making of South Africa's International Borders, 1900 to c.1950' PhD Thesis, University of Cambridge, 2012.

Makambe, E. P., 'The African Immigrant Factor in Southern Rhodesia, 1890–1930: The Origin and Influence of External Elements in a Colonial Setting', PhD Thesis, University of York, 1979.

Milford, Ismay, 'Harnessing the Wind: East and Central African Activists and Anticolonial Cultures in a Decolonising World, 1952–64', European University Institute, 2019.

Mudeka, Ireen, '"We faced *Mabvuto*": A Gendered Socio-economic History of Malawian Women's Migration and Survival in Harare, 1940–1980', PhD Thesis, University of Minnesota, 2011.

Nkhoma, Bryson, 'The Competition for Malawian Labour: Wenela and Mthandizi in Ncheu District, 1935–1956', MA Dissertation, Chancellor's College, University of Malawi, 1995.

Phiri, Kings M., 'Chewa History in Central Malawi and the Use of Oral Tradition, 1600–1920', PhD Thesis, University of Wisconsin, 1975.

Sakala, M. M. J., 'The Experiences of Ex-Migrant Workers in Mzimba District, 1956–2006', History Seminar Paper, Mzuzu University, 2006.

Scarnecchia, Timothy, 'The Politics of Gender and Class in the Creation of African Communities, Salisbury, Rhodesia, 1937–1957', PhD Thesis, University of Michigan, 1993.

Stuart, Ossie W., '"Good Boys", Footballers and Strikers: African Social Change in Bulawayo, 1933–1953', PhD Dissertation, SOAS, University of London, 1989.

Yoshikuni, Tsuneo, 'Black Migrants in a White City: A Social History of African Harare, 1890–1925', History PhD Thesis, University of Zimbabwe, 1989.

Internet Sources and Reports

Delius, Peter, 'The History of Migrant Labour in South Africa, 1800–2014', *Oxford Research Encyclopedia for African History* (2017). https://doi.org/10.1093/acrefore/9780190277734.013.93.

Dube, Rumbidzai, 'Identity, Citizenship and the Registrar General: The Politicking of Identity in Zimbabwe', A Report by the Research Advocacy Unit, Harare (2012).

Manby, Bronwen, Report on Citizenship Law: Zimbabwe, January 2019, available online: http://hdl.handle.net/1814/60436.

Robert Mugabe's Address to the Nation. 4 March 1980. http://www.politicsweb.co.za/politicsweb/view/politicsweb/en/page71619?oid=164016&sn=Detail (1 July 2014).

Rossi, Benedetta, 'Migration History and Historiography', *Oxford Research Encyclopedia for African History* (2018). https://doi.org/10.1093/acrefore/9780190277734.013.325.

Sande, Akwete, 'The golden glitter of South Africa is gone', *Pambazuka News*, 12 June 2008. Available at: https://www.pambazuka.org/land-environment/golden-glitter-south-africa-gone.

Zimbabwe Human Rights Bulletin, Issue 5, September 2001.

Zimbabwe Lawyers for Human Rights, 'The Path to Disenfranchisement', *Pambazuka News*, 21 March 2002.

Index

Z. R. Groves, *Malawian Migration to Zimbabwe, 1900–1965*, Cambridge Imperial and Post-Colonial Studies Series,
https://doi.org/10.1007/978-3-030-54104-0

The manufacturer's authorised representative in the EU is Springer Nature Customer Service Centre GmbH, Europaplatz 3, 69115 Heidelberg, Germany. If you have any concerns regarding our products, please contact ProductSafety@springernature.com

Printed and bound by CPI Group (UK) Ltd, Croydon, CR0 4YY
30/09/2026
02225443-0006